Image, History and Memory

This book discusses the active relationship among the mechanics of memory, visual practices and historical narratives.

Reflection on memory and its ties with historical narratives cannot be separated from reflection on the visual and the image as its points of reference which function in time. This volume addresses precisely that temporal aspect of the image, without reducing it to a neutral trace of the past, a mnemotechnical support of memory. As a commemorative device, the image fixes, structures and crystallises memory, turning the view of the past into myth. It may, however, also stimulate, transform and update memory, functioning as a matrix of interpretation and understanding the past. The book questions whether the functioning of the visual matrices of memory can be related to a particular historical and geographical scope, that is, to Central and Eastern Europe, and whether it is possible to find their origin and decide if they are just local and regional or perhaps also Western European and universal. It focuses on the artistic reflection on time and history, in the reconstructions of memory due to change of frontiers and political regimes, as well as endeavours to impose some specific political structure on territories which were complex and mixed in terms of national identity, religion and social composition.

The volume is ideal for students and scholars of memory studies, history and visual studies.

Michał Haake is Professor and Art Historian at the Adam Mickiewicz University in Poznań, Poland. His research interests focus on history of European painting from medieval to contemporary art and art history methodology. His publications include *Figuralizm Aleksandra Gierymskiego* (*Aleksander Gierymski's Figuralism*) (2015) and *Obraz jako obiekt teoretyczny* (*Image as the Theoretical Object*) (as co-editor, 2020).

Piotr Juszkiewicz is Professor and Art Historian at the Adam Mickiewicz University in Poznań, Poland. His publications include *Od rozkoszy historiozofii do "gry w nic". Polska krytyka artystyczna czasu odwilży* [From the Bliss of Historiography to the "Game of Nothing". Polish Art Criticism of the Post-Stalinist "Thaw"] (2005) and *Cień modernizmu* [The Shadow of Modernism] (2013).

European Remembrance and Solidarity Series

The recent crisis of the European project (the Euro, migration, Brexit, the rise in national populism) has brought about new questions about the direction of EU integration. The debate on a common European memory and identity has been equally dramatic, and in particular since the expansion of the EU towards the east, as pleas for proper recognition of the 'new' Europe within a common European historical awareness have emerged. With a number of volumes studying social memories in connection to art, religion, politics and other domains of social life, the series editors wish to contribute to the debate on European memory and identity and shed fresh light on the region of Central and Eastern Europe and Europe more broadly, a region stretched between the past and the future in the negotiation of identities – both national and transnational. The editors encourage comparative studies of two or more European countries, as well as those that highlight Central and Eastern Europe in reference to other regions in Europe and beyond.

The book series is developed in cooperation with the European Network Remembrance and Solidarity (www.enrs.eu).

Editorial Board of the book series: Marek Cichocki, Peter Haslinger, Catherine Horel, Csaba Gy. Kiss, Dušan Kováč, Elena Mannová, Andrzej Nowak, Attila Pók, Marcela Sălăgean, Arnold Suppan, Stefan Troebst, and Jay Winter.

Coordination: Małgorzata Pakier, Ewelina Szpak

Image, History and Memory
Central and Eastern Europe in a Comparative Perspective
Edited by Michał Haake and Piotr Juszkiewicz

Memory and Religion from a Postsecular Perspective
Edited by Zuzanna Bogumił and Yuliya Yurchuk

A New Europe, 1918–1923
Instability, Innovation, Recovery
Edited by Bartosz Dziewanowski-Stefańczyk and Jay Winter

For more information about this series, please visit: https://www.routledge.com/European-Remembrance-and-Solidarity/book-series/REMEMBER

The European Network Remembrance and Solidarity

The European Network Remembrance and Solidarity is an international initiative the aim of which is to research, document and enhance public knowledge of the 20th-century history of Europe and European cultures of remembrance, with particular emphasis on periods of dictatorships, wars and resistance to political violence. The members of the Network are Germany, Hungary, Poland, Romania, and Slovakia, with representatives from Albania, Austria, the Czech Republic, Estonia, Georgia, Latvia and Lithuania present in its advisory bodies.
More information: www.enrs.eu

ENRS is funded by: the German Federal Government Commissioner for Culture and the Media, the Ministry of Human Capacities of Hungary, the Ministry of Culture and National Heritage of the Republic of Poland, the Ministry of Culture of Romania and the Ministry of Culture of the Slovak Republic.

Image, History and Memory
Central and Eastern Europe in
a Comparative Perspective

**Edited by
Michał Haake and Piotr Juszkiewicz**

LONDON AND NEW YORK

First published 2022
by Routledge
2 Park Square, Milton Park, Abingdon, Oxon OX14 4RN

and by Routledge
605 Third Avenue, New York, NY 10158

Routledge is an imprint of the Taylor & Francis Group, an informa business

© 2022 selection and editorial matter, Michał Haake and Piotr Juszkiewicz; individual chapters, the contributors

The right of Michał Haake and Piotr Juszkiewicz to be identified as the authors of the editorial material, and of the authors for their individual chapters, has been asserted in accordance with sections 77 and 78 of the Copyright, Designs and Patents Act 1988.

All rights reserved. No part of this book may be reprinted or reproduced or utilised in any form or by any electronic, mechanical, or other means, now known or hereafter invented, including photocopying and recording, or in any information storage or retrieval system, without permission in writing from the publishers.

Trademark notice: Product or corporate names may be trademarks or registered trademarks, and are used only for identification and explanation without intent to infringe.

British Library Cataloguing-in-Publication Data
A catalogue record for this book is available from the British Library

Library of Congress Cataloging-in-Publication Data
A catalog record for this book has been requested

ISBN: 978-1-032-20624-0 (hbk)
ISBN: 978-1-032-20625-7 (pbk)
ISBN: 978-1-003-26446-0 (ebk)

DOI: 10.4324/9781003264460

Typeset in Bembo
by Apex CoVantage, LLC

This publication was financed by the European Network Remembrance and Solidarity. ENRS is funded by: the German Federal Government Commissioner for Culture and the Media, the Ministry of Human Capacities of Hungary, the Ministry of Culture and National Heritage of the Republic of Poland, the Ministry of Culture of Romania and the Ministry of Culture of the Slovak Republic.

 Federal Government Commissioner for Culture and the Media

 MINISTRY OF HUMAN CAPACITIES

 Ministry of **Culture** and National Heritage of the Republic of Poland

 MINISTRY OF CULTURE

 MINISTRY OF CULTURE OF THE SLOVAK REPUBLIC

This volume has been written in partnership with the
European Network Remembrance and Solidarity and
the Adam Mickiewicz University, Poznań.

Contents

List of figures	xiv
List of tables	xvii
Notes on contributors	xix

Introduction   1

PIOTR JUSZKIEWICZ

PART 1

Forms of memory and oblivion   5

1 **Dis-remembered and mis-remembered: a confrontation with failures of cultural memory**   7

MIEKE BAL

2 **Matejko: how did he do it?**   22

WOJCIECH SUCHOCKI

3 **The devotional image as a medium of memory: the case of the painting of the *Divine Mercy* by Eugeniusz Kazimirowski**   36

MARIUSZ BRYL

4 **Images *in cito*, *in situ*, *in extremis*: visual testimonies from the "Holocaust by bullets"**   51

ROMA SENDYKA

5 **The stratified image: medium, construction and memory in Frank Stella's *Polish Villages***   66

FILIP LIPIŃSKI

xii *Contents*

6 Against illusion: Kuno Raeber's thoughts on the power
of material and the art of Karl Rössing   75
DOROTA KOWNACKA

7 The past, memory and oblivion   84
TADEUSZ J. ŻUCHOWSKI

8 A leap: operations of memory between sketch and
picture in Piotr Potworowski's painting process   92
ŁUKASZ KIEPUSZEWSKI

9 Smiling in Auschwitz: instagram selfies and historical
representation at the Auschwitz-Birkenau Memorial
and Museum   105
ROBBERT-JAN ADRIAANSEN

10 Image world, memory space: photographic
spectatorship as a mode of remembrance   121
ROBERT HARIMAN

PART 2
Memory and identity   131

11 The memorial topography of the Holodomor between
cumulative and cultural trauma: a genealogical approach   133
VITALII OGIIENKO

12 Building the Finnish national mythos: photographs
from the Russo-Finnish Winter War of 1939–1940 and
their post-war use   151
OLLI KLEEMOLA

13 Archived and mediated: trauma and "sense memory"
in *Son of Saul*, *Warsaw Uprising* and *Regina*   162
BEJA MARGITHÁZI

14 Memory, history, image, forgetting: *Obrona Warszawy*
(*The Defence of Warsaw*) by Zygmunt Zaremba and
Teresa Żarnower   178
STANISŁAW CZEKALSKI

Contents xiii

15 **Pictures and history: art exhibitions as a tool for the validation of communist authority in Poland** 189
MICHAŁ HAAKE

16 *Hungary in Flames*: **photographic, cinematic and literary memories of the Hungarian Revolution of 1956, and their impact on the history of ideas** 201
TAMÁS GERGELY KUCSERA

17 **Pictures for the Fathers: Baselitz's *Heldenbilder* as anti-images of the socialist and fascist body** 213
JUSTYNA BALISZ-SCHMELZ

18 **The everyday life in the GDR in individual, cultural and political memory** 224
MARIA KHOROLSKAYA

19 **Between memory and myth: the images of Joseph Stalin in new Russian media** 232
ANDREI LINCHENKO

Index 241

Figures

1.1	Installation in Freud Museum London, *Saying It*, curated by Joanne Morra, The Freud Museum, London, 20 September 20–19 November 2012	13
1.2	Installation *Anacronismos*, Guggenheim Bilbao Museum, for exhibition *The Golden Age of Dutch and Flemish Painting from the Städel Museum*, curated by Jochen Sander, 7 October 2010–23 January 2011	13
1.3	Descartes "mad", played by Thomas Germaine, in *Reasonable Doubt*	16
1.4	The first meeting of Descartes and Kristina at Nieborów Castle, Poland	17
1.5	Elisabeth (Johanna ter Steege) consults Kristina (Marja Skaffari) after Descartes's death (fiction)	18
2.1	Jan Matejko, *Rejtan at Sejm of 1773*	24
2.2	Moritz von Schwind, *Dumouriez arrests the members of Convention*, in Edouard Duller, *Erzherzog Carl von Oesterreich*, 1847, p. 137	26
2.3	Artur Grottger, *Forced Recruitment* (cycle "Polonia"), 1863	28
2.4	Artur Grottger, *Widow* (cycle "Warsaw II"), 1863	29
2.5	Jan Matejko, *Rejtan at Sejm of 1773*, 1866	30
2.6	Santi Gucci, Stefan Bathory's tomb, 1594–1595, Cracow, Wawel Cathedral	32
2.7	Michelangelo, *Creation of Adam*, c. 1511	33
3.1	Eugeniusz Kazimirowski, *Image of the Divine Mercy*, 1934	37
3.2	Adolf Hyła, *Image of the Divine Mercy*, 1944 (present state)	40
3.3	Adolf Hyła, *Image of the Divine Mercy*, 1944 (state until 1954)	41
3.4	Ludomir Sleńdziński, *Image of the Divine Mercy*, 1954	43
3.5	Eugeniusz Kazimirowski, *Image of the Divine Mercy*, 1934 (state 1987–2003)	46
3.6	Michał Nowicki, *Photo of the Image of the Divine Mercy by Kazimirowski*, 1940	47
4.1	Walls in the fort in Pomiechówek with the signatures of victims	53
4.2	Cut-outs in bark at the site of the death of denounced Jews	54

4.3	Fragment of the display *Drawings on the Scraps of Life*	57
4.4	Jakub Guterman, Drawing, recto, Warsaw, Jewish Historical Institute, inv. no. B-513/3	59
4.5	Jakub Guterman, Drawing, verso, Warsaw, Jewish Historical Institute, inv. no. B-513/3	60
5.1	Franks Stella at his West Houston Street Studio, New York, with works from the *Polish Village* series, 1974	68
5.2	Bogoria synagogue: view from the northwest	70
8.1	Heston Aircraft flight suitcase containing six volumes of Piotr Potworowski's sketchbooks from 1952 to 1961	93
8.2	Page from volume III	94
8.3	Page from volume IV	95
8.4	Page from volume V	96
8.5	Page from volume V	97
11.1	Memorial in the village of Kalanchak, Kalanchatskyi district, Khersonska oblast	135
11.2	Monument in the village of Targan, Kyiv oblast	140
11.3	The Black Board Alley at National Museum of the Holodomor-Genocide	143
11.4	The Candle	144
11.5	The Altar	145
11.6	*Bitter Childhood Memories* sculpture	146
12.1	The bomb-ravaged Luther Church in Helsinki (SA-kuva 1547)	155
12.2	A staged picture of a mother with her child hiding in the wintry forest during the bombing (SA-kuva 10825)	156
12.3	Remains of the destroyed Soviet 44th Division on Raate Road in January 1940 (SA-kuva 2984)	156
12.4	A Finnish ski troop during the Winter War (SA-kuva 4706)	157
12.5	The Finnish National Monument of the Winter War	159
13.1	Sonderkommando photograph no. 280 framed by the gas chamber's visible door frame (1944)	167
13.2	Watching the inspection of the miraculously surviving boy in Nemes's *Son of Saul*	168
13.3	Filming the gunfights from the protection of a window in Komasa's *Warsaw Uprising*	169
13.4	One of the two surviving photographs of Regina Jonas (1936)	172
13.5	Young Jewish woman in *Regina*	173
14.1	Teresa Żarnower, *Obrona Warszawy. Lud polski w obronie stolicy (The Defence of Warsaw. The Polish people in defence of the capital)*	181
14.2	Teresa Żarnower, *On the Road of Death*, photomontage, in *Obrona Warszawy. Lud polski w obronie stolicy (The Defence of Warsaw. The Polish people in defence of the capital)*, Polish Labor Group, New York 1942	184

xvi *Figures*

14.3 Teresa Żarnower, *Days of Horror*, photomontage, in *Obrona Warszawy (The Defence of Warsaw. The Polish people in defence of the capital)*, Polish Labor Group, New York 1942   185

15.1 Aleksander Gierymski, *Sandblasters*, 1887   192

15.2 Wojciech Gerson, *The Capture of the Wends, (1147)*, 1866   194

15.3 Aleksander Lesser, *The Death of Wanda*, 1855   195

15.4 Jan Matejko, *The Battle of Grunwald*, 1882   196

15.5 *1000 Years of Art in Poland*, exhibition poster, 1970   198

17.1 Georg Baselitz, *The Modern Painter*, 1965   217

17.2 Georg Baselitz, *The Shepherd*, 1966   218

17.3 Georg Baselitz, *Economy*, 1965   219

17.4 Georg Baselitz, *Picture for the Fathers*, 1965   220

Tables

9.1 Top 10 used hashtags according to frequency (case insensitive)   111

9.2 Frequency distribution of the number of lines per post in the
sample of Instagram posts (hashtags excluded)   113

Notes on contributors

Robbert-Jan Adriaansen

Assistant Professor in the theory of history and historical culture at Erasmus University Rotterdam. His research focuses on conceptions of history and historical time, in the past and in the present. He published the monograph *The Rhythm of Eternity: The German Youth Movement and the Experience of the Past, 1900–1933* (2015). He is working on two projects about the representation of violent pasts in contemporary historical culture, focusing on representations on Instagram and in historical re-enactments.

Mieke Bal

Professor, co-founder and lifelong affiliate of the Amsterdam School for Cultural Analysis (ASCA). She focuses on gender, migratory culture, psychoanalysis and the critique of capitalism. Her 40-some books include a trilogy on political art: *Endless Andness, Thinking in Film, Of What One Cannot Speak. Emma & Edvard Looking Sideways* demonstrates her integrated approach to academic, artistic and curatorial work. She co-made documentaries on migratory culture and "theoretical fictions". *A Long History of Madness* argues for a more humane treatment of psychosis and was exhibited in a site-specific version, *Saying It*, in the Freud Museum in London. *Madame B* was combined with paintings by Edvard Munch in the Munch Museum in Oslo (2017). *Reasonable Doubt* explores the social aspects of thinking (2016). She exhibited a 16-channel video work *Don Quixote: Tristes Figuras* (2019). Her latest film, *It's About Time! Reflections of Urgency*, was produced in Poland (2020).

Justyna Balisz-Schmelz

Adjunct Professor at the Department of History of Modern Art and Culture of the Institute of Art History at the University of Warsaw. She is the author of the book *Przeszłość niepokonana. Sztuka niemiecka po 1945 roku jako przestrzeń i medium pamięci* [The Insurmountable Past. The German Art Post-1945 as the Space and Medium of Memory] (2018). She has published articles in scholarly journals, including *Jahrbuch der Deutschen Akademie der*

Wissenschaften zu Berlin, RIHA Journal, View. Theories and Practices of Visual Culture, Quart and in collective works, including *Polish Avant-Garde in Berlin* (2019) and *Cold Revolution. Central and Eastern Europe Societies in the Face of Socialist Realism, 1948–1959* (2020). Her scientific interests focus primarily on German art after 1945, bilateral German–Polish and German–German artistic relations. She also examines the possibility of applying the cultural theory of collective memory to the field of visual arts.

Mariusz Bryl

Professor at the Institute of Art History, Adam Mickiewicz University in Poznań, Poland. His fields of interests are history of art history, history of European art of the 19th and 20th centuries, contemporary visual culture, and art history methodology. He has published, among others, books such as *Cykle Artura Grottgera. Poetyka i recepcja* [Artur Grottger's Cycles. Poetics and Reception] (1994); *Suwerenność dyscypliny. Polemiczna historia historii sztuki od 1970 roku* [Sovereignty of the Discipline. Polemical History of Art History since 1970], (2008). He has also translated into Polish many art historical books and studies, among others, by such authors as H. Belting, H. Bredekamp, M. Brötje, N. Bryson, M. Fried, W. Kemp, R. Krauss and G. Pollock.

Stanisław Czekalski

Associate Professor at the Institute of Art History, Adam Mickiewicz University in Poznań. His research interests focus on methodology of art history, theory and hermeneutics of the image, photography and visual culture. He is the author of *Awangarda i mit racjonalizacji. Fotomontaż polski okresu dwudziestolecia międzywojennego* [*The Avant-Garde and the Myth of Rationalization. Polish Photomontage 1918–1939*] (2000), *Intertekstualność i malarstwo. Problemy badań nad związkami międzyobrazowymi* [*Intertextuality and Painting. Problems of the Analysis of Interpictorial Relationships*] (2006); *Obrazy mocne/obrazy słabe. Studia z teorii i historii badań nad sztuką* [*Strong Images/Weak Images. Studies in Theory and History of Art Research*] (as co-editor, 2018).

Michał Haake

Professor at the Institute of Art History, Adam Mickiewicz University in Poznań, Poland. His research interests focus on history of art history, history of European painting from medieval to contemporary art and art history methodology. He published the books *Portret w malarstwie polskim u progu nowoczesności* [Portrait in Polish Painting at the Threshold of Modernism) 2008; *Przemyśleć wszystko . . . Stanisława Wyspiańskiego modernizacja pamięci zbiorowej* [Think Over Everything . . . Modernization of Collective Imagination by Stanisław Wyspiański] (as co-editor), 2009; *Oko i myśl. O Zdzisławie Kępińskim* [Eye and Thought. On Zdzislaw Kępiński], (as editor, 2012); *Figuralizm Aleksandra Gierymskiego* [Aleksander Gierymski's Figuralism], 2015; *Utracone arcydzieło. Losy obrazu Targ na jarzyny Józefa Pankiewicza*

[Lost Masterpieces. The Fortune of Józef Pankiewicza's Painting "The Vegetable Market", 2020; *Obraz jako obiekt teoretyczny* [*Image as the Theoretical Object*] (as co-editor), 2020.

Robert Hariman

Professor of rhetoric and public culture in the Department of Communication Studies at Northwestern University. His book publications include *Political Style: The Artistry of Power* (as co-authored with John Louis Lucaites, 1995); *The Public Image: Photography and Civic Spectatorship* (2016); *No Caption Needed: Iconic Photographs, Public Culture, and Liberal Democracy* (as co-authored with John Louis Lucaites, 2011). He edited or co-edited books on popular trials, political judgement, political realism and catastrophe. Book chapters and journal articles include work on parody, allegory, image appropriation and other modes of public address. His work has been translated into Arabic, Chinese and French.

Piotr Juszkiewicz

Art historian and a professor at the Adam Mickiewicz University in Poznań, where he lectures at the Institute of Art History. His interests include 20th-century art history, contemporary art and art criticism in the 18th–20th centuries. He is the editor of publications including *Melancholia Jacka Malczewskiego* [The Melancholy of Jacek Malczewski] (1998) and *Perspektywy współczesnej historii sztuki* [Perspectives on Contemporary Art History] (2009] as well as the author of several books: *Wolność i metafizyka. O tradycji artystycznej twórczości Marcela Duchampa* [Freedom and Metaphysics. On Artistic tradition of Marcel Duchamp's Art] (1995); *Od rozkoszy historiozofii do gry w nic. Polska krytyka artystyczna czasu odwilży* [From the Bliss of Historiosophy to the "Game of Nothing". Polish Art Criticism of the of the Post-Stalinist "Thaw"] (2005); and *Cień modernizmu* [The Shadow of Modernism] (2013). He also has numerous texts in *Artium Quaestiones*, *Centropa*, *Rocznik Historii Sztuki* and *Journal of Victorian Culture*.

Maria Khorolskaya

Research fellow at the Primakov National Research Institute of World Economy and International Relations, Russian Academy of Sciences (IMEMO). She has a PhD in political science. Her PhD thesis was devoted to the problems of the integration of the new federal states (the former GDR) in the reunited Germany. Her current interests include problems of the eastern federal states in FRG, representation of the history of the GDR, German foreign policy, Russian–German relations and German political parties. Maria Khorolskaya is the author of several articles in Russian, including "Differences in the political culture of West and East Germany in the context of the EU crises" (2017) and "Problem of treatment and perception of history of GDR in united Germany" (2017). She is also the co-author of the collective monographs *Economy and Politics of Germany: A Year After the*

Election (2019) and *Strategic Autonomy of the EU and Prospects for Cooperation with Russia* (2020).

Łukasz Kiepuszewski, art historian and painter, Professor at the Institute of Art History, Adam Mickiewicz University. His selected publications include *Obrazy Cézanne'a. Między spojrzeniem a komentarzem* [Cézanne's Paintings. Between a Gaze and a Commentary] (2005); *Niewczesne obrazy. Nietzsche i sztuki wizualne* [Untimely Images. Nietzsche and Visual Arts] (2013); *Historia sztuki po Derridzie* [Art History after Derrida] (as editor 2006); Obrazy mocne – obrazy słabe [Strong Images – Weak Images] (as co-editor, 2018); *Obraz jako obiekt teoretyczny* [Image as the Theoretical Object] (as co-editor, 2020).

Olli Kleemola

Postdoctoral research fellow in the Department of Contemporary History at the University of Turku. His research interests focus on visual history; photographs and history; and new military history. His doctoral thesis is titled "The Photograph in War. Soviet Soldiers, Soviet Population and the Soviet Union in Finnish and German War Photographs 1941–1945" (2016). He co-edited the book *Photographs and History: Interpreting Past and Present through Photographs* (2018).

Dorota Kownacka

Art historian, Assistant Professor at the Institute of Art of the Polish Academy of Sciences. She published the book *Rainera Marii Rilkego teksty o sztuce* [Rainer Maria Rilke's texts on art] (2016). Her research projects are focused on brilliant men of letters, poets and writers and their dilettante approach to artistic phenomena. By exploring the potential of juxtaposing both language and image, her works offer genuine and unique refreshment in the perception of art.

Tamás Gergely Kucsera

Art theorist writer, historian of ideas, filmmaker, Associate Professor at Károli Gáspár University of the Reformed Church in Hungary, Research Professor at the University of Győr and Honorary University Professor at the University of Pécs. He is the Chairman of the Documentary Judging Committee of the National Film Institute of Hungary. Among his main works are *Drafts About Funding Practice of Hungarian Higher Education Between 1990–2013* (2015); *Federalist Concepts in the 19th and 20th Century* (2007); and *Beyond Art, Beyond People* (2019).

Andrei Linchenko

Associate Professor at the Financial University under the Government of the Russian Federation. He is the author of *The Wholeness of Historical Consciousness: An Introduction to the Study of the Problem* (2013); *Conceptual foundations*

xxii *Notes on contributors*

of the politics of memory and the perspectives of post-national identity (as co-editor, 2019), *Myths about the past in the media: actual practices, mechanisms of influence, prospects for use* (as co-editor, 2020). His research interests lie in studying the philosophical aspects of the historical culture and cultural memory studies, the transformation of historical consciousness of young people in the contemporary world, the narrative strategies of the autobiographical memory of the Russian-speaking migrants in the European Union, modern Soviet mythologies in the Russian historical culture and politics of the memory.

Filip Lipiński

Art historian and Americanist, Assistant Professor (PhD) in the Department of Art History, Adam Mickiewicz University in Poznań, Poland. His academic interests concern American art and the theory and methodology of art history, and his current research focuses on the relationship between art history, film and film studies. He is the author of the book *Hopper wirtualny. Obrazy w pamiętającym spojrzeniu* [The Virtual Hopper. Images in a Remembering Look] (2013). He is also finishing another book project titled *Ameryka. Rewizje wizualnej mitologii Stanów Zjednoczonych* (America. Re-visions of Visual Mythology of the United States, 2021).

Beja Margitházi

Assistant Professor at the Institute for Art Theory and Media Studies, Department of Film Studies at Eötvös Loránd University (ELTE) in Budapest, Hungary. She is the author of the book *Az arc mozija. Közelkép és filmstílus* [The Cinema of the Face. Close-up and Film Style] (2008) and co-edited *Vizuális kommunikáció* [Visual Communication] (2010). Her research and teaching interests include classic and cognitive film theory, visual studies, theory of trauma and documentary film. She is the editor of *Metropolis* Hungarian journal of film theory and film history, and has edited the issues of *Film and Emotion* (2017) and *Trauma and Documentary Film* (2018). Her articles and critical essays have been published in Hungarian, Romanian, German and English in different periodicals and anthologies.

Vitalii Ogiienko

Lead Specialist of the Ukrainian Institute of National Remembrance from Kyiv. He received his PhD in history from Taras Shevchenko University of Kyiv. He works on the project *Holodomor as a historical trauma*, which studies how the experience of original trauma has influenced the development of a cultural memory of the Holodomor and how this memory has been transmitted over generations. His research interests include trauma studies, memory studies, genocide studies and history of the Holodomor. He is an author of the books *Nationalna ta istorychna pamiat: slovnyk kluchovych terminiv* [National and historical Memory: glossary of key terms] (as co-editor, 2013) and *Studii pamiati v Ukraine* (as co-editor, 2013).

Roma Sendyka

Director of the Research Center for Memory Cultures and Associate Professor in the Anthropology of Literature and Cultural Studies Department at the Faculty of Polish Studies, Jagiellonian University, Krakow. She specialises in criticism and theory, visual culture studies and memory studies. Her focus is on relations between images, sites and memory, and she currently works on a project on clandestine sites of trauma in Central and Eastern Europe and Polish bystanders observing Holocaust. She recently authored an analysis on uncommemorated post-violence sites in Poland: *Beyond Camps: Non-sites of Memory* (2021).

Wojciech Suchocki

Art historian and Professor at the Institute of Art History at Adam Mickiewicz University in Poznań (retired). Director of National Museum in Poznań (2010–2018). He is the author of the books *Składniki genetyczne malarstwa Piotra Michałowskiego i osobista synteza jego sztuki. Z zagadnień dialogu obrazów* [Genetic components of Piotr Michałowski's painting and a personal synthesis of his art. On the issues of image dialogue] (doctoral thesis, 1982); *Śladem myśli o sztuce Martina Heideggera* [*In Place of Conscience. In the Wake of Martin Heidegger's Thinking on Art*] (1996); and *Libri veritatis Atanazego Raczyńskiego*, Vol. I–II (as editor, 2018).

Tadeusz J. Żuchowski

Professor of art history at the Adam Mickiewicz University in Poznań, Poland. He teaches and publishes on European art and architecture from late antiquity until today in its global context, and on the heritage and culture of remembrance. He is an authority on German romantic painting, sculpture and drawing technique. Among his many publications are *Patriotyczne mity i toposy. Malarstwo niemieckie 1800–1848* [Patriotic Myths and Topoi. German Painting 1800–1848] (1991); *Pałac papieski na Watykanie od końca V do początku XVI wieku: ceremoniał a ewolucja kompleksu rezydencjonalnego* [The Papal Palace in the Vatican. The ceremony and the evolution of the residence complex] (1999); *Poskromienie materii. Nowożytne zmagania rzeźbiarzy z marmurem kararyjskim. Michał Anioł, Bernini, Canova* [Taming of Matter. Sculptors' Struggle with Carrara Marble in the Modern Age. Michelangelo, Bernini, Canova] (2010); *Visualisation of the Topographical Space in Europe on Manuscript Maps from the Eighteenth Century* (as co-author with Beata Medyńska – Gulij, 2018); and *In the Shade of Berlin and Warsaw* (as co-editor, 2010).

Introduction

Piotr Juszkiewicz

In 1958, during the second stage of a competition announced by the International Auschwitz Committee for a memorial located in the former concentration camp, the jury chaired by Henry Moore gave the first prize to a design submitted by Oskar Hansen, Jerzy Jarnuszkiewicz, Julian Pałka, Lechosław Rosiński and Tadeusz Plasota. Their design was very different from the idea of a figurative or abstract piece of sculpture placed in an open space, which would activate, articulate and support the remembrance of the war atrocities either in a narrative manner or through an expressive form. Oskar Hansen's team proposed a memorial that abandoned the concept of a vertical monument connecting the object of commemoration with universal temporality. The road-memorial, as their proposal was called, replaced the usual vertical form with a horizontal dimension of human experience and memory. Its main element was a broad concrete road which was to run diagonally across the area of the camp regardless of the logic of its former functional arrangement, engulfing the remains of the barracks and latrines. The historic remnants of the camp were to disappear under the pressure of nature, gradually obliterated by erosion. After some time, the road would become a mediated trace of the past, with its meaning determined by the steps of all those who would wish to walk along it and leave on it a stone, the Jewish sign of memory placed on tombs, as a sign of their individual remembrance. Thus, the road–memorial would articulate a social and individual process of remembering, in which the commemorated reality vanishes irrevocably, always mediated, but at the same time lasts in the specific form that is the effort of remembering, the ritual of memory, where the bygone reality is replaced with a completely different materiality and different activity, de facto inclined towards the future, although that would be impossible without understanding the past.

This one example shows that reflection on memory, and on its links with historical narratives, cannot be separated from reflection on the visual and the image as its points of reference which function in time. Hansen attempted to replace a single image with a temporal process, reaching beyond the modernist exclusion of the temporal from reflection on the painted or photographic image.

DOI: 10.4324/9781003264460-1

2 *Piotr Juszkiewicz*

In proposing the links between image, memory and history (or perhaps historiography) as the topic of this book, we wanted to address precisely that temporal aspect of the image, without reducing it to a neutral trace of the past, a memory aid, a mute and immobile testimony to past events arranged in a narrative frame of history. The idea of the book reflects our intention to discuss the active mutual relationship between the mechanics of memory, visual practices and historical narratives. Of course, this is a complex issue, comprising a number of fundamental questions and answers from various areas of reflection, depending on their relations to different theoretical models of memory (from phenomenology through psychoanalysis to cognitive science) and their reception in today's humanities, in reference to the concepts of subjectivity, identity, consciousness and the unconscious, defined in terms of cultural construction. Focusing more narrowly on the study of images, motivated in various ways, we may also ask about the reception of our own tradition of such reflection, that is, the continuation of Walter Benjamin's thinking or Aby Warburg's idea of the *Nachleben* of images. Among the more crucial questions, one must certainly distinguish those which refer to the status of "picture memory" and the status of the image as a medium of memory formation and functioning. As a memorative device, the image fixes, structures and crystallises memory, turning the view of the past into myth. Having the power to demythologise, however, it may also stimulate, transform and update memory, functioning as a matrix of our interpretation and understanding of the past, as well as an alternative to the forms of its discursive emplotment.

Another cluster of questions concentrates on the tension between the materiality of the image and the virtual quality of its memorised form, which brings us to the problem of the fluidity of the image, its susceptibility to transformations and its specific mode of existence in time, marked by anachronicity and preposterousness (Walter Benjamin, Georges Didi-Huberman, Mieke Bal). On the one hand then, there is the continuity and perseverance of the pictorial tradition, defined as a certain totality, an enormous repertoire of visual schemata repeatedly applied to articulate historical events; on the other, the continual changing, updating and filtering of history through contemporary visual culture, which shapes contemporary visual memory. Finally, there is a whole set of questions regarding the extent to which the functioning of the visual matrices of memory can be related to a particular historical and geographical range, that is, to Central and Eastern Europe, and whether it is possible to indicate their origin. To what extent are they of a specifically local and regional or Western European and universal character?

The different parts of the book are connected to those aspects of the nexus of images, memories and history which, in our opinion, seem the most significant. The first part, under the title "Forms of Memory and Oblivion", focuses on artistic reflection on time and history, and on artists' attempts to come to grips with historical narratives both as regards their historical features and in terms of dealing with them by means of a particular medium and its temporal dimension.

The second part, "Memory and Identity", is related to frequent attempts, particularly intense in Central and Eastern Europe, to reconstruct memory in connection with changes of borders, political regimes, official alliances and zones of influence, and especially to endeavours to impose some specific political structure on territories which were incredibly complex and diverse in terms of national identity, religion and social composition. In this respect, the function of art and interventions through imagery seems particularly interesting at every level of the social functioning of the image, including in conditions of censorship and the erasure of memory deemed undesirable and hence banned. This is closely related to the question of memorials and monuments and the political significance of public space. As far as memorials are concerned, particularly current is the question of the kind of social remembrance that they should sustain and the images they should use to do so, especially today, when the idea of a monument as a monumental figure placed on a pedestal has lost its relevance and appeal.

The subject of the third part of this book is strictly connected with the memory of communism – its atrocities and crimes, but also images of everyday life under communist regimes. Although the next chapter is devoted to photography as a tool for shaping social memory ("Photography as Testimony"), many essays in this book address popular culture and film as particularly effective visual modes of storing and modelling memory and compare them with historical narratives. In press photography, the digital storage of billions of ready-made pictures, popular TV serials and blockbuster movies, we are witnessing today the endless production of images which exert unprecedented pressure on the forming of historical memory. Perhaps the most important aspect of that pressure is the completeness of cinematographic and photographic images, which leaves no room for what the Polish philosopher Roman Ingarden called "concretisation" in the individual process of response. Such images occupy memory slots so tightly and persuasively that they may acquire iconic value as historical pictures. On the other hand, the fact that digital photos and films can be manipulated ruins their credibility. As Jean Baudrillard tells us, the threat of absolute illusion annuls the relations between the image and reality – in consequence, only in some cases do those two categories overlap.

I am glad that these and similar issues have attracted such great interest among scholars wishing to contribute to this book, and I hope that it will inspire many interesting discussions worth inscribing in our memory.

Part 1

Forms of memory and oblivion

1 Dis-remembered and mis-remembered

A confrontation with failures of cultural memory

Mieke Bal

Introduction: what kind of memory matters?

Memory must be understood as a cultural phenomenon as well as an individual and social one. Although the term "cultural memory" has been quite popular for a few decades now, my assumption for this chapter is that these three aspects of memory cannot be separated. All memories have an individual, a social and a cultural aspect. The distinction is only a matter of emphasis, perspective and interest on the part of the researcher, analyst, or memorising subject. This is logical, since the subjects who remember are also participants in all three of these domains. Moreover, memories have a tripartite temporality. Memory is a connection between the three times of human temporal awareness: the past, in which things happened that the memory engages – or not; the present, in which the act of memorising takes place and into which the remembered content is, so to speak, "retrieved"; and the future, which will be influenced by what the subjects in the present, together and embedded in their cultural environment, remember and do with those memories. The memories that matter are steeped in those tripartite processes. I will focus on "cultural memory"– as I said, this is a focus only; one that brings forward political aspects and the plurality of the subjects involved.[1]

What matters most, when we discuss memories, is those memories that miscarry. That is where the past is not recognised for what the present can and should do with it. This is my topic in this chapter. My contribution addresses cultural memory in its negativity, its failures, and seeks to find hints of solutions. Failure of memory is not so much *forgetting*, a very useful concept we should not "forget" when considering memory; which Aleida Assmann, in her book *Formen des Vergessen*, helpfully sums up as "a filter, as a weapon and as a prerequisite for the creation of new things". Instead, I focus on actively, albeit not necessarily purposely, *repressing* or, in a different view, *disassociating* – in other words, *dis-remembering*, on the one hand; as well as on wilfully *distorting* potentially helpful memories on the other, as *mis-remembering*. Both are devastating, wasteful – missed opportunities for the present and future. I have probed both these negatives in film projects, on which I will call sometimes. During the conference out of which this book emerged, a video installation

DOI: 10.4324/9781003264460-3

8 *Mieke Bal*

was displayed that established a dialogue between these two negative forms of memory. The two failures take shape in the cultural imagination in and with which, humans exist.[2]

The anthropomorphic imagination

The memories at issue here pertain to the cultural domain of art, through which the past is frequently recalled ("cultural heritage"). The *human figure* constitutes the primary subject matter of (figurative) literature and art, although by no means exclusively. In literature, especially narrative, the human figure takes on the propulsion of narrative thrust. As agent or patient, it carries the action that is the motor of the plot. Here, this figure is named *character*. Both figure and character can be seen as figurations: *figurative* in that they embody ideas shaped in forms, and *figures* of anthropomorphic appearance that are, do and appear. It is the convergence of figure and character in their guise of figurations that projects the terms in which we analyse art. A most emblematic manifestation is the recurrence of the self-portrait, and the memoir, autobiography or self-reflexive moments in fiction. I see in the convergence between art and its analysis the work of "the anthropomorphic imagination". This is a tendency to approach cultural artifacts through the lens or frame of frequently unacknowledged anthropomorphic concepts. The tools of analysis are thus made congruent to the objects. One such tendency is the conflation of artwork and the maker's *intention*. Another is the *unification* of the artwork to resemble a unified human being anxious to hold himself or herself together. A third tendency is the "spiritualisation", the de-materialisation or dis-embodiment of art, art-making and viewing or reading. These three tendencies will be obliquely questioned by my discussion of failures of memory.

If we attempt to bracket these three tendencies, an alternative vision of the human figure and agent will appear. The un-reflected conflation between representation of humans, human agency and humans in the flesh can be suspended. The close resemblance of human figure and character to humanity as we live it will not be denied, however. But the closeness of the human figure to bodies, and characters to agents as we know them, can only be accepted conditionally. Indeed, it can even be endorsed as semiotically and aesthetically exciting, but only if we also set them off alongside ourselves through resisting the temptation to automatically identify them by identifying *with* them. Semiotically, that closeness helps imagine solutions to memorial problems humans encounter. Aesthetically, on the basis of sensation, it becomes possible not to identify with, but to *encounter*, in the public space of art, subject-figurations that show, rather than obliterate, what went amiss; what led to dis- or mis-remembering. This alternative is the backdrop of my attempts to *figure*, in video installations, how we can engage and understand the issues of memory outside of the psychological, but instead, with the imagination as our most important tool.

I cast the discussion of memory's failure at the interface between figure and character that the personification of artistic agency comes to enact. In theory, this discussion would open the question of the anthropomorphic imagination through the fragmented, synecdochic body. Body parts deployed as synecdoches dispense mastery over the objects: "voice" (of the narrator), "hand" (of the artist) and "eye" (of the connoisseur/viewer). As we have learned from Barthes and Foucault in the 1960s, all three serve to identify in order to bestow authority on the "owner" of the body part – the "whole" person of which the body part is only a part; that authority that unifies, conflates work with intention, and due to its deceptiveness, de facto *dis*-embodies those figures; in the act, de-materialising the artwork.[3]

Keeping the need to avoid that bestowal of authority in mind, I will primarily probe the anthropomorphic imagination in its disembodying thrust. The operations of an anthropomorphic metaphor that reduces the figure to its "fleshless" essence serve various interests such as realism, rigidified images, exclusion, repression and the exploitation of violence along with the repression of its remembrance. These interests will be countered by proposals for a deployment of the same metaphors in a less anthropomorphic, unified and unifying analysis based on the dispersal of these concepts over all parties of the artistic process. One can think of, respectively, "body", "character", "psyche", "spirit" and "person"; all these not unified, but as a disorderly part of what matters.

These aspects join forces, without unification, in the failed memories I would like to bring to the fore. They enable us to explore the possibility of a *psychoanalytic* approach to art – and what can be more anthropomorphic? – that is neither naïve about the "unconscious" status of the work's "psyche" in a consciously elaborated artwork, especially in our time, nor entangled in the problematic causality and author-centeredness of classical psychoanalytic criticism. The must-read books by Kaja Silverman remain a powerful inspiration for an alternative deployment of psychoanalysis as a mode of reading. The following statement is, for me, emblematic of what a psychoanalytic perspective can contribute outside of the drawbacks of the anthropomorphic imagination:

> If, in trying to make sense of this strange account of unconscious memories, I am unable to avoid attributing to them the status of a subject, that is because subjectivity itself is in its most profound sense nothing other than *a constellation of visual memories* which is struggling to achieve a perceptual form.[4]

The beautiful metaphor of memories struggling to accede to form, hence, *visibility*, converges with psychoanalyst Christopher Bollas's similar metaphor, who applies it to thought, to ideas, not memories:

> I often find that although I am working on an idea without knowing exactly what it is I think, I am engaged in thinking an idea struggling to have me think it.[5]

10   *Mieke Bal*

But to make cultural memory really *work* for a visual aesthetic that helps the plight of the dis-remembered, the last words of Silverman's invocation of visual habitus must be taken up: perceptual form. Ideas, too, must achieve form. This is where the writing we, as academics, curators and students attempt to do to articulate ideas, and the "constellation of visual memories" that we are, as subjects, come together. Perhaps this struggle to achieve perceptible form and articulated thought can also be considered an adequate definition of art. The form of the multiple-screen installation gives shape to that struggle.[6]

Acts of memory

The psyche has been a commonsense anthropomorphism; interpretations based on untheorised psychology are pervasive in scholarship on art and literature. Following the lead of the two psychoanalytic theorists quoted earlier, I propose to examine what is possible if we displace the anthropomorphism of the psyche in favor of a more aesthetic metaphor while remaining, or not, within the psychoanalytic paradigm. "To be inside someone else's memory" (Silverman's phrase) is an act of solidarity. It is the impossible formulation that connects the psyche to no one in particular – no biographical author, no specific audience, no hypothetical mind of the text, so that the vacant position is open for every cultural participant to endorse. This is a *memorial* equivalent to the concept of fiction. I argue for this conception of cultural memory art, with and through the figures in these videos, asking how the viewer comes to concretely partake of the direction of the memory-alias-artwork, and how this affects visual analysis of and for cultural memory. The title of a collective 1999 volume suggests that the best concept concerning memory is not memory as an abstraction but "acts of memory".[7]

This is a concept of the kind I have been discussing in my book *Travelling Concepts in the Humanities*. This phrase-concept comprises a set of characteristics that, together, form a mini-theory that makes the concept a suitable methodological basis for analysis. With the term "mini-theory" I mean that the concept implies the elements and the syntax that form a theory; the concept can be seen as a summary of a theory. This makes it possible to use it for analysis in precise ways to reach its political potential, as simple words cannot. Paul Patton explains: "Philosophical concepts . . . fulfill their intrinsically political vocation by counter-effectuating existing states of affairs and referring them back to the virtual realm of becoming". The Deleuzian verb form "becoming" resonates perfectly with the two "struggles" just quoted. It finds its basis in the tripartite temporality of memory.[8]

The concept of "acts of memory" also seeks to be specific in that it links memory to narrative. As psychoanalysts Onno van der Hart and Bessel van der Kolk formulate it, quoting Freud's contemporary Pierre Janet, "Memory is an action: essentially, it is the action of telling a story". Traumatic memory thus gives insight, through contrast, into the formation of "normal", narrative memory. This implication of narrative in the concept is relevant for the art

Dis-remembered and mis-remembered   11

form of video installation. More importantly, it is crucial for the understanding of its failure in traumatic (non-) memory.[9]

Thus, the concept encompasses, while privileging the middle one, the three kinds of memory I have disentangled in the introduction to *Acts of memory*:

> Automatic, routine memory, that is as crucial to our everyday functioning as it is uninteresting to bring to consciousness. If such unreflected habitual memories are worth mentioning, it is to distinguish them from narrative memories.
>
> Narrative ("normal") memory specifically recalls events from the past that have some bearing on or relevance for the present, and suggest possibility for the future.
>
> Traumatic memories remain present for the subject with particular vividness and/or totally resist integration. In both cases, they cannot become narratives, either because the traumatizing events are mechanically reenacted as drama rather than synthetically narrated by the memorizing agent who "masters" them, or because they remain "outside" the subject.[10]

With the phrase "acts of memory", I seek to condense the mini-theory that turns "memory" from a word into a concept. Memory, this theory says, is a *verb*, a transitive one; and its mode is active. It is something we do; it has a subject and an object. And that act takes place in the *present*. The phrase thus encapsulates a theory of memory; hence, its status as a concept. This twofold characteristic – activity and present tense – in turn imports into the concept aspects of cultural utterances such as performativity and duration. The former implies that the act of memory has consequences for its "second persons" – which may be the memorising subject herself or others who are affected by the memory; the latter, in that it takes, occupies or gives *time*.

This engages viewers of these videos to insert themselves into the thoughts, psyches or fictions of the figures presented, in an interactive mode. With this conception of the act of memory, there is no better place to seek inspiration for this thought-on-the-move than the world of art. Indeed, along with inspiring philosophers and scholars, I find in the process of analysing as well as making artworks that the refinements, the assessments of the consequences and potential and the politics of memory come to the fore. The video installation, as an art form, comprises figurative images, and these, whether or not they convey movement technically, are *moving* by definition. One of the aspects of movement is *affect*. This moving quality is activated in space and mediates effects that are not bound to the traditional ways of meaning making. It is in the intersection between movement and space that the political potential of figuration in installation resides. Video presents movement, and installation, space. The question of how this mediation occurs refers us to the bond between meaning and affect. Images do not evince a one-on-one relationship between signs and meaning. I deploy the phrase "thinking in film" to unpack these connections in discrepancy.[11]

Failing the past

With this chapter and the installation that accompanied the lecture, I present, for reflection, a confrontation between two failures of cultural memory to meet the needs of a number of individuals but, as a consequence, of society as whole. The first of these failures, shaped in one part of the installation, derived from the film project *A Long History of Madness*, based on *Mère Folle* by French psychoanalyst Françoise Davoine (1998). In this book, the author develops a theory of the analytical treatment of trauma-induced psychosis – something Freud claimed to be impossible – using fiction as a mode of thinking.[12]

We – co-director Michelle Williams Gamaker and I – call this "theoretical fiction". This term is borrowed from Freud, who used it to defend his bizarrely speculative, indeed totally fictional book *Totem and Taboo*, a fiction that enabled him to discover the Oedipus complex – I am tempted to see it as an early instance of "artistic research". Davoine's book and the film project based on it have acts of memory at their heart: the memories of old, medieval traditions of revolutionary street theatre; the memories of violence, in wars and within homes, sometimes going back several generations; failed memories, in the acts of negligence of collective forgetting as looking the other way; and memories of dreams and delusions that help insight to become possible when social companions listen, believe and support.

As an act of inter-temporal dialogue, we installed a version of this work as an interventionist exhibition in the Freud Museum London, where a monitor at the foot of Freud's iconic couch performed a visual dialogue with the master of psychoanalysis. As we visually argued, the condition of proving Freud wrong and setting past wounds right is that the analyst behaves like a *therapôn*, or companion, mate or buddy, *with* whom the traumatised subject can come to achieve narrative form. In the video installed at the foot of the couch, the analyst and patient are sitting side by side on a couch – a set-up strongly at odds with Freud's clinical method of which it is a counter-method yet remaining within the psychoanalytic paradigm. This is the important difference between the propositions "counter-" and "anti-", the latter implying wholesale rejection.[13]

To aid the recollection of the dis-remembered without falling back into a disingenuous and exploitative identification, then, I advocate the deployment of anachronism to connect, in the inter-temporality that is indispensable for memory, not only times but also experiences and forms of expression. Sometimes, a contemporary perspective can bring to life something we might not otherwise have seen. A simple example is the contemporary idea of "music therapy", in two canonical old-master paintings, a Rubens and a Rembrandt, in our installation *Anacronismos* in the Guggenheim Bilbao Museum in 2010. The physiognomy of Rembrandt's *Saul* depicts paranoia according to 17th-century iconography, which Rubens's does not. But also, David's hand displays "music-making" and, together with his barely outlined, *de facto* blind face, attunes the viewer to look *synaesthetically* so as to "see hearing". Then, look

Figure 1.1 Installation in Freud Museum London, *Saying It*, curated by Joanne Morra, The Freud Museum, London, 20 September 20–19 November 2012

Source: photo by Michelle Williams Gamaker

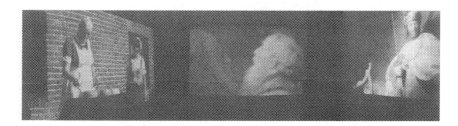

Figure 1.2 Installation *Anacronismos*, Guggenheim Bilbao Museum, for exhibition *The Golden Age of Dutch and Flemish Painting from the Städel Museum*, curated by Jochen Sander, 7 October 2010–23 January 2011

Source: photo by Elan Gamaker

at the tense fist with which Saul holds the lance, the other hand holding the chair's arm as if preparing to get up and kill David.

All this fits perfectly in the iconographic tradition within which this painting was made. But then, these gestures have something cinematic: predicting an action to come, they prefigure a *moving* image, in the two senses of that qualifier. Then, it becomes easier to see Saul's head also turning away, the eyes looking back. Suspense is produced, and we hold our breath, awaiting the violence to break out. And if Saul remains still, it is not only because painting is a still medium. Also, narratively, the music calms him down; he is still suspicious,

14   *Mieke Bal*

and the threat is not over yet. All that we can imagine, and hence, recall. This is a clear case of a productive anachronism – that historiographical madness.[14]

The tension between visibility and invisibility, parallel to that between remembering and forgetting-repressing, raises the question if there can be an "iconography of madness" – one that navigates the fine line between stereotyping and failing to see, while avoiding an appropriating, sentimentalising identification. Unhindered by the logic of the narrowly practical considerations of everyday life, the straightjacket of habits and routine – what we call "normal" – madness and art both are capable of transgressing the boundaries of which they thus demonstrate the arbitrariness.

The other kind of failed memory concerns the neglect of the crucial importance, for today, in the age of new, "democratically elected" dictators and the dominance of communication in Twitter-word-bites at the expense of thinking, of the contributions of earlier thinkers. These figures from the past came up with then-new ideas we consider too quickly and easily "obsolete" and strive to move "beyond". This is our failure to acknowledge that memory does not belong to the past, but to the present in view of the future. In this case, we "mis-remember" the contributions of 17th-century philosopher Descartes to rational thought, by declaring ourselves hastily "post-Cartesian". By reifying the strenuous thinking efforts of the first rationalist philosopher of the modern age, René Descartes, and reducing them to a dualism that, in fact, he spent his life challenging, we have mis-remembered what he could contribute to remedy the sad situation that we have allowed the world to slip into.

This constitutes another vague of collective madness – the current rejection of reason in favour of a fanatic othering, with the abduction of the word "radical", formerly indicating endeavours to go all the way, to firmly and consistently follow the logic of a position, such as Descartes attempted. This word, before our very eyes, has been transformed and is now a synonym of "terrorist" – the terrorist being the cultural other. The traumatised mad and the "father of rationalism" are not so "radically" different as we assume, if only we bother to examine the life & works with a more open mind. In the installation *Dis-remembered & Misremembered*, I combined these two neglected streams of memory. And the first thing we noticed is that Descartes, too, was subject to psychotic episodes, which totally undermines the opposition we have based our view of his thoughts on.[15]

Analysing the heritage of the traumatised "mad" and Descartes's work audiovisually, it was my hope that, encouraged by the installation to actively engage with the characters, visitors would literally perform acts of cultural memory in the present, recalling the violence that has produced madness, and the great efforts of thought that can counter the resulting devastation. This temporal reversal, which I have called "preposterous", is perhaps the most literal enactment of the theoretical concept of *acts of memory in the present*. And, since they are not alone in the galleries where the installation confronts, surrounds or interpolates them, visitors also enact the social aspect of such acts. In this I seek to heed the warning by Walter Benjamin in his *Theses on the Philosophy of*

History, that for me, condenses the mini-theory implied in the visual side of the concept of cultural memory and its political relevance in the most convincing way: "[E]very image of the past that is not recognized by the present as one of its own concerns threatens to disappear irretrievably".[16]

For a different Descartes

Through the presentations of "mad" people, I have attempted to establish a connection between a past that happened long ago and elsewhere, and a present here-and-now. The endeavour is to enable cultural memory to be active and politically productive by distinguishing between *guilt* and *responsibility*. This distinction, proposed by Spinoza, eliminates an unproductive postcolonial guilt and replaces it with contemporary responsibility in and for the migratory culture that is an affective after-effect of colonialism. That *after-affect* is what needs to be remembered.

Spinoza's distinction is explained in the most useful book on his thought I have encountered, Moira Gatens and Genevieve Lloyd's lucid *Collective Imaginings*. I learned the importance of the distinction from making this video work, and this distinction helped me understand the political aspect of acts of memory as based on responsibility in the present. Here is a patchwork of some passages of their book concerning responsibility:

> "Spinozistic responsibility" is derived from the philosopher's concept of self as social, and consists of projecting presently felt responsibilities "back into a past which itself becomes determinate only from the perspective of what lies in the future of that past – in our present." Taking seriously the "temporal dimensions of human consciousness" includes endorsing the "multiple forming and reforming of identities over time and within the deliverances of memory and imagination at any one time".[17]

I find it useful to keep thought and art in each other's company. Creativity and the imagination are essential to both.

I chose Descartes when in my various readings I encountered the empty qualifier "post-Cartesian" one time too many, without any further explanation and specification. I felt disconsolate about the lack of thinking in texts supposed to be thoughtful, and I decided to look again at the work of this master of thought. Kyoo Lee's 2013 book (see footnote 15), which, alas, came to my attention after the fact, supported my sense that Descartes's memory would gain value once his madness was recognised. I was interested less in his ideas than in the way he did his thinking. I wondered if it is possible to show past thought-as-process visually, to make it accessible for everyone in the present, so as to undo the mis-remembering that made the important ideas and the social processes that generated them, invisible. I took up the project to show, in film, how thinking happens, and to do that through thinking "in" film, as in a foreign language.[18]

16 *Mieke Bal*

Figure 1.3 Descartes "mad", played by Thomas Germaine, in *Reasonable Doubt*
Source: *photo by Przemo Wojciechowski 2015*

The mis-remembering occurs in our habit of thinking in linear chronology. We speak of influence but not about the need to be in dialogue with others for thought to be even possible. Also, thinking is not done in one single way, or mode. Moreover, thinking, in spite of the alleged but misconstrued meaning of the *Cogito*, does involve the body, and moods. It also needs places, where the process can happen. The possibility to see them in installation, sculpturally dispersed throughout a space, makes the idea of "thinking *in* film" spatially concrete and precludes attempts to turn the pieces into a (linear) biography, where the anthropomorphic imagination would be allowed to take over. The Kraków-based professor of literature and cultural studies, Roma Sendyka, saw the relevance of this view and organised the première of the film in the festival "Philosophy and Film" and curated the exhibition. Wherever in the scenes one is focusing, what one has seen before becomes an amalgamation of memories. Thought, including memory, I propose, works that way, rather than in linear fashion. Each scene experiments differently with expressing the inexpressible, the subtleties and ambivalences of reason and emotion together, outside of the narrative impulse, in the process of thinking.[19]

Descartes left Western thought with a burden and a treasure. The burden is a misconstrued dualistic tradition. He accepted the dualism of the Catholic Church but fought against it all his life, torn by doubt, because it is not reasonable. The treasure is a decisive advance in rational thought that, precisely, did not excise the body nor religion for that matter. The (in)famous *Cogito* can be interpreted in the opposite direction, as an attempt to embody and *subjectify* thought. This is especially clear when we look back from his last book, *The Passions of the Soul* (1649), and see the ongoing struggle against dualism in different episodes of his life. Moreover, he left a more specific treasure. Descartes dedicated that book to another woman friend-by-correspondence, Princess Elisabeth of Bohemia. This woman had been traumatised by childhood events of a political and economic order. As she writes in her letters, Descartes truly helped her overcome a chronic affliction caused by the trauma.[20]

Elisabeth pushed him on his thoughts. Although they never met as a trio, Descartes at some point asked Kristina to help Elisabeth. I use that anecdote for the far-reaching claim that through his mode of thinking, specifically thinking *with* the other person, he "invented" psychoanalysis, in a post-Freudian form that returns that theory to re-becoming a true social science. This theory that so eminently integrates body and mind, as it was later developed, emerged not only from Descartes's thoughts about the interaction between body and mind as exposed in his book, but also from the solidarity with Elisabeth that he, as one who was also traumatised in childhood, felt and demonstrated. This also has implications for our contemporary feminism that makes us too easily consider gender relations in the past as hopelessly exclusive. The two women who thought *with* him and helped him think with them, stand for the aspect of thinking that counters the myth of the thinker as loner.

I see Descartes's thinking process in the cracks between the certainties he also proffered, when bracketing his doubt in his reasoning. To help overcome them while "recognizing it by the present as one of our own concerns", in Benjamin's line, I looked at the discrepancies between the Descartes we have abused and the

Figure 1.4 The first meeting of Descartes and Kristina at Nieborów Castle, Poland
Source: photo by Przemo Wojciechowski 2015 (cropped)

one whose meetings with others were the point of origin of the struggle for a non-dualistic mode of thinking. Conversely, Queen Kristina, on her part, was not only capricious but also philosophical, constantly thinking about life, and the bearer of the after-effects of this different Descartes. And as a conversation partner, she asks the questions the philosopher needs to ponder to make headway in his process.

Doubt for solidarity

My interest in doing this project was to remember the complexity of the rationalism these figures represent. The productivity of the dialectical relationship between reason and a certain kind of madness in both Descartes and Kristina was rarely fully recognised. I want to suggest that reason and "madness" can go very well together. Madness is the form doubt takes when it is cut off from the social bonds based on respect and dialogue, so that we can turn mis-remembering into a memorial solidarity that recognises and thus, *narrativises* trauma. This act can defeat the dis-remembering so that we can actually "cure" or, retrospectively, "make sense of" the madness. The persistent deceptive and arrogant progressivism in our thinking is fond of the qualifier "post-Cartesian", as something we have happily left behind. But it is that "post-" thinking itself, as well as the overuse of the phrase, that betrays us as, I'd say, pre-Cartesian; as failing to integrate doubt into reason. Had we really listened to and looked

Figure 1.5 Elisabeth (Johanna ter Steege) consults Kristina (Marja Skaffari) after Descartes's death (fiction)

Source: *photo by Thijs Vissia 2015; location: Palazzo Corsini, Rome*

Dis-remembered and mis-remembered 19

at him, endorsing our own madness as part of instead of rejection of reason, that vexed preposition post-itself would be used with more (Cartesian) doubt. Using audio-visual images to put this on the table is my attempt to bring thought and images together in supporting each other.[21]

The bond between movement and the image is not limited to the moving image of film, although the latter is an overdetermined instance of it. To understand why and how still images also move, the best resource remains the work of Henri Bergson (1859–1941), especially *Matter and Memory* (1991 [1896]). This "essay on the relationship between body and mind", as its subtitle has it, helps understand Descartes's search for such a relationship. It starts with the thesis that perception is not a construction but a *selection* the subject makes in view of her own interests; an act *of* the body and *for* the body. The selection that perception is, takes place in the present. Not only the interests of the perceiver motivate it, but also her memories. Bergson writes, "memory [images], laden with the whole of the past, respond . . . to the appeal of the present state" (168). At the end of the book, Bergson sums it up in these words:

> In concrete perception memory intervenes, and the subjectivity of sensible qualities is due precisely to the fact that our consciousness, which begins by being only memory, prolongs a plurality of moments into each other, contracting them into a single intuition.[22]

That coexistence of different moments (or memories) has a spatial aspect to it. This timespace is given shape in video installation in the simultaneous presence of – and, hence, the simultaneous movement on – multiple screens. It complicates narrative without cancelling it.

Reminiscent of Descartes's unsettlement in *The Passions of the Soul*, Bergson considers the body to be a material entity, and he consequently sees perception as a material practice. This makes Bergson's conception of the image synonymous with the moving image. This is a deeper level on which images move; it comes closer to affect. The image itself – not its support – is both moving and material. It implies that it is plural and functional. It *does* something. In 1907, Bergson proposed yet another aspect of movement in the image: when the perception image, as Deleuze called it, morphs into an affect-image and makes the perceiver develop the *readiness to act*. This readiness lies at the heart of the political potential of the image, film and video installation. The combination of these forms of movement is the possibility film offers when we try to think visually, in this case, "think *in* film", in order to make the dis-remembered memorable, and let the mis-remembered guide us to what we need most urgently: solidarity.[23]

Notes

1 Here are just a few important publications in this field, but there is much more. Aleida Assmann, *Formen des Vergessen*, ed. C. Raudvere (Göttingen: Wallstein, 2015); *Contested Memories and the Demands of the Past: History Cultures in the Modern Muslim World* (New York: Springer, 2016); *Cultural Memory and the Construction of Identities*, ed. D.

20 *Mieke Bal*

Ben-Amos and L. Weissberg (Detroit, MI: Wayne State University Press, 1999); Ernst van Alphen, *Caught by History: Holocaust Effects in Contemporary Art, Literature and Theory* (Stanford, CA: Stanford University Press, 1997); Marianne Hirsch, *The Generation of Post-Memory: Writing and Visual Culture After the Holocaust* (New York: Columbia University Press, 2012).

2 The installation combined screens and photographs from *A Long History of Madness,* Mieke Bal and Michelle Williams Gamaker (Cinema Suitcase), Theoretical Fiction, 120', 2011, and *Reasonable Doubt: Scenes From Two Lives,* Mieke Bal, Docu-drama/ theoretical fiction, 2016. For more information about these projects, see www.mieke bal.org/artworks/films/a-long-history-of-madness/ and www.miekebal.org/artworks/films/reasonable-doubt/.

3 The two most famous articles on this critique of the author: Roland Barthes, *The Death of the Author* in *The Rustle of Language,* ed. R. Barthes (New York: Hill and Wang, 1986), 49–55; Michel Foucault, *What is an Author?* in *Textual Strategies: Perspectives in Post-Structuralist Criticism,* ed. Josué V. Harari, trans. Donald Bouchard and Sherry Simon (Ithaca: Cornell University Press, 1979), 41–60.

4 Kaja Silverman, *World Spectators* (Stanford, CA: Stanford University Press, 2000), 89. Emphasis added.

5 Christopher Bollas, *The Shadow of the Object: Psychoanalysis of the Unthought Known* (New York: Columbia University Press, 1987), 10.

6 Again, Roland Barthes was an early proponent on video installation over theatre film. See Roland Barthes, *Leaving the Movie Theater,* in *The Rustle of Language,* trans. Richard Howard (New York: Hill and Wang, 1986), 345–346. See also Mieke Bal, *Thinking in Film: The Politics of Video Installation According to Eija-Liisa Ahtila* (London: Bloomsbury, 2013). In an important book, Eugenie Brinkema argues that affects, too, have, or seek to achieve, form. See *The Forms of the Affects* (Durham, NC: Duke University Press, 2014).

7 *Acts of Memory: Cultural Recall in the Present,* ed. Mieke Bal, Jonathan Crewe, and Leo Spitzer (Hanover, NH: University Press of New England, 1999).

8 Paul Patton, *Deleuzian Concepts: Philosophy, Colonization, Politics* (Stanford: Stanford University Press, 2010), 139; Mieke Bal, *Travelling Concepts in the Humanities: A Rough Guide* (Toronto: University of Toronto Press, 2002).

9 Onno van der Hart and Bessel van der Kolk, "The Intrusive Past: The Flexibility of Memory and the Engraving of Trauma", in *Trauma: Explorations in Memory,* ed. C. Caruth (Baltimore: Johns Hopkins University Press, 1995), 158–183.

10 See footnote 7 for reference.

11 On affect as a concept for analysing art and literature, see the recent collective volume *How to Do Things with Affects: Affective Triggers in Aesthetic Forms and Cultural Practices,* ed. Ernst van Alphen and Tomáš Jirsa (Leiden and Boston: Brill |Rodopi, 2019).

12 Françoise Davoine, *Mother Folly: A Tale,* trans. Judith C. Miller (Stanford: Stanford University Press, 2014), xiii–xxiv.

13 For more on that exhibition, *Saying It,* curated by Joanne Morra, The Freud Museum, London, 20 September–19 November 2012, see www.miekebal.org/artworks/exhibitions/saying-it/.

14 The low technical quality of this photo is adequate to the resolution on the screens of the installation.

15 For a critical reflection on this abduction of the word "radical", see Marie-José Mondzain, *Confiscation des mots, des images et des temps. Pour une autre radicalité* (Paris: Les livres qui libèrent, 2017). An important assessment of Descartes's "madness" as a source of his philosophical genius is Kyoo Lee, *Reading Descartes Otherwise: Blind, Mad, Dreamy, and Bad* (New York: Fordham University Press, 2013).

16 Walter Benjamin, "5th Thesis on the Philosophy of History", in *Illuminations: Essays and Reflecions,* edited and with an introduction by Hannah Arendt, trans. Harry Zohn (New York: Schocken, 1968), 155–200.

17 Moira Gatens and Genevieve Lloyd, *Collective Imaginings: Spinoza, Past and Present* (London and New York: Routledge, 1999), 81.
18 Before you wonder about it: the phrase "post-Cartesian" is so frequently used that it makes no sense to cite specific sources.
19 For more on the installation and the exhibition in Kraków, see www.miekebal.org/artworks/exhibitions/reasonable-doubt/.
20 On the relationship between Descartes and Princess Elisabeth, see Yaëlle Sibony-Malpertu, *Une liaison philosophique. Du thérapeutique entre Descartes et la princesse Élisabeth de Bohême* (Paris: Stock, 2012).
21 For a much more extensive interpretation of the figure of Descartes, see Mieke Bal, "Thinking in Film", in *Thinking in the World*, ed. Jill Bennett (London: Bloomsbury, 2019).
22 Henri Bergson, *Matter and Memory*, trans. N. M. Paul and W. S. Palmer (New York: Zone Books, 1991 [1896]), 218–219.
23 Henri Bergson, *Creative Evolution*, trans. A. Mitchell (Lanham, MD: University Press of America, 1983 [1907]).

2 Matejko: how did he do it?

Wojciech Suchocki

The title of this chapter probably promises too much and raises expectations that cannot be met. Unravelling the secrets of the structure and impact of even one painting by Jan Matejko is a task that goes beyond the confines of a single chapter. I will try – based on a single painting and its many varied aspects seen as particularly significant – to initiate reflection on Matejko's concept of the historical painting.

Before I present my observations on one of the works from the main cycle of his great historical canvases, painted over three decades of his life (he died at the age of 55), I will recall, as a kind of a long motto, a comprehensive, oft-quoted record of his "programmatic" statement.

> It may, or rather must, be true that a painting can present only one material moment of some issue, but it should conceive and present this moment so that it expresses the historical incident in its entirety, with all the spiritual factors and elements that informed the event. However, rarely can we find in history a moment so completely characteristic that it would embrace and give a full account of the historical process and fact. An historical incident does not take place abruptly, out of the blue; it is triggered by a whole process of aspirations and actions of various people who were present or, conversely, did not happen to be in attendance at the moment and in the place where the event occurred. In truth, all these people acted as the forces that triggered it and brought it about, even from a distance of time or of place. Therefore, the painting, which is to show the incident in its entirety, has every right to, and indeed ought to, depict all these forces within its frame. Only then will the historical painting be a truly autonomous image rather than a slavish chronicling illustration; it will then be a focus and an autonomous rendition of what is dispersed in the chronicles and yet belongs to the entire event. Then the painter will assume the role of an artist-as-historian, a sort of judge of both the fact itself and of all the forces and elements at work within it. . . . I cannot work as I would like to. I do not compose and do not paint in accordance with my understanding of the artistic conditions of a perfect painting. I am seeking far more important matters – I am seeking the expression of a character or the

DOI: 10.4324/9781003264460-4

Matejko. How did he do it? 23

clarity of a group more than the purity of the line and the beauty of the arrangement.[1]

And now – to the point.

Rejtan, the name of a deputy from the constituency of Novogrodek during the 1773 Parliament, or Sejm, has for a long time been part of the common parlance and has become, in rhetorical terms, an antonomasia, a proper name used to define a particular type of person or behaviour. This was due to his protest against the adoption by the Polish Sejm of treaties approving the First Partition of Poland by Russia, Prussia and Austria. Tadeusz Rejtan, who committed suicide seven years after his protest, quickly became a mythical figure. He was honoured by the Four-Year Sejm, the activities of which represented a significant attempt at regaining sovereignty and reforming the state, frustrated by the reaction of two neighbouring countries and the Second Partition of Poland in 1793. Two years later, as a result of the Third Partition, Poland disappeared from the map. The figure of Rejtan was immortalised in national memory by the greatest Polish poet, Adam Mickiewicz, in his epic poem *Pan Tadeusz*. Let us note at this point that Mickiewicz may have been Matejko's greatest inspiration.

The ample literature on Matejko's oeuvre has primarily focused on the principal motifs of his paintings, especially on their relation to knowledge of the author's time and subsequent history. Texts on Matejko's art have less often addressed the importance of the "historical incidents" which Matejko highlighted through his artistic choices as a self-styled "artist-as-historian".

The painting *Rejtan* is a case in point (Figure 2.1). On the one hand, following the artist's indications, critics and viewers referred to the named figures and pondered their roles in the painting; on the other hand, they discussed the context behind the painting, the debates that it generated and its status among assessments of the nature of the event that it depicts. The question arises as to whether all the structural components which informed the painting's meaning were considered.

In such a brief chapter, it is impossible to give an account of the history of the work's reception, to describe its construction or even to offer short presentations and descriptions of the 30 persons participating in the scene. Every single painting by Matejko, especially those of the grand historical series, offers food for thought worthy of a separate book. I will try to provide a gloss to this history, focusing on the elements which have not been scrutinised before, but which I consider to be worthy of the utmost attention. For instance, in the epoch-making book written over 100 years ago by Stanisław Witkiewicz, a painter and eminent critic, we can read about the impossibility of producing a historical painting precisely in connection with *Rejtan*:

> Painting, fatalistically doomed to present just a single moment, is incapacitated and powerless with respect to the questions addressed by history. Painting, including historical painting, made use of allegories, symbols

Figure 2.1 Jan Matejko, *Rejtan at Sejm of 1773*
Source: *1866, 282 x 487, oil on canvas, Warsaw, Royal Castle*

or even legends in the work itself, in order to supplement its message. Matejko, whose mind and talent were perfectly suited to comprehending concrete facts and tangible things, clear and evident forms, wrestled with this limited character of the means of his art, wrestled and often marred his paintings or included some naïve concepts which were supposed to supplement that part of the historical content which seethed in his mind and that which churned in his sensitive heart. . . . This time [in *Rejtan*], however, despite the mental struggle with the artistic means, the painting is perfect. Matejko's most exquisite talents include his mastery over the expression of human emotions and his ability to sense with the utmost intensity that which may occur in a human soul touched by a tragic clash between passion and the outside world; this ability resonates from each and every figure.

Matejko expressed only what the medium of painting allowed him to do: the relationship of a particular individual to a particular crowd. This relationship was based on certain emotions; the rest is beyond the realm of painting and the person to whom the entry "Rejtan" in a catalogue means nothing at all, one who cannot know or feel what we, Poles, can feel; the French actually thought that the valiant Poles were dismissing a Turkish envoy.

Yet this incomprehensibility of the anecdote of an historical painting, albeit an argument against historical painting, is not the fault of the painting and does not reduce its artistic value. If we struck all incomprehensible paintings from the list of masterpieces, few would survive. The entire

Matejko. How did he do it? 25

ceiling of the Sistine Chapel and all of Raphael, apart from the portraits, would be classified as incomprehensible curios.[2]

We might try and reflect on whether Witkiewicz did not omit some means of overcoming the difficulties under discussion available to painting; perhaps Matejko used them.

Let us recall the fundamental circumstances of the painting's origins. As the painter Izydor Jabłoński, a friend of Matejko's, noted, most likely under the powerful impact of the photographs of the casualties of the incidents in Warsaw in 1861 (the brutal crushing of demonstrations on 27 February, which killed five people, and 8 April, which left several hundred dead), Matejko decided to change his planned subjects. "I will start with the wounds", he thought.[3] This decision contributed to the painting of a triad: *The Sermon of Skarga* (1864), the unfinished *Polonia – Poland Bound* (1864) and *The Fall of Poland – Rejtan*. Another painting produced at that time was *Stańczyk*, combining a self-portrait with a portrait of a wise 16th-century court jester. *Skarga* catapulted Matejko to fame; the 26-year-old painter rose to the top and saw an opportunity to implement his great intention of rendering history in painting. *Rejtan* – much as it was admired – was met with scathing criticism.

With the proviso that the ensuing remarks are necessarily of a fragmentary nature, let us first note that Matejko, as usual, apart from choosing the event and learning as much as possible about it, had to channel that knowledge into a painting. This entailed preparing a list of the figures, so that the painting could depict, in his own words, "the historical incident in its entirety" (in line with this reasoning, the painting includes those not actually present at the event: King Stanislaus Augustus of Poland, the Russian envoy Repnin and Szczęsny Potocki; Franciszek Salezy Potocki had died the previous year, and the portrait of Catherine the Great was not displayed in the Deputies' Room at the Royal Castle in Warsaw). Yet it also called for numerous decisions related to the painting medium, not necessarily familiar to those interpreting the work.

This translation of knowledge about an event into a painting is always facilitated by the formulas and ways of representation which, stored in the memory, suddenly reveal their usefulness. Most importantly, this flash of illumination allows one to discern and sense the registers of significance which they possess and which can come into play in the new pictorial entity being constructed.

Let us start with a seemingly insignificant example, an illustration by Moritz von Schwind for Eduard Duller's book *Erzherzog Carl von Oesterreich*, published in Vienna in 1847 (Figure 2.2). The theme is not closely related to Matejko's painting (although Dumouriez arresting the Convention deputies, the history of this figure and the contemporary setting of the event [1793] call for reflection as well). First, as an illustration of a historical incident, this example gives us a hint of how Matejko looked for the sources of his painting – not only visual tokens of the era depicted in the work, but historical illustration in general. We encounter examples where Matejko does not refer to something closely related to the fact to be depicted but, rummaging through historiographic texts, which

Figure 2.2 Moritz von Schwind, *Dumouriez arrests the members of Convention*, in Edouard Duller, *Erzherzog Carl von Oesterreich*, 1847, p. 137

he leafed through rather than read (as he did not know foreign languages), finds inspiration for the construction of his painting.

More importantly, this illustration includes both the motifs used in the *Rejtan* painting and the idea for the layout of the scene, which will prove useful in Matejko's work from *Stańczyk* and *Skarga* onwards. As to the motifs, the passage to the adjacent space, drawing on the motif of the soldiers standing there, the compact group of three figures and finally the gesture of an outstretched arm, although transformed, clearly point to this inconspicuous illustration. As to the scene direction, we may suspect that we are witnesses here to the stabilisation of Matejko's imagery and the way the painting will open up for him as a potential field of action; we can observe how he will develop the surface and space of the painting and invest them with a variety of meanings.

Matejko allows the viewer to first see the space as if it were the continuation of the space in front of the painting: the slanting floor (the slanting pattern of the carpet in *The Sermon of Skarga*) intensifies the impression. However, hardly does the viewer walk a few paces forward than he will encounter an obstacle, and at the same time a suspension of the significance of spatial recognition. The path is obstructed by a crowd of figures amassed on the surface, as if projected onto a screen, and the further path to meaning entails the recognition of their mutual relations. The path leads to the feet of three full-length figures of "traitors". The foreground is filled on one side by Rejtan, thrown onto the floor, and on the other by an upturned armchair tucked on the edge of the painting space. The chair is most likely that of the Speaker of the Sejm; Rejtan tried to sit there, but it was swept up and overturned by the delia of Franciszek Salezy Potocki, who left the room as a token of protest against those acting as the authority of Parliament. We cannot omit the telling presence and materiality of the piece of furniture and the objects scattered across the floor.

Both the object in the foreground and the properties of the composition make us consider in relation to *Rejtan* another painting: *Forced Recruitment* by Artur Grottger (Figure 2.3), the opening panel (if we disregard the title page) in the *Polonia* series of 1863, inspired directly by the outbreak of the January Uprising (which Matejko supported as he best could, shipping arms to Langiewicz's camp, a unit of the insurgent army, with the historian and writer Józef Szujski). Matejko admired Grottger and invoked him more often than has been identified thus far. So the overturned chair is a kind of *repoussoire* that opens up a shallow space, a metonym of violence and the violation of domestic concord. At the same time, the space becomes enclosed, and the inward rush is offset by the motion along the surface, from one side of the field to the other. This motion is driven by the central figure, whose appearance is marked not only by a solemn gesture, but by his concise, simple and clear silhouette. The figure links what takes place both within the room and behind the open door. What is more, it sets in motion the narrative and arranges the components of the scene into the outcome of what has taken place, of what is taking place and of what will occur, which slightly reduces the register of the deficiencies of painting indicated by Witkiewicz.

Figure 2.3 Artur Grottger, *Forced Recruitment* (cycle "Polonia"), 1863
Source: cardboard, black and white pencil, Budapest, Szeptmuveszeti Museum

Matejko not only adopted Grottger's way of arranging the foreground and opening a second space, but appreciated the way he depicted the central figure, especially since he had noticed these elements in Grottger earlier, namely, in Panel 4 of *Warsaw II* (Figure 2.4), a series produced in 1862. Although the cycle was quickly bought by a private collector, this panel was reproduced in a magazine published in Vienna. Its depiction of a *Widow* foreshadows the figure from *Forced Recruitment*, or rather uses the expression of inscribing a figure into the simple shape of a right-angled triangle, with its internal dynamic divisions which show the figure not so much standing near the column as being pushed across the space of the church.

In many of his paintings, Matejko highlights some figures by inscribing them in a simple shape. In *Rejtan*, he chose for such a procedure the figure of Potocki the father (Figure 2.5), leaving the gathering with a flourish. Potocki, standing out from the crowd of figures, stressing the juxtaposition between Rejtan and the "traitors", is the third focus of the event and the only figure who looks at and extends his hands to the viewer. While nearly all the figures, especially those to Potocki's right, direct their gaze towards the depth of the painting, as if

Matejko. How did he do it? 29

Figure 2.4 Artur Grottger, *Widow* (cycle "Warsaw II"), 1863
Source: *cardboard, black and white pencil, Budapest, Szeptmuveszeti Museum*

following Poniński's gesture, he looks in the opposite direction, and the trail of his robe projects towards the viewer, under his feet, objects that provide a commentary on the scene. Once we discern the inscribing of this figure into the shape of Grottger's widow, we tend to link the painting first of all with its era, with what was taking place there and then, with Matejko's reasons for painting this picture, and we also impress onto this figure the stigma of widowhood

30 *Wojciech Suchocki*

and thus impart it with a more general meaning: Potocki is losing his son, and they resemble a cleft tree trunk, with a wedge of crowded, confronting heads between them. The figures exhibit a host of different reactions; Rejtan's companion Korsak has Matejko's facial features, and the boy in a cap with a sabre is usually interpreted as a harbinger of a future awakening and struggle.

Finally, let us focus on Rejtan. For Poles, the familiarity with the painting in our imagination makes us see his conduct as something natural and obvious. Not only does Rejtan lie on the floor and block the way to the door, but through his dramatic gesture of tearing his clothes, he stresses the extreme

Figure 2.5 Jan Matejko, *Rejtan at Sejm of 1773*, 1866

Source: 282 cm x 487 cm, oil on canvas, Warsaw, Royal Castle (fragment)

Matejko. How did he do it? 31

character of the act. This is what it should be like. This depiction of Rejtan in the painting is justified by a number of significant factors.

First, Rejtan is portrayed in a way which shows him blocking the entrance to the adjacent room on the plane rather than within the space. Even the way his body is arranged can raise doubts. The same applies to the correctness of his anatomy – for instance the leg blocking the "traitors'" path. Is it not blocking the passage for the viewers more than for those who are actually standing in the doorway? Perhaps for some reason this is precisely how Rejtan had to be posed.

Second, while obstructing the passage through the door, Rejtan is at the same time linked to something else – to the curtain which fills up the prominent right margin of the painting. Again, we are faced with doubts as to the correctness of the spatial relationship, which is no less persuasive; Rejtan clings to something which we initially treat as immaterial. We notice, however, a curtain on the other side of the door and at the opposite edge of the field, in both cases pleated and obscured – by Ksawery Branicki and by the figure merged, like a kind of backpack, with Stanislaus Augustus and the ermine on his coat.

Finally, let us look into the eyes of Rejtan himself. We will not meet his gaze, as he looks neither at us nor at the other figures in the painting. He directs his body, the torso with the clothes torn and his gaze upwards, beyond the space of the painting, at a slant. This, too, was necessary in the pose, although it seems to transcend a simple connection with the plot. At the same time, it opens up other connections. The first is that with a tombstone. We know this kind of pose also from the royal tombs in Wawel Cathedral in Cracow. One is especially noteworthy in this context: the tomb of King Stefan Batory in St Mary's Chapel (Figure 2.6) (he reigned in the years 1576–1587). This, in turn, reminds us of Mickiewicz again. In the thirty-eighth lecture of his first course in Slavic Literature at the Collège de France in 1840, published in Polish in Feliks Wrotnowski's translation, Mickiewicz refers to Batory when announcing the content of his course: "He is the ideal Polish monarch". He later elaborates on this idea:

> Stefan Batory is shown as the ideal patriot monarch . . . his policy was to withstand the barbarians, leave no peace or rest to the enemies of the Church and of freedom and dedicate himself wholeheartedly to the greatness and glory of his country.[4]

Moving on to literature by comparing King Batory with Jan Kochanowski, his court poet for a decade, but above all a poet recognised as the father of literary Polish, Mickiewicz concludes this part of the lecture by invoking the "greatest Polish man of letters and orator, Piotr Skarga".[5] Matejko made all of them the protagonists of his paintings.

However, Rejtan's pose brings to mind another work, the mention of which in connection with Rejtan may seem risky. I have in mind one of the sources of the later popularity of this pose, as it was appropriated and restored from antiquity, one that Michelangelo used for the tombstones of the Medici family,

Figure 2.6 Santi Gucci, Stefan Bathory's tomb, 1594–1595, Cracow, Wawel Cathedral

but in a most poignant way, projecting it onto a surface: *The Creation of Adam* from the Sistine Chapel (Figure 2.7). We can now ask: what does Rejtan's tearing of his clothes signify apart from its being a ritual gesture of biblical provenance, a tell-tale sign that something horrible, in particular a sacrilege, has taken place? Tearing up his clothes, Rejtan shows not only his body but the gorget on his bare chest, turning not towards what is taking place in the

Figure 2.7 Michelangelo, *Creation of Adam*, c. 1511
Source: 230, 1 x 480, 1, fresco, Sistine Chapel

painting but upwards. Yet the gesture of Adam, a memorable component of the emblem of creation, is retracted here and directed inwards; it seeks and finds, it shows something that links the two images more than anything else. That is the body, which in Michelangelo's painting of the created man is completely nude. It invokes something primary – sealed, as it were, by the gorget revealed by Rejtan on his naked chest. This dialogue between the paintings suggests a trail of meanings which we can attribute to his conduct.

Yet this is not the entire significance of Rejtan's pose. Subordinated to the plane, stretched sideways, it demonstrates an illuminated torso at the intersection of two streaks of blackness – one related to space, the other to the plane. In the former, the blockading bent knee, one side of the robe and the hilt of the sabre move towards us, nearly to the edge of the painting. In the latter, the leg outstretched along the lower edge and the section of the robe cast on the curtain map out the access route to what Rejtan merges with, in spite of the reality of the objects and space around him. He is reclining against a curtain, a prominent edge of the field, an element which offers him not so much physical as visual support. Merging with it, he guards not so much the exit from the room as the curtain itself – access to himself and to the reality which he embodies with his conduct. He defends the curtain, the evident borderline, the connection with that which cannot be adulterated by what is going on in the room, that which is behind it and that which is immutable, behind the painting, and so not yet completed, still possible and marked by what he reveals on his chest.

The curtain, which in two other places is clasped by the participants of the events, changes its status at the edge of the painting and becomes a solid support. At the same time, its way of being transcends the here and now of the event and its narrative. Rejecting and invalidating the physical state determined

34 *Wojciech Suchocki*

by the "reality" of the depiction, it may become a buttress, by existing as a revealed part of the surface, beyond the limits of time, and bringing its border into play. Therefore, the curtain cannot be clasped and moved here, but – in defiance of matter – it serves as a support.

The curtain also provokes us to look at its section on the other side of the door. The figure of Branicki screens and captures half of it. Without delving into this aspect, let us consider Poniński's gesture – forceful and dominant over the group. This is both a directing and a commanding gesture, as well as an incursion into the field of the curtain, reaching out for it. So if it reminds us of the gesture of creative contact, then the disconnection of the contact, that is Rejtan's withdrawal of his hand, demonstrates that the gesture has been desecrated. The implication of its repetition defines it as an anti-gesture, a token of usurpation, of the corruption of authority, against which the only salvation is to turn to the supreme and only legitimate power – that of the lawgiver in the face of lawlessness, begging for and expecting the restoration of the covenant.

So much for the painting. In conclusion, I will try to reflect on the extent to which the painter's oeuvre, this kind of oeuvre, and the field of signification set in motion by the term "Matejko" embody major issues related to the topic of this book.

The descriptions of these issues refer to various possible roles played by paintings; they may be witnesses to history, tangible tokens of memory, and objects making both history and the content of memory. They may appeal to the imagination and help us to visualise memories and stories from the past. In addition, Matejko's art has been credited with a possible motivational role, especially within a particular socio-political context. Finally, his renderings of key moments in Poland's history laid the groundwork for the culture of historical iconography, which was reiterated in history textbooks and other media of collective imagination.

Indeed, it is hard to find anything comparable in this respect. We can safely say that the word has become flesh. The amassed and complete knowledge about the "historical incident" is embodied literally: it is embodied by the figures, whose selection, presence and conduct demonstrate the "forces" which informed the entire incident. Matejko acts though his figures, which explains the proverbial crowds in his paintings, as nearly every figure has a role to play. It is difficult here to arrive at a hierarchy, although such efforts are prompted by our knowledge about the event. The artist, like his protagonists, is afraid that they will remain unnoticed. Today that hierarchy often eludes us, or else we cannot name the figures, but we are inclined to blame our own ignorance or to interpret, from the protagonists' actions, their role in the incident portrayed in the painting.

We can, however, in line with established custom, focus on reconstructing the artist's intentions, aided by his own words, which I quoted at the start. A historical reconstruction of the artist's intentions is an important, although obviously not the sole legitimate way of assigning meaning to a work of art. The same applies to the texts which help us to reconstruct those intentions, limited in one way or another in their selection by their relation to a given work.

Yet the history of a painting is a history of a continuous revelation of meaning, of the viewers' never-ending investment in their own experience. If some implications of the meaning of *Rejtan* seem risky to you, may they direct our attention away from criticism of Matejko towards the way of being of the work, of the painting, and *through this* towards matters related to the subject of this book.

The medium. The limited surface with which the artist must struggle and which he seems to be in control of. Still, the longer he paints, the better he recognises, appreciates and considers the scope and manifestation of its power. The surface seems to disappear under the painting, and yet it is present in the conditions which it imposes; it makes the painting continuously open or exhibiting – to (ab)use a term of the great thinker Martin Heidegger: *Jemeinigkeit* – my-own-ownness, mineness. This applies in the highest degree to those rare moments when I experience a shock in the face of a painting; and this extraverbal sense is the only sense of the work. If we try to express it in words, we must take a new interpretative path that we did not know before.

Are those paintings that seem the most open not also the most fragile?

Notes

1 Stanisław Tarnowski, *Matejko* (Kraków: Księgarnia Spółki Wydawniczej Polskiej, 1897), 466.
2 Stanisław Witkiewicz, *Matejko* (Lwów: Gebethner-Wolf, 1912), 237–238.
3 Izydor Jabłoński, *Wspomnienia o Janie Matejce* (Lwów: Altenberg, 1912), 56.
4 Adam Mickiewicz, "Literatura słowiańska. Kurs pierwszy", in Adam Mickiewicz, *Dzieła*, trans. Leon Płoszewski, vol. 8 (Warszawa: Czytelnik, 1997), 542.
5 Ibid., 543–544.

3 The devotional image as a medium of memory

The case of the painting of the *Divine Mercy* by Eugeniusz Kazimirowski[1]

Mariusz Bryl

The purpose of this chapter is to analyse Eugeniusz Kazimirowski's painting of the *Divine Mercy* as a multifaceted medium of memory (Figure 3.1). The notion of the "medium" is understood here, from the perspective of the anthropology of images, as a part of the image-medium-body triad complemented by the concept of the human being as a "store" of images.[2] All images possess their "bodies", and a human being perceiving external images disembodies them, at the same time embodying them anew and lending them his or her own body. This means that the externalised memory recorded in the medium of a picture turns into an internalised memory inscribed in the corporeal subject. This specific transfer of memory takes place in the historically changing social context in which reception takes place. Our task will be to reconstruct three modes of this transfer in relation to the first painting of the *Divine Mercy*. First, we will consider the problem of Kazimirowski's painting as a medium of memory of the revealed image. Second, we will present the story of Father Michał Sopoćko, whose body became the "store" of the memory of Kazimirowski's painting. And third, we will draw attention to the problematic status of the painting's body as a medium of memory about the painting itself.

1 The painting of the *Divine Mercy* as a medium of memory of the revealed image

Among all the representations of the Divine Mercy, exceptional status is granted, without a shadow of a doubt, to the painting by Kazimirowski, as a medium of the memory of the revealed image, painted in accordance with the guidelines from Sister Faustina, who participated in the creative process of this work of art.[3] Theologian Jan Machniak defines revelations as "experiences in which supernatural reality attains presence in a natural way, aided by the senses (hearing and seeing) and by mental faculties (imagination)".[4] Visions, on the other hand,

> are only reflections in the psyche of a mystical experience which comes into being in the most secret recesses of the soul. . . . So the subject of a

DOI: 10.4324/9781003264460-5

The devotional image as a medium of memory 37

Figure 3.1 Eugeniusz Kazimirowski, *Image of the Divine Mercy*, 1934
Source: www.merciful-jesus.com

vision is the result of the capacity of the imagination, which connects spiritual powers with the powers of the senses.[5]

The inaccessibility of the source image of transcendence means that Faustina's account, related next, refers to a "reflection" of the revealed image in the psyche, being "a result of the capacity of the mystic's imagination".

38   *Mariusz Bryl*

> In the evening, when I was in my cell – Faustina recorded in her *Diary* – I saw the Lord Jesus clothed in a white garment. One hand [was] raised in the gesture of blessing, the other was touching the garment at the breast. From beneath the garment, slightly drawn aside at the breast, there were emanating two large rays, one red, the other pale. . . . After a while, Jesus said to me "Paint an image according to the pattern you see, with the signature: Jesus, I trust in You (Diary 47)".[6]

Analysis of the "verbal image of Jesus" in the *Diary* led Izabela Rutkowska to question the conviction expressed by theologians that [Faustina's] "visions of the image of Jesus were based on a strongly visual imagination capable of reconstructing the tiniest details of the image appearing in the consciousness".[7] As Rutkowska maintains, "the images reconstructed here seem to contradict this thesis, as they are of a rather schematic and stereotypical character".[8] And yet the visual innovativeness of Kazimirowski's picture seems to contradict such a conclusion, all the more so as the picture has an advantage over an ekphrasis, as it offers direct visual access to the vision understood as the "sensual-imaginative objectivisation" of the revelation. We should remember that Faustina herself participated in the creation of the painting, which took half a year. She paid regular visits to the artist, assessed the progress made in terms of conformity to her vision and indicated any necessary corrections. Father Sopoćko,[9] who was a witness to the creative process of the painting, always emphasised that Faustina "attached great importance to the accuracy of the picture".[10]

The idea was, in line with Sister Faustina's suggestions, to depict Jesus as if he was walking and had stopped to greet somebody. That is why his left leg was to be extended forward and the right one slightly bent at the knee. The scars on Jesus's feet and hands were to be exposed. The entire figure was to be depicted against a dark background, clothed in a white garment, long, bound at the waist and slightly pleated below. His right hand was to be raised to shoulder level in blessing. The palm of his hand should be open, and its fingers straight and gently touching each other. And two fingers of his left hand, the index and the middle, opening the garment a little, near the heart, were to let out the rays of light. They should be directed towards the viewer and slightly to the sides, like irregular streaks. They were to carry light through the air to the ground and partly also onto the hands. They should be transparent, so that the garment and belt are visible through them. The saturation of the rays with red and white should be most intense at their source, by the heart, and then it should gradually lessen and disperse at their very ends. Jesus's gaze was to be directed slightly downwards, just as it is when a standing person looks at a point on the ground a few steps away. The expression on Jesus's face should be one of grace and mercy.[11]

The meticulousness and precision of Faustina's verbal guidelines allows us to conclude that Kazimirowski's painting should be treated as a faithful representation of the "sensual-imaginative objectivisation" (i.e. vision) of the revealed

The devotional image as a medium of memory 39

image. Opponents of awarding Kazimirowski's picture such a status usually point to Faustina's discontentment with the work in progress expressed in her *Diary*: "Once when I was visiting the artist who was painting the image, and saw that it was not as beautiful as Jesus is, I felt very sad about it" (Diary 313). However, we must juxtapose this fragment with the account of Father Sopoćko, according to which, on completion of the picture, Faustina was "generally satisfied and did not complain about its lack of verisimilitude".[12] So Faustina's critical remarks document only one particular stage in the work on the painting.

Kazimirowski's painting met with Faustina's affirmation, and she acknowledged that its appearance corresponded to her vision embodied in her body as a medium. In her later entries regarding subsequent visions, Faustina not only used phrases such as "I saw the Lord Jesus as He is represented in the image" (Diary 420), but she also documented the experience of the painted image being brought to life: "When the picture was displayed, I saw a sudden movement of the hand of Jesus, as He made a large sign of the cross" (Diary 416) and "the image came alive" (Diary 417).[13] Faustina's internalisation of Kazimirowski's painting as a medium of memory of the revealed image meant that she endowed to it her own body as a medium to the limits of indistinguishability. From then on, the two images occupied the same place in her body as a medium, ready for the reception of further medium externalisations. Kazimirowski's painting as a medium of the memory of the revealed image occupied a special place not only in Sister Faustina's body as a medium, but also in that of Father Sopoćko – a place which, as we will see, required special protection, the essence of which was to defend the integrity of the image of Merciful Jesus.

2 A human being as a "place of images": the case of Father Michał Sopoćko

Although the pictures of the Divine Mercy created in the Vilnius region during the Second World War differed from the original in their precision of replication and degree of workmanship, they did not deviate radically from it.[14] The need to defend the original's integrity occurred soon after Sopoćko left Vilnius for Poland in September 1947.[15] Almost immediately, he went to Łagiewniki to see a painting by Adolf Hyła,[16] which had enjoyed cult status for several years. One should remember that this painting was different to Hyła's current version (Figure 3.2). Here, Jesus was depicted with a landscape in the background (Figure 3.3). The artist followed the guidelines of Father Józef Andrasz,[17] in accordance with which "the Saviour . . . is walking on this poor land of ours" wearing a white garment as a symbol of "his great readiness to heal the sickness in humankind with his Mercy".[18] As Sopoćko recalls:

> When I saw it in September 1947, I did not find in it much similarity to the image described by Faustina. Mr Hyła did not react to my remarks,

Figure 3.2 Adolf Hyła, *Image of the Divine Mercy*, 1944 (present state)
Source: www.faustyna.pl/zmbm

and he made many (approximately 200) paintings which were not accurate (rays like ribbons or even cords point towards the ground, while they should be directed towards the viewer; the eyes are looking at the viewer with a playful, piercing gaze, while they should be looking downwards; the hand in a gesture of blessing, which should be outstretched to shoulder

The devotional image as a medium of memory 41

Figure 3.3 Adolf Hyła, *Image of the Divine Mercy*, 1944 (state until 1954)

Source: repr. after: Paweł Szweda, *Adolf Hyła – malarz w służbie Bożego Miłosierdzia* [Adolf Hyła: a painter in the service of the Divine Mercy] (Warsaw, 2009)

level, is raised too high; the entire figure assumes a pose as if it were about to dance, while it should be depicted as walking; the background of the picture ought to be dark . . ., while Hyła's pictures had varied backgrounds: flowers, meadows, mountains, the sea, factories, etc. . . . My protests had no effect.[19]

42 Mariusz Bryl

The image of Jesus in the Łagiewniki picture was so different from Kazimirowski's prototype that Sopoćko remained Hyła's intractable foe till the end of his days.[20] He fought against Hyła's images, as they "were not those of Sister Faustina"[21] and presented a "distorted" image of Merciful Jesus.[22] One should remember that Sopoćko's fight for visual accuracy in paintings of the Divine Mercy was part of a wider battle in which the establishing of the cult of the Divine Mercy by the Church was at stake. In 1951, when the first (unsuccessful) process of Faustina's beatification was initiated in Rome, Hyła's paintings, as Sopoćko maintained, were an obstacle to the Vatican's recognition of the cult of the Divine Mercy.[23] So he decided to convince the Polish Episcopate that the image of the Divine Mercy "may be treated as depicting the Saviour at the moment when the sacrament of penance was established – a moment based on a public revelation (John 20:19 NIV)".[24] As a result of a competition organised in 1953 under the auspices of the Episcopate, Ludomir Sleńdziński painted a picture of the Divine Mercy representing Jesus against the background of the door to the Upper Room at the moment when he appears to the Apostles, greeting them with the words "Peace [be] with you" (Figure 3.4). After the Episcopate's approval of the picture, Sopoćko sent colour photographs of it to all the dioceses in the country and to the centres of the cult of the Divine Mercy abroad with a request that the cult of the Divine Mercy be separated from the revelations of Sister Faustina".[25] Although this operation was aimed above all at the pictures painted by Hyła, it also hit out at the prototypicality of the picture by Kazimirowski, which he had hitherto postulated.

As in the case of Kazimirowski's painting, there were two people who had contributed to the creation of the picture by Sleńdziński. One of them supplied the driving force and controlling discourse, the other the creative skills. Sopoćko replaced Faustina's discourse, in which he acted as an intermediary exercising full control over her meticulous verbal guidelines, with his own discourse, combining the former guidelines from Faustina regarding the mode of depiction of the figure of Jesus with new guidelines of his own regarding the scenery and the situational context in which the figure of Jesus was to be presented. From the moment when Sleńdziński's picture was accepted by the Episcopate, Sopoćko propagated it as the new prototype of the image of the Divine Mercy till the end of his days. In other words, he lent to it his own body as a medium and became the "place" for the image to which Hyła's picture never gained access.

The fact that Hyła repainted the Łagiewniki picture did not change anything.[26] Although he painted over the landscape, he still left the image of Jesus unchanged, and Sopoćko never gave it his approval.[27] At the end of the 1950s, when the Holy Office, banning the cult of the Divine Mercy based on the revelation of Faustina, recommended the removal of images of the Divine Mercy from churches,[28] Sopoćko saw this as an opportunity to eliminate Hyła's pictures from the sacral space and replace them with paintings which conformed to Sleńdziński's prototype. After Karol Wojtyła, the archbishop of Cracow,

The devotional image as a medium of memory 43

Figure 3.4 Ludomir Sleńdziński, *Image of the Divine Mercy*, 1954
Source: repr. after: Father Michał Sopoćko, *Dziennik* [Diary], ed. Revd Henryk Ciereszko (Białystok, 2010)

initiated the second beatification process with regard to Faustina,[29] Sopoćko turned to the archbishop with a request for support for Sleńdziński's painting as a canonical image of the Divine Mercy in the hope that Polish bishops would then accept it "as the model to follow for their dioceses".[30] Despite appearances,

44   *Mariusz Bryl*

however, the second beatification process, although much better prepared than the first, was not conducive to Sopoćko's argumentation that liturgical and iconographic independence from Faustina's revelations should speak in favour of the picture by Sleńdziński. In his letter to Archbishop Wojtyła, the postulator of the beatification stated that, despite the ban from the Vatican, "worship of the painting by A. Hyła did not wane". At the same time, he warned that Sopoćko's demand for Hyła's paintings to be replaced by those of Sleńdziński "might lead to the disappearance of the cult of Merciful Jesus".[31] Sopoćko's (rather illogical) explanations that his intention was not to "remove pictures by Hyła and by other painters from shrines but to ensure they were properly reworked in accordance with Sister Faustina's guidelines, of which he was *the one and only authentic witness* [my emphasis]"[32] did not convince Archbishop Wojtyła.

One should note that despite Sopoćko's statement, the painting by Kazimirowski vanished as a point of reference. As early as in 1959, Sopoćko wrote in a letter that this painting should be treated as "an artistic vision" which "Mr Kazimirowski transferred to canvas in accordance with Sister Faustina's guidelines".[33] Such wording indicates the endpoint of a certain process. Initially, the battle with Hyła's painting was closely bound up with the defence of the integrity of Kazimirowski's painting, for a long time identified with the struggle for the accuracy of the image of Merciful Jesus. However, in the final instance, the guarantee of this correctness was not to be found in the prototype picture but in Faustina's verbal guidelines, which, in relation to the succinctness of the ekphrasis in the *Diary*, played a decisive role. This key source of discourse was under Sopoćko's complete control, which, in the face of the crisis relating to the propagation of Faustina's revelations, paved the way for the emergence of a new discourse on the subject of iconography of the image of the Divine Mercy and for the creation of the picture by Sleńdziński as a new prototype. And so, in Father Sopoćko's body as a "place" of images, the memory of Kazimirowski's picture as a medium of memory of the revealed image slowly faded as the struggle for recognition of the prototype status of the picture by Sleńdziński continued.

3 The body of the picture as a problematic medium of memory

Looking at Kazimirowski's painting today, we see an almost ideal untouched surface, which it obtained as a result of the last thorough restoration in 2003.[34] Cameramen find this surface fascinating, as they repeatedly show the viewer close-ups of its parts, creating the impression of contact with the original from 1934.[35] At the same time, however, one witnesses the erasure of *the history of the painting's body*, which was repeatedly damaged and underwent numerous repairs. Only after getting to know the turbulent history of the picture's

The devotional image as a medium of memory   45

material body can we examine the aim of its last renovation, "to restore the painting's original look", from the correct perspective.[36]

Kazimirowski's picture was first damaged in 1937, when it was placed "in an altar during the Corpus Christi procession . . . it was partly damaged while the altar was being dismantled and the picture removed from it".[37] The picture was then renovated by Łucja Bałzukiewiczówna, a painter from Vilnius.[38] It was damaged for a second time in 1940, when it fell out of its frame while being moved.[39] After conservation in 1942, it returned to its original place in the church of St Michael.[40] It remained there until 1950, when Janina Rodziewicz removed it from the church, which had been wrecked by the communists, and hid it in the attic of a house in Vilnius.[41] In 1954, after her return from exile in Siberia, Rodziewicz noticed some damage to the picture and gave it to Vilnius artist Helena Szmigielska for renovation. So this was the third interference in the material body of Kazimirowski's picture. The fourth was connected with Sopoćko's attempt to illegally bring Kazimirowski's work from the Soviet Union to Poland, which ultimately never happened. The painting, which had been rolled up for the journey, "was seriously damaged again to such an extent that paint had come off in a number of places". So they brought in "a painter from Kaunas, and she renovated the picture". After that, the painting, again "rolled up", was deposited in the church of the Holy Spirit.[42] In 1956, Father Józef Grasewicz took it from there and placed it in the parish church in Nowa Ruda near Grodno.[43]

The next (fifth) restoration, about which, unlike the previous ones, we have quite a bit of information, came 30 years later. In November 1986, when it was brought back to the church of the Holy Spirit in Vilnius, it was declared to be "severely damaged".[44] Filipavicius, the Lithuanian artist who was entrusted with the restoration, "did a thorough job of repainting the image. . . . Unfortunately, as a result of the restoration, the face of Christ lost its former expression" (Figure 3.5).[45] As noted by the painter commissioned to carry out the last restoration, in 2003, "successive attempts to renew the painting had considerably changed the facial expression of Jesus. They were performed inexpertly and carelessly".[46] Hence, the purpose of the renovation was to "restore the original look of the painting – one which is principally known only from small pre-war pictures".[47] This refers to photographic reproductions made at Sopoćko's request by Vilnius photographer Michał Nowicki (Figure 3.6).[48] "What immense satisfaction I experienced when *the face of Jesus painted by Kazimirowski* appeared from under the layers of paint upon it!" [my emphasis].[49] Today, the "effect of Kazimirowski's original" achieved in this way plays a key role in the cult of the painting. The documentary films previously mentioned, in which Kazimirowski's work is celebrated as a masterpiece of sacral art, provide spectacular examples of this. At the centre of this celebration, there is the face of Jesus, which, after the *via dolorosa* of the picture's material body, now resembles the face of Jesus from the Shroud of Turin,[50] reinforcing the veracity of the image among the faithful.

Figure 3.5 Eugeniusz Kazimirowski, *Image of the Divine Mercy*, 1934 (state 1987–2003)
Source: www.faustyna.eu/informacje_pl.htm

The devotional image as a medium of memory 47

Figure 3.6 Michał Nowicki, *Photo of the Image of the Divine Mercy by Kazimirowski*, 1940
Source: https://tadeuszczernik.wordpress.com/2012/10/09/26857/

48   Mariusz Bryl

Notes

1 On the image of Divine Mercy, see Piotr Szweda and Andrzej Witko, *Obraz Miłosierdzia Bożego i jego tajemnica* [The Image of the Divine Mercy and its Mystery] (Cracow: Wydawnictwo AA, 2012); Ivan Gaskell, "Jesus Christ as the Divine Mercy by Eugeniusz Kazimirowski: The Most Influential Polish Painting of the Twentieth Century?", *Ars: asopis Ústavu dejín umenia Slovenskej akadémie vied*, 42 (2009), 81–91; Jane Garnett and Alana Harris, "Canvassing the Faithful: Image, Agency and the Lived Religiosity of Devotion to the Divine Mercy", in *Prayer and Spirituality*, ed. Giuseppe Giordan and Linda Woodhead (Leiden: Brill, 2013), 77–102.

2 See Hans Belting, *Antropologia obrazu. Szkice do nauki o obrazie*, trans. Mariusz Bryl (Cracow: Universitas, 2007); Ger. orig., *Bild-Anthropologie. Entwürfe für eine Bildwissenschaft* (Munich: Fink, 2001).

3 Sister Faustina Kowalska (1905–1938) – Polish nun and mystic, saint of the Roman Catholic church. See Ewa Katarzyna Czaczkowska, *Siostra Faustyna. Biografia świętej* [Sister Faustina: Biography of a Saint] (Cracow: Znak, 2012).

4 Jan Machniak, *Doświadczenie Boga w tajemnicy Jego Miłosierdzia u bł. Siostry Faustyny Kowalskiej. Studium krytyczne w świetle myśli teologicznej* [The Experience of God in the Mystery of His Mercy in the Case of Blessed Sister Faustina Kowalska] (Cracow: Wydawnictwo Naukowe Papieskiej Akademii Teologicznej, 1999), 295.

5 Ibid., 296–301.

6 *Diary of Saint Maria Faustina Kowalska: Divine Mercy in My Soul*, coll. trans. (Stockbridge, MA: Marian Press, 2005) (paragraph number marked in brackets).

7 Machniak, *Doświadczenie*, 308.

8 Izabela Rutkowska, "'Wtem ujrzałam Pana. . .' – językowy obraz objawień w 'Dzienniczku' św. Faustyny Kowalskiej" ['And then I Saw the Lord. . .': The Verbal Image of the revelations in the 'Diary' of St Faustina Kowalska], in *Język religijny dawniej i dziś* [Religious Language then and Now], ed. Paweł Bortkiewicz, Stanisław Mikołajczak and Małgorzata Rybka, vol. 3 (Poznań: Wydawnictwo Poznańskie Studia Polonistyczne, 2007), 599.

9 Father Michał Sopoćko (1888–1975) – Polish Catholic priest, blessed of the Roman Catholic church, spiritual leader of Sister Faustina, propagator of the cult of the Divine Mercy, author of numerous publications on this topic. See Henryk Ciereszko, *Ksiądz Michał Sopoćko. Apostoł Miłosierdzia Bożego* [Father Michał Sopoćko: Apostle of the Divine Mercy] (Cracow: WAM, 2004).

10 Ibid., 68.

11 Ibid., 66–67.

12 Ibid., 69.

13 On images brought to life, see David Freedberg, *The Power of Images: Studies in the History and Theory of Response* (Chicago: University of Chicago Press, 1989).

14 See Skirmantė Smilingytė-Žeimienė, "Apie Gailestingojo Jėzaus paveikslą raudonosios ir rudosios okupacijų kryžkelėje" [On the Painting of Merciful Jesus at the Crossroads of Bolshevik and Nazi Occupations], *Menotyra*, 19 (2012), 1; Barbara Cichońska, *Historia trzech obrazów Jezusa Miłosiernego autorstwa Ludomira Slendzińskiego* [The Story of Three Images of Merciful Jesus Painted by Ludomir Slendziński], *Biuletyn Konserwatorski Województwa Podlaskiego*, 14 (2008); Wiesław Józef Kowalski, *Ikona Jezusa Miłosiernego* [The Icon of Merciful Jesus] (Płock: Koło Czcicieli Jezusa Miłosiernego im św Faustyny Kowalskiej, 2002).

15 Kazimirowski's painting then remained in Vilnius, and Sopoćko lost sight of it forever, as it turned out.

16 For more information on the artist, see Paweł Szweda, *Adolf Hyła – malarz w służbie Bożego Miłosierdzia* [Adolf Hyła: A Painter in the Service of the Divine Mercy] (Warsaw: Wydawnictwo AA, 2009).

The devotional image as a medium of memory   49

17 For more on Fr Józef Andrasz, Sister Faustina's other spiritual leader (besides Sopoćko), see Stanisław Cieślak, *Kierownik duchowy świętej Faustyny* [Saint Faustina's Spiritual Leader] (Cracow: WAM, 2011).

18 Józef Andrasz, *Miłosierdzie Boże . . . ufamy Tobie!* [Divine Mercy . . . We Trust in You!] (Cracow: Wydawnictwo Apostolstwa Modlitwy, 1947), 24–25.

19 Father Michał Sopoćko, *Dziennik* [Diary], ed. Revd Henryk Ciereszko (Białystok: Wydawnictwo św. Jerzego, 2010), 123–124.

20 The term "prototype" was used by Sopoćko; for example, regarding the guidelines given to Hyła by Fr Andrasz, Sopoćko wrote that "he was not able to convey them properly, as he had not been present at the painting of the prototype" (ibid., 123).

21 Kowalski, *Ikona*, 20.

22 Sopoćko, *Dziennik*, 123.

23 One should add that the postulator of this process, Fr Stanisław Suwała, announced in 1953 that "the picture of Merciful Jesus painted by Adolf Hyła to be found at the chapel of the Sisters of Our Lady of Mercy in Cracow-Łagiewniki is the picture endorsed by the postulator" (Andrzej J. Gorczyca, *Kult obrazu Jezusa Miłosiernego w Narodowym Sanktuarium Bożego Miłosierdzia w Stockbridge (USA)* [The Cult of the Image of the Divine Mercy at the National Shrine of The Divine Mercy in Stockbridge (USA)] (Opole: Wydawnictwo Wydziału Teologicznego Uniwersytetu Opolskiego, 2015), 23).

24 Sopoćko, *Dziennik*, 124.

25 Ibid.

26 It is assumed that this happened as early as 1952 (see Szweda, *Adolf Hyła*, 102); it is possible, however, that it was only in 1954, after a competition for a new prototype was announced. Cf. Andrzej Witko, *Nabożeństwo do Miłosierdzia Bożego według świętej Faustyny Kowalskiej* [A Religious Service for the Divine Mercy according to Saint Faustina Kowalska] (Cracow: WAM, 2004), 155.

27 The radicalism and durability of the rejection of the image of Jesus in the painting by Hyła on the part of people who have been influenced by Father Sopoćko testifies to the words of Maria Winowska (a Polish writer living in Paris) regarding the image: "Here, before my eyes, I have paintings that are so lacking in artistic talent, not to mention ugly and pretentious, *like that of a young man with the swooning look of a Hollywood star*" [my emphasis], Maria Winowska, *Prawo do miłosierdzia. Posłannictwo Siostry Faustyny* [The Right to Mercy: The Mission of Sister Faustina] (Paris: Éditions Dembinski, 1974), 11.

28 On this subject, the Holy Office first passed a decree (unpublished) of 19 October 1958, the content of which was communicated to Primate Wyszyński in a missive dated 28 November 1958; this was followed by a notification, published in *L'Osservatore Romano*, 7 March 1959. See Ciereszko, *Ksiądz Michał Sopoćko*, 172–174.

29 The function of postulator was performed by Fr Antoni Mruk SJ. See Antoni Mruk, "Trudna droga procesu beatyfikacyjnego Sługi Bożej siostry Faustyny Kowalskiej" [The Difficult Path of the Beatification Process of Sister Faustina Kowalska, Servant of God], in *Posłannictwo siostry Faustyny* [The Mission of Sister Faustina], ed. Czesław Drążek SJ (Cracow: Wydawnictwo Archidiecezji Krakowskiej, 1991), 9–22.

30 Sopoćko, *Dziennik*, 222.

31 Ciereszko, *Ksiądz Michał Sopoćko*, 233.

32 Ibid., 235.

33 Ewa Katarzyna Czaczkowska, "Kłopoty z kultem Bożego miłosierdzia w korespondencji Marii Winowskiej w latach 1958–1975" [Problems with the cult of the Divine Mercy in the letters of Maria Winowska 1958–1975], *Polonia Sacral*, 2018/3, 13.

34 Conservation work was conducted by Edyta Hankowska-Czerwińska, from Włocławek; see Edyta Hankowska-Czerwińska, "Konserwacja obrazu Jezusa Milosiernego z kościoła pw. Świętego Ducha w Wilnie" [Conservation of the painting of Merciful Jesus from the Church of the Holy Spirit in Vilnius], *Niedziela Ogólnopolska*, 2003/46, 5.

50 *Mariusz Bryl*

35 See for example two documentary films (both from 2016): *Ufam Tobie* ("I Trust in You"), dir. Aleks Matvejev; *The Original Image of Divine Mercy,* dir. Daniel DiSilva.
36 Hankowska-Czerwińska, "Konserwacja".
37 Sopoćko, *Dziennik*, 99.
38 Ibid.
39 Ibid., 116.
40 Andrzej Witko, *Święta Faustyna i Boże Miłosierdzie* [Saint Faustina and the Divine Mercy] (Cracow: Wydawnictwo AA, 2014), 183.
41 Zbigniew Żakiewicz, "Z dziennika" [From My Diary], *Gwiazda Morza*, 1990/16.
42 Witko, *Obraz*, 44–45.
43 On the history of the painting by Kazimirowski in Nowa Ruda, see Maria Faustyna Cydzik, *Działalność Zgromadzenia Sióstr Matki Miłosierdzia w okresie okupacji i komunizmu* [The Work of the Order of the Sisters of Our Mother of Mercy during the Periods of German Occupation and Communism] (Cracow: Wydawnictwo Alleluja, 2006).
44 Witko, *Obraz*, 71.
45 Ibid.
46 Hankowska-Czerwińska, "Konserwacja".
47 Ibid.
48 In the years 1940–1945, around 150,000 reproductions were produced, in some 80 different variants. See Michał Nowicki, "Ile może jeden człowiek! Przyczynek do historii Pana Jezusa Miłosiernego" [How Much One Person Can Do! A Contribution to the History of Merciful Jesus], *Orędzie Miłosierdzia*, 1989/7.
49 Hankowska-Czerwińska, "Konserwacja".
50 Familiarity with the face of Jesus from the Shroud of Turin was already widespread at that time in Poland. See Kazimierz Pruszyński, *Prawdziwa fotografia Pana Jezusa i ślady całej męki Jego na całunie* [The Real Photograph of Lord Jesus and the Traces of Passion on the Shroud] (Warsaw: Zakłady Drukarskie F. Wyszyński i S-ka, 1932).

4 Images *in cito, in situ, in extremis*

Visual testimonies from the "Holocaust by bullets"

Roma Sendyka

In this chapter, I would like to consider the possibilities for representing the Holocaust when it developed as a decentralised set of random and rapid violent events, characteristic of the second part of the Second World War. In camps and ghettos, visual documentation developed, thanks to photographers and artists working in secret. However dire the circumstances, they still allowed for the production of visual testimonies (i.e. there was sufficient time, support and material for artists' work). What we call today "Holocaust art" is mainly constructed from such visual evidence.

I wish to explore whether the victims of events, such as forced marches, round-ups, transportations, the actions of the Judenjagd (the hunt for Jews hiding in woods or on the Aryan side[1]), Einsatzgruppen shootings,[2] bandit raids and pacifications, also managed to respond with "pictorial resistance", despite the limited time and resources. If so, how did they present the events? What media did they use? What happened to that visual testimony? If it exists, what is its status today?

In my research into small-scale and uncommemorated post-genocide sites, I seek to understand their ontology, as well as their impact on the processes of remembrance.[3] Exploring the visual testimony of the "Holocaust by bullets" produced by the victims, I would like to focus on historical visual representations of sites that are now often overlooked or contested.[4] There are numerous visual documents, mostly photographs, produced by the perpetrators from execution squads in the East. But are there victims' images that may allow us to visualise those wartime events which occurred at the sites in question (now overgrown, abandoned and uncommemorated)? We know that victims were occasionally able, in the chaos of resettlement, to pass on brief notes, which were sometimes scattered in the hope of reaching some kind-hearted passer-by, as evidenced by the exhibition *Czego nie mogliśmy wykrzyczeć światu* (*What we've been unable to shout out to the world*) at the Jewish Historical Institute in Warsaw.[5] So perhaps sketches, drawings or maps were also left on those same scraps of paper? Perhaps there are other sources that visually convey what happened "outside the camps"?

DOI: 10.4324/9781003264460-6

"Hobbled" images

For at least three decades, in the field of visual culture, research has been developing into "images" – any objects characterised by a relationship of similarity defined by Charles Sanders Peirce as "iconic".[6] Today, even objects with very limited visual information have been effectively brought to attention and study: imprints, mirror images and cuts or reliefs, as well as schemata, graphs, geometric figures or indeed letters (one of the key stimuli for the new, expanded field of the visual has been "Jacques Derrida's critique of logocentrism in favour of a *graphic* and *spatial* model of writing"[7]). If we calibrate our research tools with greater sensitivity, then, in this new, more egalitarian and inclusive scopic field, we will be able to include many images "from the Holocaust" not hitherto investigated as pictorial objects but which were used by the victims of sudden acts of violence.[8]

Published on the website of the Yad Vashem research project The Untold Stories: The Murder Sites of the Jews in the Former USSR was a photograph found in the pocket of an item of female clothing from a killing site in Antanašė in Lithuania. (In 2009, 101 locations of shootings of Jewish people in former Soviet republics was revealed.[9]) The photograph was of a piece of paper bearing the following words: "My dearest one, before I die, I write these few words. We will die very soon – five thousand innocents. They shoot at us without mercy. Kisses for everyone. Mira".[10] Four sentences, scribbled down in a hurry by someone risking their life, words from the vortex of the Holocaust. They were born of the same extreme effort to bear witness as the "four pieces of film snatched from hell" that Georges Didi-Huberman wrote about in his well-known essay *Images in Spite of All*. His interpretation inclines one to consider this piece of paper from the area around Rokiškis as a visual message. With its torn-off corner, hesitant handwriting, and larger and larger letters, hurried and separate, it is an icon, but also a symptom and an indicator of what was happening, a rare case of a document *in situ* (drawn up at the scene of the crime), *in cito* (in the course of the violence) and *in extremis* (in life-threatening circumstances).[11]

Today we know of more relics of this kind.[12] In *Les graffiti du camp de Drancy. Des noms sur les murs*, prepared by Mélanie Curdy, Denis Peschanski and Thierry Zimmer under the supervision of Benoit Pouvreau (2014), we find inscriptions left on the walls of the transit camp for Jews in Drancy, near Paris, documented just after the war, rediscovered in the 1980s and then during the most recent renovation in 2011. (Today this is the site of a branch of the Paris Shoah Memorial Museum.) The writing style catches our attention: it is impeded by the irregular rhythm due to the uneven wall underneath, the breaking writing equipment (lead and coloured pencils), the uncertainty of the random sharp tools for etching away at the wall and finally – the emotional state of those imprisoned. The letters are outlined, underscored, corrected. On the more than 150 pages of the album presenting the relics from the wall, there are also human figures (Nazis and functionaries, p. 31), religious images

(p. 58), portraits (pp. 64–65, 115, 146, 149) and stylised initials. Viewing it from a distance, we can see half-abstract images produced by multiple authors naturally emerging on the walls – a sum of graphics, records, numerical tables, haphazard markings and cuts in plaster left by the victims occupying that space (Figure 4.1).

Similar material can be found at other sites of isolation: a case in point is the fort at Pomiechówek (part of Modlin Fortress, used during the war as a transit camp and remembered for the especially cruel groups of Volksdeutsche recruited from the neighbouring areas).[13] Cuts on the walls, although merely names or numbers, have a powerful visual dimension communicating the outrageous circumstances of imprisonment. Also the research team investigating the area of wartime action and the forced POW labour camp in Chycina (located 130 km from Poznań) discovered cuts in trees made by prisoners.[14] Had it not been for renovation work, we could also investigate the writing on the synagogue in Kowel.[15] (Etched marks and writing can also serve as a record of eyewitnesses, made during or after acts of sudden wartime violence to mark a site of murder. While investigating a killing site in Redecznica, our research team discovered a cross and a Star of David cut into a beech tree, made by a witness to the burials that followed the shooting of victims who had been caught hiding in a bunker (Figure 4.2)).

If the scope of the research includes "all visual work created by witnesses or victims in the period of the Holocaust"[16] – and I agree with Luiza Nader that it should – we will need a new research procedure covering expression at "the level of performance, image, form or content, including the material aspect".[17]

Figure 4.1 Walls in the fort in Pomiechówek with the signatures of victims
Source: photograph by Roma Sendyka, 2016

Figure 4.2 Cut-outs in bark at the site of the death of denounced Jews
Source: photograph by Roma Sendyka, 2016

The rhythm of the hand and the position of the person cutting into the wall or bark becomes evident to the researcher studying a relief, offering insight into the past experience of someone working hastily, under the pressure of time and the threat of death. Despite their material limitations, these objects provide a deep understanding of the affective and existential dimension of the experience they were a part of.

"Most images are not art", writes James Elkins in a text about "hobbled images": deficient, incomplete, feeble images in which expressive merit has been replaced by the task of conveying information:

> There is no good name for such images, which include graphs, charts, maps, geometric configurations, notations, plans, official documents, some money, bonds, patents, seals and stamps, astronomical and astrological charts, technical and engineering drawings, scientific images of all sorts, schemata, and pictographic or ideographic elements in writing: in other words, the sum total of visual images, both Western and non-Western, that are not obviously either artworks, popular images, or religious artifacts. In general, art history has not studied such images, and at first it may appear that they are intrinsically less interesting than paintings. They seem like half-pictures, or hobbled versions of full pictures, bound by the necessity of performing some utilitarian function and therefore unable to mean more freely. Their affinity with writing and numbers seems to indicate they are incapable of the expressive eloquence that is associated with painting and drawing, making them properly the subject of disciplines such as visual communication, typography, mathematics, archaeology, linguistics, printing, and graphic design.[18]

I would claim, however, that the examples previously presented, the distorted images "from the Holocaust", are full of expression, representing a particular kind of "hobbled" image: too technically limited to be art, often no more than scribblings or sketches of purely informative value. Only by recognising them as being unusually effective as emotional messaging can we connect them with artistic expression. The appreciation of these kinds of object, their communicative and visual properties, may perhaps allow us to include in our research into the representations of the Holocaust an extensive list of hitherto disregarded "half-images", thereby leading to new openings for research into the visualisation of the Holocaust.

Image scraps

Sometimes found among "hobbled images", as the research in Drancy shows, are sketched, unfinished, figurative images made by the victims. There is a remarkable record from occupied Poland – an example of a hurried, figurative sketch from a genocide site that links visual elements with textual testimony. We have 18 drawings documenting the period of the "Erntefest" operation (1943), targeting Jews who had survived operation "Reinhard". These are "drawings on the scraps of life", as the curators of the Majdanek State Museum exhibition, Krzysztof Banach and Lech Remiszewski, put it when presenting these images to the public in November 2017.[19] The author

56 *Roma Sendyka*

signed the drawings with the initials JR. There are at least three accounts as to how the sketches reached the collection of the Ghetto Fighters' House in Israel.[20] Until 2018, it was not known who the author actually was, but it was assumed, following the notes of the museum's founder and first curator Miriam Nowicz, that it was a Jewish man, Józef Richter, who had been hiding on the Aryan side.[21] Jakub Chmielewski, a researcher at the Majdanek Museum, recently discovered the statement of one Aleksander Paszko, an interwar dental technician, who gave an account of the help his family had given to a Józef Rychter.[22] Aryan papers, clothes and food enabled him to function and go by the name of Zbigniew Zaprzalski in Baudienst. After 1944, Paszko lost contact with Rychter; there are a few hypotheses as to the circumstances of his death.[23] It is highly likely that JR is actually Rychter-Zaprzalski, a Polish-speaking and assimilated photographer from the Chełm area (Figure 4.3).[24]

According to discovered testimony, Rychter "drew records on anything he had to hand. When he had some paper, he drew on paper; when he had a newspaper, he drew on the newspaper".[25] He made his pencil drawings on small pieces of torn wartime newspapers (the dimensions are random, the sides usually ten to 15 centimetres in length), and some larger ones on posters torn in two. Eight of the works on paper are of the same size – around 19 x 16 cm. These "recycled materials" were produced in the years 1940–1944. The dates on the back of the sketches are 1942 and 1943. The depicted scenes relate to the operation of the camps in Sobibór, Trawniki and Majdanek. The locations given on the back are Sobibór, Uhrusk and Lublin, but not all the locations featured have been identified. Also on the back, Rychter wrote laconic notes:

> Jewish-French women with children sort potatoes; I saw the camp by the station from the window. Stop on the way to Sobibór.

> Lublin. here Jews were loaded out of cars into cargo wagons (or perhaps the other way round).

> Window in a wagon. They ask for water. The guards watch over, we sit in the train on the other track. I quietly draw on a newspaper.

> Transport went to Sobibor, we stand by the track in railwaymen uniforms with railway tools (shovels, podboykas and slewing bars). We stand motionless and in a visible place, so they don't take us for Jews jumping out. In the distance, piles of burning corpses are smoking. This is a forest beyond Stulno.[26]

The steady hand of the notes on the sheets of paper stands out from the shaky records on the torn-off corners of newspapers, posters and printed notices

Images in cito, in situ, in extremis 57

Figure 4.3 Fragment of the display *Drawings on the Scraps of Life*
Source: The State Museum at Majdanek; photograph by Katarzyna Grzybowska, 2017

58   *Roma Sendyka*

ordering the public to gather berries from the forest. With the date and location of the production and with explanations that identify the position and actions of the author ("I am drawing quietly on a newspaper" . . .), the drawing scraps suggest, by means of their precarious materiality and the type of record used, the directness of visual notation – created in accordance with the criteria mentioned earlier: *in situ, in cito, in extremis*. It is, however, uncertain that the sketches were really drawn suddenly: the transport from 1943, for example, is sketched on a newspaper with a much later date, March 1944.

Due to the work he was carrying out, Rychter documented train routes: the area surrounding the tracks, stations, junctions, ramps in the camps and whatever was visible from the locomotives. He documents the working of the camps of the "Reinhard" operation but also – which makes this cycle of images of great significance in the search for visualisations of the "Holocaust by bullets" – sites of shootings, escapes and random executions. At least four of the 18 works concern wayside sites of the murder of Jews right next to train tracks (perhaps one of the most common among the subgroups of uncommemorated sites): the work of "Uhrusk 43", with the description "Hand which lay on the tracks after the passing of the transport to Sobibor"; pencil drawings from 1943 –

> Stulno forest, Ukrainian children wait by a dying Jewish woman, so as to be able to rob her. The transport was apparently from Belarus, Jews jumped into the forest.

> Forest near Sobibor; she fled the transport convoy, on the last wagon there is a machine gun, the forest is not thick with trees.

> The same Jewish woman that fled has a broken arm – no longer alive.

The fifth work is somewhat different, more dynamic. Three persons are depicted: someone is kneeling down (in civilian clothes); a soldier is turning towards that first person, with a rifle on his back, while a third figure has his back to the other two as he digs a burial ditch. The description is long, detailed and achieves intensity by means of its brief sentences, concentrated like an image in a lens – a dramatic scene with dialogues and a laconic but precise characterisation of the *dramatis personae*.

> At the Uhrusk station an old Jewish woman with a broken arm fled. German Grenzschutz (Austrians) did not want to finish her off. The Ukrainian police did that. One of them digs her grave by the tracks while the other waits to shoot her, she begs, "At least a drop of vodka".[27]

"Drawings on scraps" (of life, of newspapers, pieces of paper that were to hand) are drafts, unfinished work; the pencil lines are sometimes smudged, as if someone had dirtied the image or wiped it with a hand. The basic sheets have been prepared in a hurry and torn apart carelessly. The pieces of paper which share the same dimensions have uneven upper edges, as if they were torn out of a pad. The sketches on newspapers sometimes overlap with the newspaper text. I claim that such "works from the Holocaust by bullets" – of uncertain origins, made "not entirely sure when" and on "whatever was to hand", left to "whomsoever", written or drawn – are crucial reports and evidence of genocide.

Induced imaginings

Thanks to his forged papers, Rychter had a dual status: he was a victim (a Jew) but also a bystander (as long as Zbigniew Zaprzalski was taken for a Pole, he observed the Holocaust from a relatively safe distance). So the visual testimony from the "Holocaust by bullets" may involve the ambiguity of a dual point of view. This feature is shared by a remarkable work from the archive of the Jewish Historical Institute – a case which complicates further still the perspectives we have historical visualisations of killing sites. I have in mind the drawing by Jakub Guterman (Figures 4.4, 4.5).

Guterman, born in 1935, survived the war in the Płock ghetto, then later on the Aryan side in Ostrowiec and Warsaw, among other places. Under the

Figure 4.4 Jakub Guterman, Drawing, recto, Warsaw, Jewish Historical Institute, inv. no. B-513/3

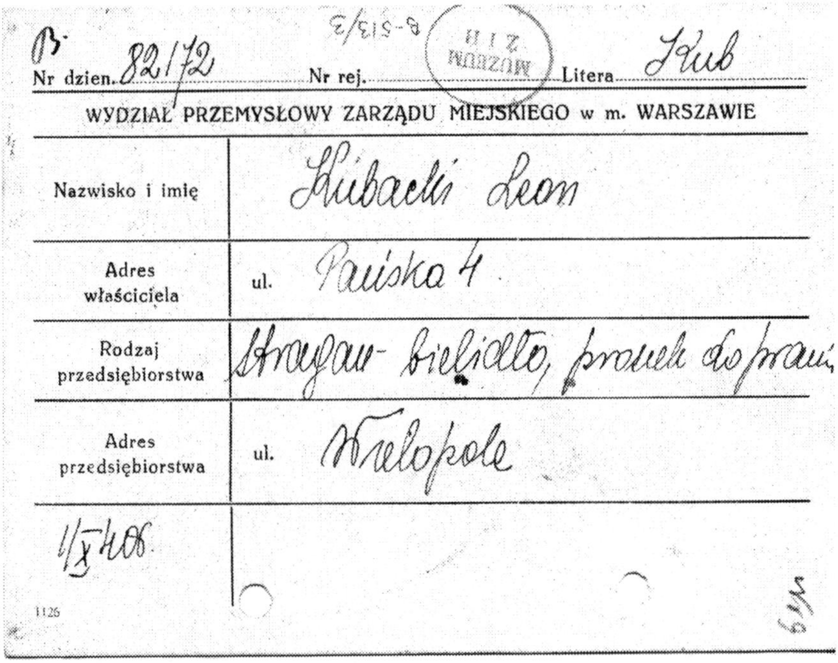
B· Nr dzien. 82/72 Nr rej. .... Litera Kub

WYDZIAŁ PRZEMYSŁOWY ZARZĄDU MIEJSKIEGO w m. WARSZAWIE

Nazwisko i imię	Kubacki Leon
Adres właściciela	ul.
Rodzaj przedsiębiorstwa	
Adres przedsiębiorstwa	ul.

1126

Figure 4.5 Jakub Guterman, Drawing, verso, Warsaw, Jewish Historical Institute, inv. no. B-513/3

name Staszek Duda, he was saved, hidden by a Polish family near Łowicz and by sisters of the Mariae Vitae congregation. After the war, in 1950, he emigrated to Israel. He worked as a teacher, illustrator and anti-war campaigner. He came back to Poland for a short visit in 1988.[28] We know more about how he survived because he recorded his family's fate in the introduction to the diary (*Leaves from Fire*) of his father, Symcha Guterman, which was recovered after the war due to a series of remarkable circumstances. His father was a craftsman and a playwright who died, having joined the Polish underground, on the first day of the Warsaw Uprising.[29] Jakub and his mother survived on the Aryan side.

This work is now archived in Warsaw. It is not an effect of direct observation or a work produced by the artist out of personal motivation. It is an effect of external encouragement to recall and document past events. As Guterman writes:[30]

> This took place in 1945, in Warsaw. A gentleman, a stranger to me, a Jew (perhaps someone from the Jewish Historical Commission) gave me these small cards and a few German forms, so I could use their reverse sides to

Images in cito, in situ, in extremis   61

draw "what I could recall from the times of the occupation". I was ten at the time. Those subjects were stuck in my memory and my soul, and for many a year my thoughts ran back to them.[31]

The drawing was made on a record card of a municipal institution from the pre-war period, which had continued operating during the occupation, the card being filled in on 1 October 1940. The drawing depicts the scene of a shooting which the viewer observes from behind the backs of the Germans. Three small groups of people are standing in the background under a tree. Bullets are flying out of the barrels of three rifles. The space between the weapons and the people is marked with colour. The figures of the victims and one of the murderers are barely drawn, while the details and proportions of the two Germans standing closer are enhanced and pronounced.

The scene is so suggestive that with time it came to be regarded as a drawing from nature made by an eyewitness who did not survive. Jakub Guterman recalled a surprising incident:

Returning to Poland for the first time in many years (1988), I was taken aback to see these pictures at an exhibition of the Jewish Historical Institute. I don't know how they got there. It was written there that the drawings had been made by "the little ten-year-old Jakub Guterman from Płock, who died in the Warsaw ghetto".

In the case of this expressive scene from the "Holocaust by bullets", we are dealing with a work of the imagination, or more precisely – imaginative memory. When asked if he had actually seen the shooting, Guterman explained the circumstances behind his work:

I drew that execution, but I was never the witness of a real execution. That's right, I was never an eyewitness, but you need to understand that "executions" were a genuine part of our daily lives. It penetrated our being, threatened us, like a sword of Damocles hanging over our heads. Executions were talked about, they struck terrible fear in our hearts.

So Guterman's testimony – put together in a similar way to Rychter's, on recycled material, by means of simple sketching tools and using a realistic, accessible aesthetic – is an imagining: a summing up of experiences of fear, information about the details of wartime danger, hearsay and wartime visual communication. Deriving, as it does, from imagination, it cannot be taken as a documentary snapshot of what happened. Nevertheless, it does bear profound, intense witness, coming straight "from the Holocaust".

So this testimony, drawn on a company registration form, is paradoxical. It is genuine, because it encapsulates a real-life experience, and yet it does not denote any specific event. It is belated and yet contemporary to the violence, because wartime reality has not been invalidated and closed-off in the past of

62 *Roma Sendyka*

the victims' lives. This reality is a construction, in which the Germans evidently play the key role as terrifying "anti-superheroes" from childhood imagination. Yet it continues to bear witness to those represented in the background by the small, schematic figures of falling victims.

***

Images from the "Holocaust by bullets", created in a place, time and circumstances of continuous murder, were made at great risk to life. Guterman accounts for the lack of more numerous visual documentation:

> Any documentation of the cruelties of the occupation (including artistic records) was punishable by death, which is why not much has remained; in any case, under those awful circumstances, people were concerned with what was most important for them: saving lives, their own lives and the lives of their dear ones. It was, simply, a fight for survival.

That is why these scenes, preserving what had been recorded by memory, were produced after the events, days or even years later. They resurface when artists develop the historian's urge to document the event or when they are recalled by a researcher documenting post-war trials. These scenes might recur beyond the individual's control, in the form of traumatic after-images. Though they reveal a motivation to record facts, they are merely drafts of factual testimony – inexplicit, imprecise, blurred. Their dating is uncertain; descriptions of locations are unclear. In place of realistic scenes, the "Holocaust by bullets" leaves its visual imprint in mural writings, scratches and sketches lacking an unquestionable connection with the corresponding events. The media of these images are materials that were free-of-charge, easily available and not typically used for artistic communication: bark, an uneven wall, scraps of newspapers, torn posters, old official record cards. Everything seems to suggest that this ontologically "weak" evidence from the "Holocaust by bullets" cannot possibly outweigh the documentary, evidential realism of the photographs taken by the perpetrators.

Nevertheless, in my opinion, it is exactly these imprecise, indeterminate, frail images that provide a fuller insight into what happened outside the camps. They are more relevant than photographs taken by the perpetrators, which usually serve as the primary visual source of the Holocaust in the East. To recognise these testimonies, however, requires a certain recalibration of expectations: abandoning the norms developed by and inherited from the history of art, aesthetics and modes of historical documentation. To receive a message that has been *transformed* by memory, imagination, wartime experience, children's perception, dreams or illness requires an augmented interpretative procedure, so as to acknowledge, without reservation, the full creative agency of the extremely precarious subjects who authored these works (unknown people, minors, the traumatised, people not trained for professional artistic work). To receive this testimony, we must treat seriously all the random "hobbled" media

Images in cito, in situ, in extremis   63

used to convey a testament to the past, and to read a sketch not as an initial gesture, but as a final and complete affidavit, so that its frequently damaged, precarious state be accepted as part of its meaning. And we must suspend the expectation of the temporal and topographical immediacy of visual testimony (perfectly accomplished by photography), so that images produced later, and elsewhere, may be acknowledged – despite all their deficiencies – as preserving their forensic agency.

It is, I claim, precisely the image-scraps from the "Holocaust by bullets" that should be the stellar witnesses to what happened outside the camps and ghettos. I see the particular value of this visual messaging in a feature which they share: they are images containing diverse properties – the power of factual testimony as well as the extreme impact of the situation here and now and the framework of violence in which the witness had to function. These are images in which suffering, regret, fear, mourning, pain and powerlessness come together in a complex emotional conglomerate that is inscribed in their materiality, challenging the viewer to develop more inclusive approaches that will allow us to place these objects within historical and artistic discourses.

I would like to express my gratitude for the support and cooperation of the author and of Michał Krasicki and Anna Duńczyk-Szulc from the Jewish Historical Institute in the course of this research. Courtesy of the artist and the JHI.

Notes

1 Jan Grabowski, *Hunt for the Jews: Betrayal and Murder in German-occupied Poland* (Bloomington, IN: Indiana University Press, 2013).
2 For a comprehensive account of the Einsatzgruppen "killing sites", see David Silberklang, Piotr Trojański, Juliane Wetzel and Miriam Bistrovic, eds., *Killing Sites: Research and Remembrance* (Berlin: Metropol, 2015).
3 Project: Uncommemorated Genocide Sites and Their Influence on Collective Memory, Cultural Identity, Ethical Attitudes and Intercultural Relations in Contemporary Poland (National Programme for the Development of Humanities 0121/NPRH4/H2a/83/2016). Key positions on the phenomenon of non-sites of memory have been developed in the following articles: Roma Sendyka, "Sites That Haunt: Affects and Non-Sites of Memory", trans. Jennifer Croft, *East European Politics and Societies*, 30/4 (2016), 1–16; Roma Sendyka, "A Prism: Understanding a Non-site of Memory (non-lieu de memoire)", in *EuTropes. The Paradox of European Empire*, ed. John W. Boyer and Berthold Molden (Chicago: University of Chicago Press, 2014). A preliminary sketch of this article was presented in the EHRI Newsletter: Roma Sendyka, "Holocaust by Bullets: Expanding the Filed of Holocaust Art", https://ehri-project.eu/holocaust-bullets, accessed 8 May 2020.
   For a study on literary accounts of the "Holocaust by bullets", see Sue Vice, " 'Beyond Words': Representing the 'Holocaust by Bullets'", *Holocaust Studies. A Journal of Culture and History*, 25/1–2 (2019).
4 Patrick Desbois, *The Holocaust by Bullets: A Priest's Journey to Uncover the Truth behind the Murder of 1.5 Million Jews*, trans. Catherine Spencer (New York: Palgrave Macmillan, 2009).
5 "Czego nie mogliśmy wykrzyczeć światu" [What We've Been Unable to Shout Out to the World], curators: Paweł Śpiewak and Anna Duńczyk-Szulc, 2017.

64 *Roma Sendyka*

6 William J. T. Mitchell, "Visual Literacy or Literary Visualcy?", in *Visual Literacy*, ed. James Elkins (New York: Routledge, 2008), 11–14.

7 Ibid.

8 According to Luiza Nader, art "from the Holocaust" would be first-hand testimony from victims, whereas art "about the Holocaust" would be testimony from bystanders. See Luiza Nader, "Polscy obserwatorzy Zagłady. Studium przypadków z zakresu sztuk wizualnych – uwagi wstępne" [Polish Observers of the Holocaust. Case Studies Drawn from the Visual Arts – Initial Remarks], *Zagłada Żydów. Studia i Materiały*, 14 (2018).

9 www.yadvashem.org/untoldstories/database/homepage.asp, accessed 20 August 2019.

10 Ibid.

11 On the use of the *in extremis* category of testimony, see Marta Janczewska and Jacek Leociak, "Świadectwo spisywane *in extremis*" [Testimony Recorded *in extremis*], in *Literatura polska wobec Zagłady (1939–1968)* [Polish Literature on the Holocaust (1939–1968)], ed. Sławomir Buryła and Dorota Krawczyńska (Warsaw: IBL, 2012).

12 See also *Last Letters from the Shoah*, ed. Zvi Bacharach (Jerusalem: Devora, 2004).

13 Marek T. Frankowski, *Mazowiecka katownia: dzieje Fortu III w Pomiechówku* [A Masovian Torture Chamber: The History of Fort II in Pomiechówek] (Warsaw: M.M., 2006); Piotr Oleńczak, *Siedem wieków dolinie Wkry* [Seven Centuries of the Wkra Valley] (Pomiechówek: Urząd gminy Pomiechówek, 2015).

14 See Dawid Kobiałka, Maksymlian Frąckowiak and Kornelia Kajda, "Tree Memories of the Second World War: A Case Study of Common Beeches from Chycina, Poland", *Antiquity*, 89 (2015).

15 According to the Memorial Book of Kowel, published in Tel Aviv in 1957, around 100 written records survived the war. They were made with small, sharp objects or in blood. (The book presents their contents; after the war, the writing was painted over and the synagogue used as a sewing room.) This historical landmark is mentioned in the display at the POLIN Museum of the History of Polish Jews in Warsaw, in the section *Holocaust (1939–1945)*.

16 Nader, "Polscy obserwatorzy", 169.

17 Ibid.

18 James Elkins, *The Domain of Images* (Ithaca: Cornell University Press, 2001), 3–4.

19 The State Museum at Majdanek exhibited a copy of the originals from the Israeli collection.

20 See Jakub Chmielewski, "Rediscovered – the Fate of Józef Richter during the Occupation", www.majdanek.eu/en/pow/rediscovered_____the_fate_of_jozef_richter_during_the_occupation/47, accessed 20 August 2019. Miriam Nowicz, a Museum employee, claimed she received it from an anonymous Polish man from the Chełm area; on another occasion, she said she received it from the family of Max Grodus. Another version of the story is the testimony of Aleksander (Aleksy) Paszko from near Chełm, recorded in Israel in June 1967, stating that he personally delivered the material to the Museum.

21 Krzysztof Banach and Lech Remiszewski, eds., *Rysunki na strzępach życia. Zagłada Żydów na Lubelszczyźnie w szkicach Józefa Richtera* [Drawings on the Scraps of Life: The Extermination of Jews in the Lublin Region in Józef Richter's Sketches] (Lublin: State Museum of Majdanek, 2017), 7.

22 From this point in the article, I will refer to the artist as Józef Rychter.

23 He may have died of typhus. He joined a partisan division and could have died in battle; there are also rumours of his execution following his capture for documenting the Holocaust. See Chmielewski, "Rediscovered".

24 Ibid.

25 Ibid.

26 Cited in Banach and Remiszewski, eds., *Rysunki*, 30–31, 38–39, 70–71, 80–81.

27 See Ibid., 56–57, 60–65, 78–79.

28 See the witness reports on the webpage of the NN Theatre, the "Spoken History" programme, http://teatrnn.pl/historiamowiona/swiadek/Guterman%2C_Jakub_%281935-_%29?tar=100540, accessed 20 August 2019.

29 *Leaves from Fire* was written in Yiddish but has been published in many languages: *Le livre retrouve*, 1991; *Het Opgedoken Boek*, 1992; *Le Libro Ritrovato*, 1992; *Das gerettene Buch*, 1993; the Polish edition *Kartki z pożogi* was published in Płock by Towarzystwo Naukowe Płockie in 2004. English edition: Symcha Guterman, *Leaves from Fire*, trans. Yaakov Guterman (Scotts Valley: CreateSpace Independent Publishing Platform, 2015).

30 I quote Jakub Guterman from our private correspondence. I reveal the contents of emails from August 2019 and personal details with the consent of Jakub Guterman, who also kindly agreed to me presenting his visual work alongside this text.

31 The gathering of children's testimonies was a common practice after the war: see *Wojna w oczach dziecka* [War through the Eyes of a Child], ed. Katarzyna Iwanicka and Marek Dubas (Warsaw: KAW, 1983). A new research approach to this material (recognising it as key evidence in court) is presented by Hannah Meszaros Martin; see www.macba.cat/es/arquitectura-forense-seminario, accessed 10 November 2017; 2 hours 3 minutes into the recording.

5 The stratified image: medium, construction and memory in Frank Stella's *Polish Villages*

Filip Lipiński

Frank Stella's series of works titled *Polish Villages*, produced between 1971 and 1974, marks a special stage in his career, when he diverted from his critically acclaimed monochromatic striped – and later polygonal, multicoloured – paintings. Many critics were surprised at the new project: it involved a radical change of formal structure and a diversification of the material support and the underlying principle of construction: the paintings differed but could be generally described as a combination of architectural objects, as collages or reliefs. Despite Stella's statements asserting his interest in construction and complete control over the process,[1] his new series of works was no longer guided by modernist analysis of the immanent, purely pictorial or physical conditions of art and its materials. In this chapter, I propose to look at *Polish Villages* as an experiment in the figuration of the complicated work of remembering, an analogue to the stratified[2] and fragmentary structure of cultural – both collective and individual – memory.[3]

Let us recap the basic facts first.[4] *Polish Villages* consists of more than 130 predominantly large-scale acrylic, hard-edged painted collages and mixed media constructions, preceded by more than 40 drawings made in 1970. The main body of the project can be divided into 43 small groups of works, each with a main large-format piece, often executed in several versions, bearing the name of a Polish village where a wooden synagogue stood before the Second World War. Each main work was additionally accompanied by a constellation of sketches, preparatory models and smaller versions. The immediate pretext for this immense body of work consisted of photographs and architectural drawings of wooden synagogues in pre-war Poland, reproduced in a 1959 English edition of Maria and Kazimierz Piechotka's book *Wooden Synagogues* that was presented to Stella by the architect Richard Meyer.[5] The starting point for this publication consisted of the interwar photographs by Polish art historian Szymon Zajczyk and other, often unnamed, photographers surveying extant Jewish wooden architecture on Polish soil. This documentation was commissioned as material for research carried out at the Jewish Art Studio on the Department of Polish Architecture run by Professor Oskar Sosnowski at Warsaw Technical School. All of the photographed, inventoried and analysed buildings were destroyed, mostly during the Second World War, as a result of military action

DOI: 10.4324/9781003264460-7

The stratified image 67

and Nazi policies aimed against the Jewish race and their cultural heritage. Also at that time, a significant part of the archive, including negatives and scholarly work on the synagogues, perished or went missing. What remained became the basis for the book that reached Stella.

Consequently, any examination of *Polish Villages* should pay attention to more than just what meets the eye – the sequence of mediations and strata of various kinds that laid the foundations for the project: the actual places of worship which stood for the histories of the diasporas that attended them, their photographic representations, architectural drawings, the creation of an archive, followed by the unfortunate dispersal of the archive and simultaneous destruction of its real-life referents, the reassembling of the remaining materials into the form of a book; at the end of this sequence, we find Stella's series of works. Importantly, it is also difficult to unequivocally determine the original referent, as it may be simply the architectural form and/or what the architecture stands for – Jewish culture and history, encompassing the past and, as will be shown later – the future.

Stella himself emphasised his predominantly formal interest in the architectural elements of these wooden constructions and described his work as a variation on those forms, which determined the nature of his procedure. For Stella, *Polish Villages* was a way to "start all over again", because he did not know how to improve or move forward with what he had been doing up to that point (Figure 5.1). Commenting on the project, the artist said:

> Struggling through the Polish pictures opened things up for me so that I was able to use my gift for structure with something that modernism hadn't really exploited before, the idea that paintings could be constructed, made by picture-building. . . . Building a picture was something natural for me. Build it and then paint it. It was a job I was well suited for.[6]

The dominant feature of *Polish Villages* as a whole is the diversification of the materials. A good example is the group *Bogoria*, from 1971 to 1974. Stella used different materials in different phases of his work, such as paper, bristol and corrugated board, plywood, wood (painted or natural), felt and even aluminium. While the preparatory works are usually materially homogeneous, the material structure of the main, large paintings is much more diverse: they are collages of elements whose physical provenance, due to the use of colour, often seems unclear. In contrast to Stella's classical, geometrical works, although geometry still plays an important role in *Polish Villages*, these works are formally more varied, unsymmetrical and less orderly. More importantly, the combination of collage and relief creates a spatial arrangement of incorporated elements, enriches the experience of the work with a haptic, textural quality and generates an impression of overlapping, interconnected layers, which sometimes are ruptured and continued elsewhere, as in *Olkienniki III* (1972). As a result, Stella relinquished the minimalist exaltation of material purity and the fetishised medium specificity, opticality and pictorial flatness of modernism in

Figure 5.1 Franks Stella at his West Houston Street Studio, New York, with works from the *Polish Village* series, 1974

Source: © Nancy Crampton

favour of what Andrzej Turowski described as "the structure of superimposed color planes"[7] – a structure that was much less modular and predictable, less formulaic or regulated, untamed, if you will, and, in consequence, despite its hard-edged quality, more difficult to classify, describe and interpret within the modernist paradigm. Moreover, as Mark Godfrey noted, viewing *Polish Villages* frontally does not do full justice to its textural and spatial complexity: a series of formal dislocations displaces the ideal, stable modernist subject to make room for "a subject in crisis, unable to experience a clear sense of presence before the work, unable to know its limits and unsure of their own position in turn".[8] This kind of anamorphic dislocation made it impossible to experience the "grace of presentness" in front of a picture,[9] and it obscured and destabilised not only the subject but also the object and its material status. Godfrey claims that the complicated or even chaotic structure of the final works reflects the process of their creation, hence concentrating viewers' attention on the work itself and blocking out external references or contexts.[10] But this "either/or" logic seems flawed, because it excludes the possibility of concentrating on the work *and* seeing its formal solutions as signifiers – or symptoms – of what I would describe as not so much external references as virtual layers of attendant images and discourses which seem to have formed and *in*formed the ultimate shape of Stella's material objects, thus becoming an indirect, immaterial, but effective

The stratified image 69

and active element of the resulting work.[11] The expanded, virtual referential field which formed in these constructions becomes part of our contemporary experience; it is open and continues to expand, due to cultural mediation and the ongoing work of remembrance. As a result, the *Polish Villages* is temporally heterogeneous or even anachronistic – its overwhelming physical presence, first internally fractured on the level of materially differential versions, virtually extends towards the past, gathering layers of its visual and cultural pre-texts which I listed previously, and brings them back to contemporary viewers only to subsequently gravitate towards the future.

Until recently, the issue of memory in relation to this body of work was either overlooked or treated very generally. That was certainly due to the interpretative framework imposed by Stella, who minimised his attachment to any aspect of the project not related to formal considerations. The authors of more recent texts, even if they do discuss the question of memory, seem to take it for granted and have not theorised the way in which memory translates into formal solutions and is signified by them. The aspect of memory was taken up more extensively by Clifford Chanin, who wrote that it is difficult to describe *Polish Villages* in terms of a memorial, but that they definitely constitute a remnant of traumatic history; they are "the art of the afterward".[12] Carol Solus noted that along with the problems of construction and what the artist called the "interlockingness" of architectural wooden elements that was of special interest to him, the series "can function as a symbolic reminder of the culture of Eastern European shtetl" and "it has been interpreted as serving as a metaphor for Stella's empathy for the lives once flourishing in those buildings in pre-World War II Poland".[13] True as it may be, the previous comment fails to give us much of a clue about any principle underlying what Piotr Jamski describes as "the miracle of memory"[14] or how this is connected with the actual objects, with the process of construction, with what Stella terms "building" a painting, or with how they trigger remembrance today.

Discussing *Polish Villages* in mostly formal, artistic or architectural terms was indeed prefigured in the approach adopted in their book by the Piechotkas, who concentrated on the architectural form and on preserving knowledge about it. This, however, implicates an omission which consequently appears even more telling: the bracketing of historical events and layers of memory, virtually located in between these images, which haunt and saturate *Polish Villages* with a special affective dimension and seem to inform its structure. As for the often-misleading search for similarities between Stella's constructions and actual architectural structures (the mimetic motivation for connecting a photograph or drawing of a synagogue to a specific work by Stella), leaving aside the general principle of interlocking parts and predominant angularity, in Stella's paintings one can, in fact, notice several persuasive analogies to the architectural elements of synagogues. *Bogoria* and *Odelsk* serve as good examples in this respect. However, rather than providing evidence of superficial mimetic resemblance, I propose that they should be regarded as a residue of the work of memory: worked-through material, memory-traces, which activate a dialectic of a distant and feeble connection in time and space on the one hand and irreversible displacement, loss and absence on the other, thus indirectly signifying the historical fortunes of the synagogues and what they stood for. Stella was working on material that was a few times removed, leading back to the lost communities, already visible in the photographs, mostly emptied of any human presence, as if prefiguring the Nazi "final solution".

These photographs and their referents, the buildings with their histories, situate the beginning of the *Polish Villages* project long before it was actually embarked on (Figure 5.2). I believe that the "subject in crisis" which Godfrey talks about, the unstable position and dislocation of an observer, can also describe the position of the artist who, regardless of his intentions and statements, finds himself in front of an archive of images that preserved the look of something which was out there but *would have been* destroyed and something which, from Stella's standpoint, *was already long gone*, an experience of the future anterior, in terms of not just the material destruction of architecture but also the loss of Jewish culture and human lives. What comes to mind here is Roland Barthes's commentary on Alexander Gardner's 19th-century photograph of the young convict Lewis Payne: he notices the *punctum*, external to the image itself but affecting it, which is the imminent and unavoidable death of the man, something bound to happen and that already belonged to the past.[15]

Figure 5.2 Bogoria synagogue: view from the northwest

Source: photo by Stanisław Rakowski, 1913, print size 4.7 x 6.69 in, IS PAN

The stratified image   71

The status of the photographs under discussion as documentary and scholarly material was additionally strengthened by architectural drawings and by its institutional framing – the Department of Architecture at the Warsaw Technical School. During the Second World War, not only did the referents of the photos disappear, but the archive itself was greatly affected: photographic negatives, some architectural drawings and scholarly notes became scattered or destroyed. In 1957, much of the remaining – and partially complemented – material was reproduced in the Piechotkas' book and as such – in its English edition – later came to Stella's attention. These photographs shock the viewer with a paradoxical combination of stability, the craftsmanship of their referents and the unrepresentable fragility – located in the temporal folds of each image – and ultimate erasure of their objects. As a result, they activate the work of remembering their destruction and the tragic history behind it, a ruin always already inscribed in the photographic medium.

Stella's collage-like and layered structures can be read as literal images of somewhat "structured" debris. But again, this facile parallel opens up another level: these irregular constructions – or rather de-constructions – appear to be a result of the mediation and attendant interpretation of memory; they not so much make us remember the appearance of synagogues as act as a pictorial/architectural analogy of their complex history seen from our contemporary viewpoint, to become, as one critic has put it, the "architecture of memory".[16] I would say that *Polish Villages*, the process of its creation and reception, is an example of dealing with what James E. Young describes as the "vicarious past", the variously activated and mediated memory of something that could not possibly have been experienced.[17] Dominick LaCapra comments on a similar issue: "the experience of trauma may be vicarious or virtual, that is, undergone in a secondary fashion by one who was not there or did not go through the traumatizing events themselves".[18] This type of mediated traumatic memory is paradoxical, because its formal realisations reveal the conditions of unavoidable failure to remember, *the work of memory* rather than actual remembrance. Stella seems to have framed or shielded this vicariously experienced past in his present in a way that he was most familiar with – solving the issues of construction, medium and materiality. At the same time, the result of his process, over which he allegedly was in total control, are works which look as if memory of the traumatic events – unrepresented but implicated in the photographs – burst open the formal seams of his earlier striped or polygonal works, resulting in a paradoxical "constructed ruin" of *Polish Villages*.

Another strictly connected perspective that sheds light on *Polish Villages* as stratified figurations of memory is the perceptual experience on the part of the viewer, who virtually tries to "peel off" the layers of the actual, physical work in a process of the differential projection of diverse associations and materials known to him or her. Such a situation is facilitated when Stella's works are encountered in the context of a comprehensive exhibition where the large versions are accompanied by the photos and drawings of synagogues, preparatory sketches and models. Exhibitions, like the one at the POLIN Museum of

72   *Filip Lipiński*

Polish Jews in Warsaw in 2016, become opportunities to discover that while these physically overwhelming, impressive structures could possibly be discussed in terms of formal solutions, they were far more persuasive when one actually let the discourse of memory ingrained in the accompanying materials play a part in the act of their perception and interpretive reading.

The complementary connection between the perception of images or objects, on the one hand, and the images, memories or associations that are thereby activated, on the other, has been discussed by numerous thinkers. In my view, the most compelling account was offered by Henri Bergson, who claimed that "there is no perception which is not full of memories. With the immediate and present data of our senses, we mingle a thousand details out of our past experience",[19] which, in the 20th century, would also involve mediated experience. At the same time, memories – belonging, in his view, to the domain of the virtual – affect and transform perceptual data. As a result, "Perception is never a mere contact of the mind with the object present; it is impregnated with memory-images which complete it as they interpret it."[20] Much more recently, from an anthropological perspective, an inalienable connection between memory, images and media was postulated by Hans Belting: images, as carriers of memory, undergo intense technological re-mediation and dissemination. Complicating the distinction between individual and collective memory, they open previously inaccessible spatial and temporal dimensions and allow us to face the "pictorial presence of absent places":[21] "Instead of visiting pictures at their given geographical places, we prefer now to visit places in pictures".[22] Belting says that we internalise and mix individual and collective images, which we appropriate as our own – if vicarious – memories. We use first- and second-hand images of lost places suffused with various temporal dimensions to defend ourselves from the loss of space and the absolute passing of time. In consequence, a differential act of metamorphosis takes place, from the seen to the remembered, from disembodied external images that we absorb to their subsequent re-embodiment, one concretisation of which consists of works of art. In the meantime, our psychological apparatus transforms, fragments, displaces or hides this material, depending on our affective investment in it. Consequently, we could generally say that our perception is always already "a productively remembering look", to borrow the term coined by Kaja Silverman.[23] In narratives about art that we – as art or cultural historians – produce, we can acknowledge that this look, infused with memory, is our own, even if it necessarily consists of borrowed material, or we can put ourselves in a more comfortable and less responsible position and virtually assign it to the author of the object. Actually, both of those ways, on different levels, work for Stella's *Polish Villages* and are not mutually exclusive.

In this short account, I did not claim to know what Stella must have thought when he was working on *Polish Villages*. Instead, I retrospectively projected a possible scenario of impulses governing such an unexpected shift in his art. More importantly, though, I tried to describe and theorise my own, and possibly other contemporary viewers', experience of these works as objects

The stratified image   73

shaped by and so figuring the work of vicarious memory. As a result, Stella's famous dictum "what you see is what you see" does not hold water here. The constructivist-minimalist reification of a work of art has been annulled for the sake of a temporalised, stratified construction, full of internal tensions, which contains much more than what is visually and physically given. Or to put it differently: the visual and material qualities of Stella's works activate an inseparable process of seeing and remembering, perception saturated with the memory of photographs of synagogues and the histories they imply. *Polish Villages* demands such a virtually extended field of vision, where what you see is what you see but only when you accept the layered, ontologically varied structure of visuality that neutralises the distance between the virtual and the material, the past and the present.

Notes

1 "The Polish pictures were well designed and very tight in terms of engineering", Frank Stella quoted in William Rubin, *Frank Stella 1970–1987* [cat.] (New York: Museum of Modern Arts, 1987), 37.

2 This geological metaphor of stratification or layering has been used in various discussions on memory. Just to give a few examples: Sigmund Freud often resorts to this structural metaphor when comparing the process of psychoanalysis and reaching the unconscious to "the technique of excavating a buried city" (Sigmund Freud, "Studies on Hysteria", in *Complete Works*, ed. Ivan Smith, 2010, 125, www.valas.fr/IMG/pdf/ Freud_Complete_Works.pdf, accessed 2 September 2019. Marianne Hirsch describes her experience of post-memory as a picture whose "power to overshadow my own memories derives precisely from the layers – both positive and negative – that have been passed down to me unintegrated, conflicting, fragmented, dispersed". Marianne Hirsch and Leo Spitzer, *The Ghosts of Home. The Afterlife of Czernowitz in Jewish Memory* (Berkeley: University of California Press, 2010), 9. Van der Kolk and van der Hart discuss layers of memory in the context of the vertical layering of the mind as exemplified by repression – pushing downward and hiding the unwanted content. They also identify the mechanism of dissociation, which "reflects a horizontally layered model of mind: when a subject does not remember a trauma, its 'memory' is contained in an alternate stream of consciousness, which may be subconscious or dominate consciousness, e.g. during traumatic reenactments", B. A. van der Kolk and Onno van der Hart, "The Intrusive Past: the Flexibility of Memory and the Engraving of Trauma", quoted in *Acts of Memory. Cultural Recall in the Present*, ed. Mieke Bal, Jonathan Crewe and Leo Spitzer (London: Dartmouth College Press, 1999), ix.

3 According to Mieke Bal, "the term cultural memory signifies that memory can be understood as a cultural phenomenon as well as an individual or social one . . . cultural memory . . . links the past to the present and future". Mieke Bal, "Introduction", in ibid., vii.

4 For a comprehensive and up-to-date source of information on the history and origins of Stella's project, see Artur Tanikowski, ed., *Frank Stella and Synagogues of Historic Poland*, published in Polish and English (Warsaw: POLIN Museum, 2016).

5 Maria Piechotka and Kazimierz Piechotka, *Wooden Synagogues* (Warsaw: Arkady, 1959).

6 Frank Stella, quoted in *Frank Stella and Synagogues of Historic Poland*, 65.

7 Andrzej Turowski, "Simulated Constructivism in Frank Stella's Minimalist Game", in *Frank Stella and Synagogues of Historic Poland*, 29. Unfortunately, Turowski neither elaborates on nor theorises this formulation.

8 Mark Godfrey, *Abstraction and the Holocaust* (New Haven: Yale University Press, 2007), 110.

74 *Filip Lipiński*

9 I am referring here to Michael Fried's famous argument against minimalism in Michael Fried, "Art and Objecthood", in *Art and Objecthood. Essays and Reviews* (University of Chicago Press, 1998), 148–172.

10 Godfrey, *Abstraction and the Holocaust,* 110.

11 I use the term "virtual" to designate the immaterial, mental, memory or fantasy-related images. I elaborate on this issue later. See also Filip Lipiński, "The Virtual as 'Dangerous Supplement' of Art (History)", in *DeMaterializations in Art and Art-Historical Discourse in the Twentieth Century*, ed. Wojciech Bałus and Magdalena Kunińska (Cracow: IRSA, 2018), 171–189.

12 Clifford Chanin, "Frank Stella's *Polish Villages* in Poland", in *Frank Stella and Synagogues of Historic Poland*, 94.

13 Carol Solus, "Frank Stella's Polish Village Series and Related Works: Heritage and Alliance", *An Interdisciplinary Journal of Jewish Studies*, 28/2 (2010), 149–150.

14 Piotr Jamski, "Frank Stella's Polish Villages and Their Photographic Inspirations", in Frank *Stella and Synagogues of Historic Poland*, 93.

15 Roland Barthes, *Camera Lucida*, trans. Richard Howard (New York: Hill & Wang, 1996), 94–97.

16 Godfrey, *Abstraction and the Holocaust*, 111.

17 James E. Young, "The Holocaust as Vicarious Past: Restoring the Voices of Memory to History", *Judaism*, 15/1 (2002), 71–87.

18 Dominick LaCapra, *History in Transit. Experience, Identity, Cultural Theory* (Ithaca: Cornell University Press, 2004), 125

19 Henri Bergson, *Matter and Memory*, trans. Nancy Margaret Paul and William Scott Palmer (New York: Zone Books, 1991), 33.

20 Ibid., 133.

21 Hans Belting, *An Anthropology of Image: Picture, Medium, Body*, trans. Thomas Dunlap (Princeton: Princeton University Press, 2014), 42.

22 Ibid., 41.

23 Kaja Silverman, *The Threshold of the Visible World* (New York: Routledge, 1996), 181.

6 Against illusion: Kuno Raeber's thoughts on the power of material and the art of Karl Rössing

Dorota Kownacka

Raeber's attitude to art

The Swiss lyric poet, writer, novelist and critic Kuno Raeber (1922–1992), regarded by many as a "great stranger"[1] because his work is only recently and gradually coming to the attention of a wider audience, contemplated art and its role in the modern world. Born in Switzerland and settled in Munich, he was a brilliant historian and political thinker, an advocate of southern European culture: "Though undeniably conditioned by his native country, he is preoccupied with the destiny of Germany and even more with that of Europe. He is convinced that the Europeans are doomed unless they create a United States of Europe".[2] So he returned to the origins of the Old Continent.

> He is not particularly fond of modern Western technology and industrialism; his mind and his heart go out to the Mediterranean countries, especially Italy (southern Italy, Sicily) and Greece, where he likes to travel as often as he can. But his true spiritual home is, despite his Roman Catholic background, the Mediterranean civilization of antiquity, and he is on intimate terms with ancient Greek mythology.[3]

At once both pessimist and optimist, aware of myth, history and common culture, he focused on the differences between seeing, writing and thinking related to timeless things, to some extent visible but invisible by nature. He believed in abiding in a truth that issued from mythological reality, which allowed art to remain authentic, due to the existence of a pre-existential dimension.

Material turn

Focused on artistic expression and on celebrating the power of poetic creation, he intended to elaborate a special language making it possible to analyse the consistency and variability of an object's meaning and refer to the inviolable element of the eternal idea hidden in its material construction. He tried to discover how artists had succeeded in elaborating a genuine compromise between illusion, abstraction, material and history, and understanding that it is

DOI: 10.4324/9781003264460-8

76 Dorota Kownacka

possible only beyond the object, but within its essence. His remarks may suggest that he succeeded in creating a logical and factual world as a conceptual model of the material world. In 1956, he stressed that art and literature, seen as freedom, impudence and a daring attitude to life, was like a game played with the "endless world of matter".[4] And he once confessed: "For me, poetry is a masquerade where there is no unmasking but only the trying-on of ever new masks".[5] These two short sentences refer to a very important idea in Raeber's theory of art memory. Things are never the same, because thoughts are never the same. Nevertheless, there must be something that ensures continuation, even if it occurs in a way that is impossible to articulate in human language and remains only characteristic of the material world. Meanings are always influenced by the present moment, culture, place and individual experience, so real meaning does not exist; one cannot reveal the true appearance of things, because everything is open-ended and there always appears another mask that opens up a space for new observations. Raeber's main interests refer to the potential of material and its natural ability to accumulate meanings organically in its structure, somewhere beyond the storyline, and to keep them in an undisturbed vacuum as a repository of forms untouched by external circumstances. It has been said that Raeber is "a poet through and through; even his stories, his novels, and his essays are, fundamentally, poems in prose".[6] Those "prose poems" offered a material turn, which should be compared with an iconic or pictorial turn, because they did not present an illusion or narrative possessing the inner truth of a work, but, in keeping with the principles of an open structure, allowed for constructive chaos. Paul Klee begins writing about "Infinite natural history" with a definition of a balanced space between chaos and cosmos:

> Chaos as an antithesis is not complete and utter chaos, but a locally determined concept relating to the concept of the cosmos. Utter chaos can never be put on the scale, but will remain forever unweighable and unmeasurable. It can be Nothing or a dormant Something, death or birth, according to the dominance of will or lack of will, of willing or notwilling.[7]

It seems that Raeber chose chaos as a form of controlled balance between realities – established, but invariably astonishing. Most of his poems, but also his narrative works, are laconic. We can read a characterisation of his writing in *Willkommen und Abschied, Studies in German Literature Linguistics and Culture* (2005):

> The body of Kuno Raeber's poetry shows constancy as well as development. The earlier poems tend to be more narrative, ornamental, emotional, and regular; the later ones, according to the author himself, show their objects "as the shadows on the wall in Plato's cave": reduced to the basic forms, simplified to such an extent that one may deplore the absence of richness, color, and corporealness.[8]

In these circumstances, the material became more real than its interpretation, and the word acquired a substantial dimension. In *Auto da fé* (1964), Raeber emphasised that language interested him only as material.[9]

The degradation of material

George Didi-Huberman, in his essay about aesthetic and material order,[10] noted that regardless of the origins of philosophy, Platonic or Kantian, material remains permanently in opposition to other values, to matter or form, and it is always subordinate to them as a passive and secondary factor. He also emphasised that material is often perceived as something abstract, without any specification or formal data. Giorgio Vasari asserted that material was subordinate to the idea, and Ervin Panofsky shared that opinion. Examining the history of wax from an Aristotelian perspective, Didi-Huberman showed its usefulness, variety of forms and ways of interpretation. His main conclusion was that a material's destiny is concealed within it, so for certain purposes a given material is more suitable, but for various reasons it cannot be used in other circumstances without being misused. Last but not least, there must exist something that one might call material memory. On the one hand, material is obedient and tractable; on the other, it shows an allegiance, which ultimately becomes its strength and potential. Gottfried Boehm stated, invoking Martin Heidegger's idea of art, that "artists always knew that their work did not consist in using certain material, but in bringing out its language".[11] Language conceived as material by Raeber shows its importance as an element affecting the expansion of an object's materiality.

Against illusion towards reality

By using old patterns and drawing on memory schemes, artists created a new pictorial language suitable and appropriate for expressing the experience of war. This potential of material makes it possible to develop a narrative hidden in its very texture, which may be compared to the crystalline constructions created and used by Paul Klee or interpreted in a slightly different way by Wilhelm Worringer. Klee noted in his diary in 1915: "In the great pit of forms lie broken fragments to some of which we still cling. They provide abstraction with its material. A junkyard of unauthentic elements for the creation of impure crystals".[12] Klee's achievements gain intellectual currency as a reflection of the world showing the foreign and reduced forms of external values.[13] Manfred Clemenz understood the relationship outlined by Klee as a metaphor of "becoming crusted" (*Überkrustung*), as the transformation of self-appraisal into inorganic crystal, as "armour plating" (*Panzerung*).

> The crystal was a common art symbol at the beginning of the last century (used mainly by the expressionists). Wilhelm Worringer, meanwhile, in the 1908 book *Abstraction und Einfühlung . . .* understood the crystal as

78 Dorota Kownacka

an aesthetic idiom of abstraction. For Worringer, abstraction is a magical incantation against human dependence on the outside world (*Außenwelt*) and a liberation from life dependencies. It is "absolute form" and represents the absolute as such. . . . Klee's argumentation was similar to that of Worringer. . . . Klee only created an explicit conception of the crystal under the sway of his impressions of the First World War (although he emphasised that the war did not take possession of him). In contrast to Worringer, however, for Klee the crystal was both an art symbol and a self-symbol. . . . As "crystal", or self-abstraction, so to speak, Klee hoped to be "immortal" in the face of adversity.[14]

This is the idea of pre-existence, origin and roots, cosmos arising from chaos. We can also find traces of pre-existence in the poetry and literature of those times, as in Hugo von Hofmannsthal,[15] who intended to use acquired wisdom, spiritual sovereignty and an understanding of the platonic vision of the eternal idea. He posited that the flesh appeared after the spirit, and this would be crucial for establishing the sequence to the inner organisation of the phases preceding the existence of an object, in this case, the work of art. Raeber followed the influence of material on artists. He discovered specific progress from external works of art, *Außenbilder*, to spiritual, immaterial pictures of the soul, or the imagination, *Seelenbilder*, similarly to Hans Belting, who believed that the body was the only space where internal and external pictures could meet.[16] Between those two extremities, there was a place for the aspiration to a non-illusory experience of the truth, based on the deconstruction of the object and its meaning and on reconstruction adapted to the new condition of the world. The power of hidden values appears in the very structure of material. A true work of art is always to some extent incomplete and indicates a hidden source of cognition. Short-term memory replaced by perspective vision enables the artist to adopt a clear position with regard to the object in order to comprehend the essence in its structure. This pure recognition no longer offers any scope for illusion.

Too close to recognise the object

Kuno Raeber, hoping for the unification in an object of its message and the features of its constituent material, devoted one of his essays to the art of Karl Rössing, in particular his experience from working in woodcut and linocut. In the 1920s, and after 1945, Rössing (1897–1987) developed a highly inventive method: he juxtaposed contrasting elements of a picture, the natural with the artificial, and, taking them from different cultures and ages, employed the so-called combinatorial principle (*Das Prinzip des Kombinatorischen*). He did not intend to disconcert the viewer, like the surrealists, or to create in his late work a reconstructed world of new reality (*Neue Sachlichkeit*), but he wanted to open multiple levels of cognition and interpretations occurring in untouched spaces. He succeeded in creating operating fields for wartime experiences. In

Against illusion 79

Raeber's opinion, this represents an attempt to focus illusion by means of a very haptic, material and strict approach to a potential object, the presentation of a phenomenon hidden behind the current represented scene. It is something like an object without an object. Raeber stated in *Die Bildwelt von Karl Rössing*:

> Art is always memory; the more absolute it is, the purer is that aspect. Only in the evocation of familiar things does something new arise. There is a reason for this. As soon as abstract art loses its initial element of surprise, it starts to be boring. As a game with form and colour, undeniably illuminating but empty, it may be very amusing for the eye and satisfactory for a refined sense of art. That is why it means nothing. Abstract art, important as a reflection of pure structure, never tempted Karl Rössing, because it contained too much *Weltstoff*.[17]

In this passage, Raeber recognised that abstract art could be empty, appealing only to the eye, not rooted in the material, but lying on the surface of the medium, without any insight into the essence, which remained absolutely inaccessible and also absent in such art. In his preface to Worringer's *Abstraction and Empathy*, Hilton Kramer explained the aim of abstraction:

> to wrest the object of the external world out of its natural context, out of the unending flux of being, to purify it of all its dependence upon life, i.e. of everything about it that was arbitrary, to render it necessary and irrefragable, to approximate it to its absolute value.[18]

Raeber did not find absolute value in art that was not historically anchored, deprived of a phase of pre-existence.

Examining Rössing's art as visual evidence of growing in continuity, Raeber once mentioned that: "The critic and scepticism are overcome. They are replaced by wisdom. Yet this wisdom contains not a hint of resignation. Late Rössing attained a state in which, without excluding himself from the world, he discovered its essential nature".[19] Raeber explains that the artist had earlier seen his own presence from too close a perspective, and as soon as he stepped back from the objects in their essence, he succeeded in comprehending them in their structures.[20] For Raeber, Karl Rössing's transition from woodcut to linocut was crucial in his process of maturing. As a young artist, Rössing acted against his time,[21] but he produced at that time external works (*Außenbilder*) inspired by external circumstances. It was only in 1950, when he began to work in linocut, that he managed to cultivate a distance from everything external. Raeber talks about the realism of the woodcut. It is the material and the technique that determine the very haptic and profound work on the provenance of a thing, with its sharp edges and deep shadows, and the need to fight for the form that the present world should assume. The possibility of understanding all these factors degrades the truth concealed in the structure. It is only history that enables commentators to advance abusive interpretations.

80   Dorota Kownacka

In the case of linocut, the viewer is given a surface with some marks on it, so he or she can follow the manifestations of an art that is eternal and independent of the ingenuity of the mind. One can choose either current tricks of the imagination or the timeless aura of art, relinquishing the current meanings of phenomena caused by the lack of productivity of the post-war object.

Raeber noticed that the artist no longer wanted to present objects in their common form; he preferred to rebuild them, and experience of the new conditions of an object ought to refer to the new world.

> It is an artistic process . . . familiar figures detached from their classical anchorage gain a new freedom by being reset in an archaic context, where everything is still undetermined, still flowing, easy and ambiguous; it is a new peace. The viewer of these pictures realises that the things which he or she has encountered so many times as enduring clichés are hidden in his soul. . . . The art of Karl Rössing, even if it cited classical – and so untouchable – symbols, is anti-classical with regard to their procedures. It is art of associations in the psychoanalytical sense. This also implies that the transmitted signs are combined with objects of the modern technical civilisation, with references to current social and political processes.[22]

Raeber concentrated his characterisation on simple remarks, on calling things by their name, as in *Fahrrad im Schnee*, in which a bicycle is lying in snow next to the body of a sphinx. The viewer ought to understand the uncomplicated message of a picture. Everything is real, so it does not evoke any illusion; although the described situation is strange and rarely has a chance to occur in the real world, the juxtaposing of particular nouns taken from different orders shocks and moves. There is no room here for perspective or any other elements of composition; the description should be unreal, in contrast to the multidimensional work of art referring to origins and previous events.[23] Rössing remained faithful to ancient culture:

> The artistic legacy of the antiquity of Mediterranean art is a reminiscence of our memory, like a gold mummy that will turn to dust at the slightest movement, and that dust contains magical ingredients. There is no other substance of such delicacy, of such quality.[24]

This magic power of ancient times enabled Rössing to continue the eternal work. Rössing comes across as naïve, but he was a wise man as well, who succeeded in returning to the source, not as an intellectual value, but as a vision of pre-existence.[25] Raeber noted that Rössing repeatedly used the same motifs. Some of them appear as dreams, wings, butterflies, female statues, a sphinx, a winged lion with female head and a creature half-man, half-bird. Raeber interprets those motifs as being responsible for "liberating form from material limitations, from the pressure of stone and walls, statues, torsos, which always remind one of overcoming, permeating, shaping, penetrating".[26] Death

Against illusion 81

is understood as transfiguration.[27] At the end of the essay, Raeber wrote that Rössing's works were based on "confrontation and struggle, reunification and reconciliation. That is the peculiarity of these pictures, their double face, now frightening now delightful".[28] Raeber argued that

> there is no possibility of retreat, because there is a crack in the gigantic edifice of the world; it cannot be repaired or closed any more, but the despair in Rössing's works offers us hope and a remedy, to which we just have to turn.[29]

One may say that the remedy contains the permanent memory of the material. At the foundation of woodcut and linocut technique, we find serial activity and multiplication that immediately takes account of the memory of a process-action; so physical memory, traces of production. Raeber's thinking regarding memory and culture was broad, mainly thanks to his general approach to history: he was inspired by ancient culture because of the timeless potential of material that it offered, especially since it was already tried and tested. He represented the view that ancient works of art were not empty, but resistant, in contrast to current art, which uses old patterns but without the old truth. This can only occur beyond the object, beyond current memory, within the material; we should experience the symbiosis of material with its organic foundation. Merleau-Ponty similarly differentiated between mental and physical paintings. He also distinguished, from the phenomenological perspective, internal and external, visible and invisible pictures.[30]

I wanted to highlight the importance of Raeber's idea of art, which he understood, in terms of material, as a remedy for illusion, which is not a sufficient counterweight to post-war realism, but rather an antithesis to Gottfried Semper's theory of material and to the adaptation of some motifs in another material.[31] One must distinguish the materiality that is purely concealed in the structure of material.

> Material as *such* he said, need not be a factor that appears in the work of art, but "the form, the idea that has become an appearance (a phenomenon), must not contradict the nature of the material in which it is shaped". . . . I may venture to say that materials showed him the limits of our imagination. Whatever we conceive as purpose and form, the material shows us what can, and what cannot, be materialized, and what purpose can be realized in which material. Semper treated four basic materials, and the media and techniques of producing art objects corresponding to them. They were textile art, ceramics, woodwork, and work in stone. What you could do in one medium and material, you could not do in another. Attaining one's purpose depended on the nature of the material.[32]

Semper discovered the foundations of current patterns in primitive art.[33] Others were also pondering materiality. Barasch, examining Alois Riegl,[34] concluded

82   *Dorota Kownacka*

that he should be seen as an advocate of material because of the spatial distance that he avoided to gain some insight into the "continuous material solidity of the object".[35]

Perspective depends on the position of the eye, but the value of material is constant, unchanging. This balance between the haptic and the optic was reached, in Raeber's opinion, in classical Greece; for Georg Wilhelm Friedrich Hegel, however, the crucial civilisation was Egypt, "in which the material character is overwhelming and determines all types of artistic creation".[36] We can discern some differences between the ideas of Riegl and Hegel, but they both built a stable foundation for material and for ancient culture, as did Kuno Raeber.

Notes

1 Dorothea Kaufmann and Heidi Thomann Tewarson, eds., *Willkommen und Abschied, Thirty-five Years of German-Writers-in Residence at Oberlin College* (New York: Candem House, 2005), 3.
2 Ibid., 6.
3 Ibid.
4 Ibid., 7.
5 Ibid.
6 Ibid.
7 Paul Klee, *Notebooks*, i: *The Thinking Eye*, trans. Ralph Manheim, ed. Jürg Spiller (London: Lund Humphries, 1961), 3.
8 Kaufmann and Thomann Tewarson, eds., *Willkommen und Abschied*, 7.
9 Kuno Raeber, *Essays und kleine Schriften*, vol. 5 in *Werke*, ed. Christiane Wyrwa and Matthias Klein (Munich: Nagel & Kimche AG, 2004), 9.
10 George Didi-Huberman, "Die Ordnung des Materials, Plastizität, Unbehagen, Nachleben", *Vorträge aus dem Warburg-Haus*, 3 (1999), 1–29.
11 Gottfried Boehm, *O obrazach i widzeniu. Antologia tekstów* [On Pictures and Seeing: An Anthology of Texts], ed. Daria Kołacka, trans. Małgorzata Łukasiewicz and Anna Pieczyńska-Sulik (Cracow: Universitas, 2006), 77–78.
12 *The Diaries of Paul Klee, 1898–1918*, ed. and trans. Felix Klee (Berkeley: University of California Press, 1964), 313.
13 Ibid., 454.
14 Manfred Clemenz, " 'Ich Kristall'. Kunstsymbol und Körpermetaphorik bei Paul Klee", *Neue Zürcher Zeitung* (10 March 2012), www.nzz.ch/ich_kristall-1.15629624): "Selbstverständlich ist das Kristalline ein zu Beginn des vergangenen Jahrhunderts gängiges Kunstsymbol (vor allem der Expressionismus bediente sich seiner). In der einflussreichen Schrift Wilhelm Worringers, "Abstraktion und Einfühlung" (1908), . . . wird das Kristalline zur ästhetischen Ausdrucksform der Abstraktion. Zugleich ist für Worringer die Abstraktion eine Art magischer Beschwörungsformel gegen die Abhängigkeit des Menschen von der Außenwelt, Erlösung von seiner "Lebensabhängigkeit" (Worringer). Abstraktion ist die "absolute Form" und repräsentiert als solche das "Absolute". . . . Klee argumentiert ähnlich wie Worringer. Explizit hat Klee seine Vorstellung des Kristallinen allerdings erst unter dem Eindruck des Ersten Weltkrieges formuliert (wobei er betont, dass der Krieg ihn "innerlich" nichts angehe). Anders als bei Worringer ist das Kristalline für Klee jedoch Kunst- und Selbstsymbol zugleich. Als "Kristall", gleichsam als Selbst-Abstraktion, hofft Klee gegen die Widrigkeiten des Lebens gefeit, "unsterblich" zu sein.

Against illusion   83

15 Hermann Broch, *Hugo Von Hofmannsthal and His Time: The European Imagination, 1860–1920*, trans. Michael P. Steinberg (University of Chicago Press, 1984), 119.
16 Hans Belting, *An Anthropology of Images: Picture, Medium, Body*, trans. Thomas Dunlap (Princeton: Princeton University Press, 2011), 15–16.
17 Raeber, *Essays und kleine Schriften*, 193.
18 Hilton Kramer, "Introduction", in Wilhelm Worringer, *Abstraction and Empathy*, X–XI.
19 Raeber, *Essays und kleine Schriften*, 189.
20 Ibid., 190.
21 Rössing created a cycle of one hundred woodcuts (1927–1931), published as *Mein Vorurteil gegen diese Zeit* (Berlin: Gutenberg, 1932).
22 Raeber, *Essays und kleine Schriften*, 190–191.
23 Ibid., 192.
24 Ibid., 193.
25 Ibid., 194.
26 Ibid., 194–195.
27 Ibid., 195.
28 Ibid.
29 Ibid., 196.
30 Maurice Merleau-Ponty, *The Visible and Invisible*, ed. Claude Lefort, trans. Alphonso Lingis (Evanston: Northwestern University Press, 1968), 12–13.
31 Gottfried Semper, *Die vier Elemente der Baukunst, Ein Beitrag zur vergleichenden Baukunde* (Braunschweig: Friedrich Vieweg, 1851), 52–99.
32 Moshe Barasch, *Theories of Art 3: From Impressionism to Kandinsky* (New York: Routledge, 2000), 203–204.
33 Ibid., 204.
34 Alois Riegl, *Stilfragen. Grundlagen zu einer Geschichte der Ornamentik* (Berlin: Georg Siemens, 1893), 186–187.
35 Barasch, *Theories of Art 3*, 153–154.
36 Ibid., 154.

7 The past, memory and oblivion

Tadeusz J. Żuchowski

When seen in terms of the social framework, remembering and not remembering are in effect two sides of the same coin. As such, they can be understood as collective memory and collective oblivion.[1] The formation of collective memory and memory sites requires the discarding or replacing of events or ideas, or unwanted views.[2]

For what goes beyond the collective memory apparently does not exist. In the process, something occurs that can be described as forgetting, the natural obliteration of a specific vision of the past, of events, people, etc., or a suppression of the unwanted ideas of the past in the collective memory. The latter is characteristic of times in which historical narratives are controlled.

The existence of alternative narratives of the past means that at least one of them is false. I call this phenomenon the "Orwellisation" of memory. The mechanism of constructing specific narratives one after another to obscure the factual knowledge and the memory of the past was described in George Orwell's famous novel *1984*. Orwell depicts a society in which an idea of memory is substituted by an idea of a transformed narration. In effect, in Orwell's story, the knowledge of real events has been lost for years; the facts have not been remembered. Here the danger lies in the fact that by substituting the memory of the past with changing narratives, we lose our grasp of historical reality. The relative past is, in fact, the past without memory; it is filled with forgetting, where new, updated narratives play an important role. These narratives have little in common with research into the past, because they consider the past as building blocks for a vision of the past in line with particular expectations. Especially important are narratives which spawn foundation myths, as was the case with the German collective memory after the end of the Second World War. Here the official narrative did not result from psychological repression but aligned itself with the pragmatic goals of reconstruction and with social expectations.

Collective memory finds its expression in monuments and memorials. Monuments cannot function without an element of remembrance, so if there is no memory of an event to recall, the monument loses its raison d'être. Thus, the monument is testimony to a particular interest in the past, regardless of whether it is dedicated to a person or to an event, as broadly understood. A monument

DOI: 10.4324/9781003264460-9

The past, memory and oblivion   85

is nothing but a specific synecdoche rhetorically addressing the past. It is like a nail that fixes a memory to a certain place. That relationship between the past and the act of remembering is all important for the considerations here.

Because monuments speak to the public, the intention here is to create a specific narrative addressing collective, not individual, memory. It is hardly surprising that a special role in monument discourse is held by ideas deriving from Maurice Halbwachs's theory. As such, the discourse on monuments is framed within the ideas proposed by Halbwachs.

The histories of countries are inscribed in monuments. It might seem that the past exists only as the time of wars or of tragic and traumatic experiences, but monuments are also erected to promote national pride or express communal gratitude. The narration of the past is a continuing process evoked especially by monuments, with their transforming and modifying power. Because history lives, changes and is constantly rewritten, monuments which refer to particular narratives become redundant or undesirable.

The complex phenomenon of rejection is seen in countries where the control of monuments belongs to official institutions rather than to the community. There, memorials that are no longer accepted by the authorities become vulnerable to destruction, while monuments which represent that authority may be removed and even destroyed at times of upheaval. Monuments become repositories of false representations, which aim to erase and negate memories.

However, the notion of history based on loosely construed facts or events eventually becomes a formation that seems to give a true account of real events. It is precisely this idea that continues to be perceived and interpreted as a manifest historical explanation. Memory of the past is an expedient and seductive subject of myth creation or mythologisation. However, myth-making is a rhetorical, non-cognitive process, the purpose of which is – in this case – to persuade the viewer of a specific version of the narrative. Roland Barthes writes that the myth as a device is barely hidden in the narrative, because its goal is to distort, not to hide.[3] That is why – according to Barthes – facts, images and texts are only the raw material, constantly reworked and transformed in the process of myth-making. The dominant narrative is usually supported by distorted fragmentary accounts of past events. Therefore, when historical sources are referenced in foundation myths, their factual reality is obscured and often forgotten.

If collective memory is understood as a distinct narrative of amalgamated remembrances which are generated by the community, then we need to acknowledge the significance of the narrative to this community – the creators of collective memory – and the specific process of the fashioning of visual memories. Before a monument takes shape, someone needs to choose a subject to commemorate, be it a specific person, a group of people or an event, and the outcome of this choice becomes a key component of memory.

A memorial, whether in a visual form or as a written text, continues its constantly reworked and altered existence. Monuments, although assumed to be spaces of collective memory, are rarely created by agreement, because their

86 Tadeusz J. Żuchowski

narrative is subordinated to a specific ideological goal. For this reason, it would be more appropriate to introduce the term cultural or artificial memory. Cultural memory is a social construct prepared for a specific version of culture with specific values. Culture as part of the social structure does not exist in an historical vacuum and needs to be authenticated if it is to provide an appropriate framework for memory.

Here we arrive at an important point. Collective memory is naturally flexible and uncontrollable when it derives from personal knowledge of the past, from individual memories, and as such it is not useful in the process of myth-making.

However, memory remains one of the fundamental abilities of an individual. There is no easy way to forget. Forgetting may involve the avoidance of places or of recollections of events that have been removed from everyday memory.

So what is collective memory? Well, I understand it as a set of experiences that were effectively accepted by the dominant collective at a given time. Collective memory needs to be seen as just one of the possible sets, beyond which there exist other objectives that can form a different set of collective memories. It is also clear that the "dominant" collective is not a demographic majority, but – here building on Michel Foucault's concept of power, knowledge and truth – that collective fabricates a successful narrative of the past.[4]

The collective memory thus possesses a specific collective value. It is a memory of many individuals who subscribe to a common emotional perception of "what it was like back then".

Cultural memory needs certain conditions to appear. Collective memory is formed by the crystallisation of the natural processes of remembering on the part of individuals, in the same way as we recall the tastes or smells of childhood. Memory acquired in this way is of a natural character. However, the concept of collective memory, which forms the foundation for Pierre Nora's model of memory spaces, has only limited value here, because memory spaces hardly ever arise from collective agreements. They more often result from filtering processes of culture.

This means that what are generally referred to as memory spaces actually represent a system of cultural topoi which allow for the creation of an artificial collective memory. In this case, a reliance on facts is not essential, and neither is a connection between collective and individual memory. This means that historical narratives can be easily constructed and that each one of them can bring about similar results to those of the natural collective memory. A key point needs to be made here: in the natural collective memory, the crucial goal is the preservation of the memory of the past; in the case of false narratives, meanwhile, the goal is mostly a misrepresentation or obliteration of natural memory.[5]

Sometimes the aim is to degrade the past and to disgrace its custodians, the bearers of memory, who transmit the historical memories.

Collective memory is not an inclusive construct. Beyond it, there exists its opposite: collective oblivion. So it is fascinating to ask how we can talk about this *oublie collective*. Some findings from the field of psychiatry may be helpful for clarifying concepts of collective oblivion. They refer to the mechanisms by which an individual accepts specific events, how those events are preserved in active memory and how they are erased in the process of forgetting.

The process of forgetting involves different phenomena: individual forgetting, which is by nature inactive, and the construction of oblivion, which is an artificial creation.

On the other hand, various models of contrived remembering do not differ in their effect from the cultural remembrance formed in the natural process.

Cultural or collective paramnesias are nothing more than agreed versions of the past. The main task of these versions is the suppression of real remembrances, that is, those formed in the natural process. It is evident that sometimes the process of suppression is repeated in the layering of subsequent versions; successive paramnesias inhibit previous ones, which leads to total mystification.

The adaptation of terms from the field of psychiatry obviously has its consequences. The convergence can never be comprehensive, because the collective memory has no similar psychiatric counterpart. The same can be said about collective oblivion or non-memory, which can be defined as the opposite of remembrance or memory. For these considerations, it remains essential to see whether the categories of psychiatry can help an enquiry into forgetting in the collective.

Well, certainly useful are such categories as negative and positive memory, the repression and distortion of memory and illusions, and, above all, paramnesia (false memory).[6] In psychiatry, these categories are used to describe the mechanisms of the acceptance of particular events in the life of the individual, that is, either their preservation in active memory or their elimination from memory and transfer into oblivion. In terms of psychiatry, the process of individual forgetting and the creation of non-memory are two very different phenomena. The former is inactive, while the latter is an artificial creation. In cultural memory, the different varieties of substitute memory become equivalent to natural memories. Substitute memories are intellectual constructs that establish an idea of the past built on memory illusions. Cultural or collective paramnesia is no different from an agreed version of the past, a version that is taken as the natural one, but where the "actual" memory is suppressed. Sometimes, as a result of the stratification of subsequent versions and paramnesias, the suppression process leads to complete bewilderment.

If memory and knowledge of the past function together in precise narrative frameworks, it becomes possible to substitute one particular memory for another, more convincing narrative.

In the case of contradictory narratives, there is a need to determine which one of them is the appropriate version. The social body which presides over the quality of historical narration includes – or at least should include – scholars and historians. Contradiction, however, is a peculiar arena in which the factual material (the evidence) is used to forge a binding narrative, usually not as it was, or is, remembered, but as it should be agreed on, or at least how the people should remember it.

88 *Tadeusz J. Żuchowski*

The creation of narratives that repress the past is an obvious manifestation of the post-truth era, although any relative utterance that formulates a fixed definition must be a logical error (the paradox of Epimenides). In the post-truth era, where such concepts as truth and fact are relative, the accepted narrative dominates the established fact. When the concealing narrative is more effective and sometimes more attractive than the natural memory, it is necessary to re-evaluate the memory and the story. It is important, then, to establish which aspects of the past should receive a "new" binding narrative and what historical image of knowledge should be created in its place. The management of memory (the past) is as important to the state as the management of energy, or the economy in general. Well-managed memory supports social order, while ill-managed memory may be ineffective and even harmful. The role of the authorities is very important to the successful management of memory.

Specialists of all disciplines who research the past constitute an essential element in the administration of memory. Certain institutions can also act as authorities.

The emergence of the authority of memory is a unique concept in European culture, predominantly developed through organised force and accompanying violence. The standing of "figures of authority" often derives from their position within an academic hierarchy or their popularity, especially in the media, but it may also result from their "anointment" by other authorities.

If a version of remembrance arises from contradictory statements and has no universal character, but its popular character indicates that it was created by a collective body of authorities, then it is a variant narrative, a substitute remembrance. If the authorities maintain a cohesive relationship, it would be more appropriate to call these narratives a corporate memory. Such memory, the work of a corporate actor, usually arises within a specific ideological context, and although it is presented as a universal collective memory, its goal is to repress those historical narratives which would be uncomfortable from an ideological point of view.

Memory spaces, or *lieux de mémoire*, as a methodological concept, are based above all on the concept of history about history, that is, narrative about narrative. So we need to consider the narratives created by historiography, literature and works of art.

Thus, *lieux de mémoire* become crystallised and situated in events, places, people, ideas and so on. They are said to constitute a time capsule, from which an idea can be summoned. That is why they are more than just narratives; they contain the facts (the truth), and as such they avoid empty appearances. Effectively, however, the past, with its "most important" topoi, recorded for "our" memory, becomes a mythologised narrative, and the matter of truth is relegated to the margins of discourse.

Researchers who use the term "memory spaces" are unanimous about one thing: the *lieu* is not a real topographical place or a real event, but an effective abstract construct. Such a memory space can be too close to myth, and

The past, memory and oblivion 89

a rumour is not far from both. Just as narratives can be alternative or parallel, there can be parallel memory spaces or indeed, in contrast, spaces of forgetting.

It is one thing to explore memory spaces and another to recreate them. Although researchers distinguish between remembrance and history, the two are closely connected. Too often in recent times historians have framed memory spaces in historical knowledge. The creation of maps of such spaces should be seen as a dangerous exploitation of history. From a position of power, the authorities censure the past and evaluate memory. This leads to the boundary between knowledge and memory becoming obscured. The term *lieux d'oubli* refers not only to what a person knows nothing about, but also to what a person does not talk about.[7] "*Lieux d'oubli*" are sites removed from the collective memory. When a discussion raises a question regarding the absence of a particular event from common memory, it is easy to answer "they still write about it", "they have already written about it" or "why talk about it at all!"

Collective memory, which is built through official historical narratives, is nothing other than a form of memory suppression, or oblivion.

The state of official oblivion, or non-existence, is reflected in the example of Katyn, near Smolensk. The Katyn massacre saw more than 22,000 Polish officers, government officials and intellectuals killed on the orders of Stalin. After the discovery of some of the mass graves in Katyn, in 1943, the Soviet government blamed the Germans for the massacre. This official narrative was common in all socialist countries for decades. Every instance of someone pointing to the real perpetrators was regarded as an anti-state standpoint and persecuted as a crime.

That is not all. In the former village of Khatyn, near Minsk (Belarus), during Soviet times, a big memorial to victims of the Nazis was created after the war. In this village, Schutzkomando 118, composed mostly of Ukrainians and Russians (for a long time they were referred to as Nazis or Germans), burned alive almost 150 people. The village of Khatyn was chosen as the main site of communist memorialisation not because it was the site of such terrible events, but due to the similarity of the name Khatyn with Katyn. In Soviet Belarus, more than 100 villages were completely burned down by the Germans, and in each of them, more inhabitants were killed than in Khatyn. However, Khatyn was singled out for a large memorial.

The documents proving the Soviet Union's undeniable guilt in Katyn came to light in 1990, but according to many recent polls conducted by both Russians and Poles, the collective memory retains the fiction that the massacre was committed by the Germans. At present, in the collective memory of Russians, the murderers from Katyn are still Germans, just as in Khatyn they are Germans or Ukrainians.

Katyn and Khatyn are very interesting examples of memory, its distortion and paramnesia, and Katyn is a special instance of the *lieu de memoire* and at the same time *lieu d'oubli*.

False memory is only an illusion that substitutes a natural memory with actual events. The Katyn case proves that the weakness and limitation of Nora's

90 *Tadeusz J. Żuchowski*

theory lie in its voluntarist approach, which is popular with many derivative methodologies that experiment with stories from the past. The alternative narrative for Katyn was only a small part of an elaborate communist fabrication which aimed at obliterating a competing, fact-based version of events.

The Soviet system constructed many false narratives, aimed at creating false representations, and thus aiding the forgetting of the past. Their effect is an extraordinary number of monuments on territories which were under the sway of Soviet ideology. More than 5,500 monuments to Lenin were built in Ukraine alone up to 1991. Over the next 20 years, 3,500 of them were removed. The scale of the phenomenon can be gauged from the fact that a separate term was applied to the removal of the monuments to Lenin: *Leninopad* ("Lenin falls down").

It comes as no surprise that in Ukraine, the historical narrative about the past was very strong and enduring and was represented in monuments to figures of authority, historical events which were important from the perspective of power and national heroes, in a convention approved by the officials. Their lasting legacy is a landscape of memory. According to a declaration of 2015, all communist monuments in Ukraine must be removed.

In the US, a variety of initiatives have arisen seeking to redress the memory of the American Civil War, with the desired effect of removing Confederate memorials from public spaces. This large-scale phenomenon includes monuments to Confederate leaders, monuments to women supporting the Confederates and even roadside stones commemorating fallen Confederates.[8] We can be certain that in time, these memorials will be withdrawn from the collective memory and paramnesia will take over.

The previous considerations show that it is impossible to define what memory is without reflecting on its counterpart: forgetting. If the opposite to memory is oblivion, if the opposite to the *lieu de memoire* is the *lieu d'oubli*, why not refer to these anti-structures which evoke paramnesias as "falliments" (from the Latin verb *fallo*, i.e. cheat, mislead, remain hidden)?

However, natural memory is unpredictable. It reveals itself through a monument and often comes alive with unexpected intensity. To destroy monuments is to destroy memory. Monuments are created in a specific context which not only defines the space but also enriches it. As a result, the space changes with the monument's history. Even when the monument is removed, the trace of a nail will remain in the pedestal – barely visible, but still felt, like a healed wound.

Notes

1 Maurice Halbwachs, *The Collective Memory* (New York: Harper & Row Colophon Books, 1980); Jan Assmann, "Collective Memory and Cultural Identity", trans John Czaplicka, *New German Critique*, 65 (1995), 125–133.
2 Pierre Nora, "Les lieux de mémoire", in *Les lieux de mémoire*, vol. 1, ed. Jacques Le Goff and Pierre Nora (Paris: Gallimard, 1984), XIX–XXI; Pierre Nora, "Between Memory and History. Les lieux de mémoire", *Representations*, 26 (1989), 7–24.

3 Roland Barthes, "Myth Today", in *Mythologies*, trans. Anette Lavers (New York: Noonday, 1991), 121.
4 Jacques Rollet, "Michel Foucault et la question du pouvoir", *Archives de Philosophie*, 51 (1988), 647–666.
5 Tadeusz J. Żuchowski, "Lieux d'oubli", in *Kulturerbe verpflichtet*, ed. Guido Hinterkeuser et al. (Berlin: Lucas, 2017), 88–89.
6 Matthew Hugh Erdelyi, "The Unified Theory of Repression", *Behavioral and Brain Sciences*, 29 (2006), 499–551.
7 Żuchowski, "Lieux d'oubli", 91.
8 The removal of Confederate monuments and memorials is a subject of extensive Wikipedia entries in English and Italian.

8 A leap

Operations of memory between sketch and picture in Piotr Potworowski's painting process

Łukasz Kiepuszewski

The suitcase

Among the many ways in which one can analyse the relationship between painting and memory, the most interesting consists of those painting practices in which memory becomes the driving force of the creative process. These somewhat elusive memory mechanisms can be partly revealed when we have access to the sketches made by the artist, which can be seen as instruments of the mnemotechnical process that underpins the creative act.

Sketches performed these very functions in the case of Piotr Potworowski (1898–1962), who developed an idiom of landscape painting that proved significant for Polish art.[1]

In the poetics elaborated by Potworowski in his mature years, combining the language of abstraction and figuration, particular motifs originated in acts involving both memory and perception. For the artists of the so-called KP[2] group (working in the 1920s and 1930s in Paris), to which Potworowski belonged, the postulate of sketching and free note-taking of various manifestations of the surrounding reality was not just part of their artistic programme but also the result of a broader ethical imperative assuming a constant *sensitivity* to the visible world.

The practice of sketching from the very beginning of one's career in painting took on new dimensions during the post-war period, when Potworowski continued his work in Great Britain. This is also when a sketch, on the one hand, became a more specific element of a complex artistic procedure and, on the other, adopted the function of a mark inscribing itself in a sequence of existential experiences.

These aspects emerge more clearly in Potworowski's corpus of sketches from the years 1952–1961 intended as a complete collection and included in six volumes of 500 pages each (Figures 5.1–5.5). These drawings and studies, mainly aquarelles and inks, are accompanied by notes reminiscent of an intimate diary. The texts mixed with pictures are diverse in character, intermingling personal notes, fictitious scenes and reflections on his own creative process. Their material form is just as interesting, because large books, measuring 22 x 28 cm, were placed in an old aluminium suitcase by The Heston Aircraft Company.[3]

DOI: 10.4324/9781003264460-10

Figure 8.1 Heston Aircraft flight suitcase containing six volumes of Piotr Potworowski's sketchbooks from 1952 to 1961

Source: deposit National Museum in Warsaw (fot. Ł. Kiepuszewski)

The form of this suitcase takes on a new meaning when we consider that the sketchbooks contain numerous traces of the artist's travels and his return to Poland from emigration in England in 1958. Each of the volumes contains a table of contents reminiscent of a list of chapters citing the ports of call reached by the painter, such as towns in Tuscany, the Aeolian Islands, northern Spain, Provence, Cornwall and the Baltic coast. The sketchbooks gathered in the suitcase represent a kind of collection of places, with related affective sensations and intuitions expressed in words and images. In this sense, the content of the suitcase constitutes an archive of the last ten years of the artist's life. It takes the form of a biographical mythography, in which the circulation of observations, reflections, sensations, impressions and expression runs between existence and artistic creation.[4] The sketchbooks containing the artist's records of his peregrinations that typify his biography not only serve as material for his later pictures but also define the logic of Potworowski's landscape painting. We can say, therefore, that the accumulation of sketches in the volumes of the collection indicates the transitional structure of the artist's mature works. Another important fact is that the artist's notes in the volumes of the sketchbooks include some ideas regarding particular aspects of the creative process in which the issue of memory – though rarely referred to directly – is an important motif. Potworowski's creative process took on a mature form in the

Figure 8.2 Page from volume III

Source: 26.8x 21.5 cm; watercolor, pencil, paper, cat.nr. rysw 13014_1–501 (0723), deposit National Museum in Warsaw

1950s. It was shaped according to the tradition of painting practices developed by French painters and modified considerably in a dialogue with representatives of post-war British painting from the St Ives school in Cornwall. An aspect significant for those practices was a phenomenological way of understanding the relationship between the subject and the world in which the connection between eye, body, place and the act of painting manifests itself. In contact with one's surroundings, there appears an impulse towards which the artist – as Potworowski wrote – must be "nothing but a transparent desire. I turn my face towards the white surface and work hard to bring out the marks which explore the mystery of space".[5]

In the practice of landscape painting, the starting point for the painting process consisted of wanderings in a chosen area. The natural and cultural qualities of a given place encountered on such strolls penetrate the senses of the subject. While moving around, the painter does not search for a single point of view providing a perspective panorama but makes many micro-observations of the surroundings. In this mode of experiencing a landscape, connected with

A leap 95

Figure 8.3 Page from volume IV

Source: 26.8x 21.5 cm; watercolor, crayon, pencil, paper, cat.nr. rysw 13014_1–500 (0965), deposit National Museum in Warsaw

immersion in it, other senses which provide evidence of its realness, such as touch and smell, become significant.

These signals,[6] and so, as Potworowski wrote, "all that my organism has absorbed from a given emotion of the visual world",[7] are multi-sensual in character, which partly explains how the resulting picture "does not appeal to the eye alone". Piotr Potworowski's painting act is a process of particularly intense "absorption" of the surrounding world. In this process, image synthesis (as it may be called) is possible in the first place due to the mechanisms of

Figure 8.4 Page from volume V

Source: 26.8x 21.5 cm; watercolor, pencil, paper, cat.nr. rysw 13016_1–499 (0699), deposit National Museum in Warsaw

memory: "I must walk more than a dozen kilometres to see at least a part of this country as a certain whole, with a head and a tail".[8]

This attitude towards a place is particularly well suited to the concepts developed by Hermann Schmitz within the framework of the so-called New Phenomenology.[9] From that perspective, human feelings are analysed not so much as private states of the subject, but as special qualities which spread and permeate our corporality.

A leap 97

Figure 8.5 Page from volume V

Source: 26.8x 21.5 cm; watercolor, crayon, pencil, paper, cat.nr. rysw 13016_1–499 (0451), deposit National Museum in Warsaw

Schmitz assumes that these qualities are not set only in the mind or body, but they achieve their own presence in space. According to the philosopher, affections and emotions take on an objective shape and represent "semi-things" which radiate through the surroundings like sounds, meteorological situations or the power of earthly gravity. Place is understood in this sense as a time–space mixture of characteristics and qualities which exceeds the sum of its component parts. In this exchange, space becomes a store of affective data which can be awakened.[10] In painting practice, sketching is the stage at which the artist records his first reaction to the topographic features of a place and its saturation with sensual properties.

The pace of a sketch

Each time I start a picture, or almost every time, I try to use my sketches from nature, the sketches of objects which are the results of fleeting observations. These sketches are pretexts for something which I call a leap into

98   *Łukasz Kiepuszewski*

the unknown. The quicker in time and the more synthetic in form the sketch is, the better suited it is as the starting point for a picture.[11]

So the starting point for the painter would appear to lie in his studies in a natural open-air setting. The sketching act must be quick and limited to the receiving of a signal, and it is a phase which is subject to the power of the impulse flowing from a place. Another significant aspect is the emphasis placed on the simplification of the pattern which must act as the leaven for a work of art to come to life. In *plein-air* practice, this lasts no longer than the blink of an eye and takes place at the very moment when the painter's vision switches from the surroundings to the paper. An after-image saved under the eyelids directs the gesture of the hand, which impresses its mark on the paper. With a study, therefore, we are dealing first and foremost with micro-memory.

In many respects, Potworowski's thinking and description of his experiences are permeated with modernist temporality, in which the central dimension is the moment when something suddenly occurs and shines brightly, only to fizzle out a moment later. Although this ecstatic nature of a moment is not the only dimension of Potworowski's art, it still most fully defines the aspect of time in a sketch. At this stage, the artist plays the role of a witness recording the trace of a sudden epiphany. The sketchbook is therefore a means of recording ephemerality and immediacy.

At this point, it is worth emphasising that the reception of the signals collected by the artist occasionally requires several steps. The sketches have their own rhythm, and they appear on a number of pages constituting an entire sequence of studies. One may say that it is the phase of dwelling on the memory of the signal. The numbering of the pages and the placement in the indices is also not insignificant. Thanks to them, the sketchbook becomes a series of personal traces bearing specific dates – a private archive of glimpses stowed in a tin box. Keeping a sketchbook in this form is also in its way an act of auto-communication, in which the traces left there reciprocally mark the experience of the artist beginning work on a picture.

The power of distance

"Painting a picture can begin with almost nothing, but that 'almost nothing' is always some observation of the world, a fragment observed suddenly and intensely", Potworowski wrote.[12] And elsewhere:

> What I mean is to express the forms I noticed in the way they were sensed by my subconscious. A bridge over the sea surely entered into my being in a massive kind of way from all sides, and its image is within me, but my intelligence takes from it only those elements which I need right away. And I dream about being able to see this real wreck of a bridge which is inside me, and I will probably never make my way to it.[13]

A leap 99

This description demonstrates the difference between a sketch and the picture created from it. We already know that while the sketch is usually made "on location", the picture comes to life later – without direct contact with the initial object. So between the sketch and the picture, there is a distance in time and space where memory gets to work. The peculiarity of this statement is in the artist's suggestion that to reach the deepest deposit of the motif in his memory, he must first move away from the direct image and then return via a detour, sort of *feeling his way* based on the selected parameters distilled from the sketch. The sketch is a place of reflection and of a transition from the act of seeing to the picture proper which must reach the lower layers of the "I". A study in a sketchbook is therefore a sort of spark for the memory making a selection between the significant and the insignificant in the object evoked. And thus, it has an extraordinary ability to conjure things up through recollection – reaching the substratum of that place, motif or occurrence. In this way, memory develops an attitude to an occurrence which once was in the present but is now in the past. Thanks to the sketch, a place which has elapsed in time returns to the present with its flavour but has already been processed within the framework of autobiographic memory. And so drawing serves the purpose of going back to a past experience, yet not to its ordinary chaotic shape but rather to its most intimate parts and to what was related to deeper strata of personal memory. The value of a sketch is that it softens the direct pressure of the sign, which might make the artist a slave to accessible visibility, and creates a distance towards the motif, ensuring space for creative freedom for his subjective projections.

Work on a picture

When the artist starts painting a picture, the contents of his or her memory are subject to a complex operation described by Piotr Potworowski as follows:

> The next stage is limiting the visuality of a picture to such an extent that it ceases to materialise before one's eyes as a whole, but permeates into the deeper strata of the subconscious and only there begins to take shape.[14]

The main vector of the painter's activity while painting is the filtration and refraction of direct viewing. This weakening of the determination of the image of a motif that imposes itself on the viewer is about – as he wrote – "the skipping of everything that is obvious".[15] A recurring aspect in these statements is the weakening of the role of shapes and forms which could blur communication channels that reach deeper layers of memory. This stems from the conviction that a picture focused unilaterally on the shape of after-images would block the activisation of the artist's mind. We can therefore acknowledge that a picture should have *empty spots*, that is, *empty spaces* allowing for collective projections. In the case of a motif included in a picture, the operations which it goes through are therefore far more preconditioned by the arrangement of

100 Łukasz Kiepuszewski

the surface used as a painting medium than in the case of a sketch. While a sketch is determined by the moment of its making, connected with perception and maintaining the features of a given place, the point of gravity in a painting is shifted to the time produced by the picture itself. Therefore, the sketch is above all a trace of the act of its creation, and it cannot grasp the complexity of perception of a given object. Even if it belongs to an entire series of studies, it is still unable to offer a common setting on which particular elements intertwine, enter into a dialogue and coexist. Sketchbooks as an archive of memory subject to the logic of collecting and registering data in the course of work on a particular picture clash with the filtering and purifying temporality of the image area. Referring to Nietzsche's metaphorics, one can say that the painting area acts as the force of forgetting, becoming for a time an instrument of amnesia.[16] This is why Potworowski calls the beginning of work on a picture "a leap into the unknown", as it should be understood as an attempt to leap over the registered baggage of memory.

The time of the surface

When transferred to canvas, the picture patterns included in the sketchbook lose their former temporality and enter a new configuration of relationships. Memory traces turn into material traces of a new kind – that which belongs to the perception apparatus undergoes essential translation and gains a new substantial form. This process is certainly the most graspable in the sphere of after-image shapes which, transposed to the picture area, immerse themselves and then emerge within the matter of its surface. They become incorporated into a new kind of temporal relations resulting from their position on a picture's surface. Contents of memory now appear in the light of the mechanisms determining perception of the entire area, among which the main ones are those dependent on the *iconic difference* between figure and background.[17] In the picture, what was once seen and experienced *in the natural setting* is subject to a new location and achieves a new substantial being, impressing itself with a greater impact on the order of things. The fact that in comparison with a page from a volume of sketches the picture area is characterised by a different organisation, results, among other things, in a situation in which the images and phenomena appearing in the memory are given new directions, for instance in relation to the four points of the compass and the laws of gravity. In Potworowski's pictures, we can find compositions in which the horizon is made vertical, thus leading to a transformation of the entire pictorial world (e.g. *The River Vistula in Kazimierz*, from 1959).

The most important vector and factor of Potworowski's imaging is the matter of the colours. This brings out not only the relations between light, shade and value, but also the qualities of temperature and internal spaciousness. The surface coated with paint in a variety of ways is a layer on which the elements creating a topography of the landscape interweave in new ways. Traces of the instrument, scrapings of the surface and the subsequent layers of pigment

A leap 101

are summoned in an act of improvisation. While provoking various kinds of painting occurrences in the creative process, Potworowski conducts an affective selection of frames from his memory film.[18] This manipulation of outgoing data essential to the creation of a work of art is the result of the free and easy exchange between the painter's hand and the canvas. The painting mark storing within itself the qualities related to viewing and touching introduces distances and relations between pictorial elements which are experiences on a scale of tactile intensity. In this kind of space, particular fragments of the field acquire their disposition in a close relationship with their adjacent areas. Thanks to this, particular elements appearing in the pictorial field, orientation points (e.g. identifiable motifs), become part of more general sequences which run across the field from one border to another. In this way, what was once a sketched record, an after-image of a past experience, locates itself in a separate rhythm of the present. It is no longer just an imprint of a past experience but turns into one taking place during the looking *here and now*.

Re-staging of memory

"Painting is just a slow laborious setting of elements so that a peculiar fact can take place".[19] This means that the manual work done by the painter on the surface of a canvas leads to a *unique* leap transforming the order of the entire picture. In this act, performed in accordance with the artist's convictions, another liberation of the outgoing memory signal takes place. The picture is a surprising form, framed in new rules, of that which is remembered. The rhythm of a picture's surface is a time which can awaken those dimensions of the motif which are buried deep down in the artist's memory and which until then had been hidden even for the artist himself.

Using the language of phenomenology, one can say that as a picture is created, the physical foundation of the experience returns. So from this perspective, creative work is a technique of saturating the painting surface with a new potential of temporality, which it extracts from the layers of memory. For Potworowski, that which is most important finds its voice at the moment when the supervision of consciousness is switched off,[20] and when there is room for activating the involuntary memory of the body. It is worth noting that the painter's feelings correspond with the convictions of Merleau-Ponty, who believed that memory was the *modus vivendi* of the body determining the approach of subject to object.[21]

It should be pointed out, however, that we are talking here not just about spatial structure, but also about the complete sensual and atmospheric impression of a given phenomenon. For Thomas Fuchs, body memory does not represent the past, but it re-stages it in a particular way, going beneath presentation:[22] "Each impression, each situation is permeated with a hidden, intercorporeal memory. Autobiographic explicit memory represents only the past as a bygone time. Body memory, on the other hand, mediates the actual living contemporaneity of the past".[23] Body memory can open a passage to update

102   Łukasz Kiepuszewski

the past in a way which will allow it to become the direct present. During his work, a painter conducts a certain kind of repetition of the past, and through the making of the picture, he discovers some aspects of his past experience which until then had been kept hidden from him.

From the perspective taken in Potworowski's reflections, we can reach the conclusion that memory traces of this kind should imprint themselves on the surface of a painting. This means that memory processes permeate the picture in an almost organic way, and the contents of mental processes remain in it like a residue deposit. Painting practice is therefore a continuation of the processes which have already been initiated in the memory. Potworowski uses its mechanisms, the characteristic phenomena of decomposition and recomposition, and harnesses them for a creative act.

Summoning motifs through the image filter dependent on memory is a way of correctly recognising and capturing that which did not make its voice heard during direct viewing. Potworowski believed that only then would a picture unveil the real idiomatic sense of what touched him on seeing a scene of nature and what constitutes the lining of experienceable reality.

"In a picture the battle must go on"[24]

The previously mentioned reconstruction of the conceptualisation of a creative act formulated by Potworowski should at this point be referred to works of art. However, there is no room here for detailed analysis. Let us just focus on what can be called a dramatisation of memory experience in the compositions of this Polish landscapist.

It seems this is the very context in which we can identify the qualities of the shapes appearing in pictures such as *A Landscape from Tarragona* from 1954, *Siena* from 1955, *A Black Boat* and *A Fountain in Ostia* from 1959 and *A Waterfall in Niedzica* from 1960.

Contrary to the materiality of the objects presented in the pictures, their shapes are of such a fragile and ephemeral character that they take on features of apparitions. In the course of viewing, these forms gradually merge with adjacent areas, retreating from their potential independence under pressure from the matter which surrounds them. As a result, particular shapes do not retain their precedence over a multiple context. Not only are particular motifs not stabilised as objects, but they also do not lead to such a stabilisation. The unrestricted topography of the elements of a picture does not transform here into a ready product of imagination, but above all it becomes the subject matter of a realisation (spread out in time and possessing a changeable dynamic), which takes place in the perception of a viewer. The phenomena designed as pockmarked surfaces, or those radiating from them, retain the quality of after-image flashes. And the configuration of motifs embracing the picture as a whole is characterised by a fragile state of suspension between the possibility for related elements to bind and their tendency to disperse. This particular characteristic of the perceptive experience of Potworowski's pictures enhances, in terms of

A leap 103

value, our understanding of the mode of existence of memory contents related to objects. This means that in the previously mentioned artworks, the processes of temporal dispersal appear in the modality of disappearance and subsequent absorption.

Hence compositions of this kind present a recollection as being susceptible to re-immersion in forgetting and subjection to further transformation. While looking, viewers who approach these works, even those lacking familiarity with the meanderings of the artist's memories recorded there, experience the mechanisms employed by the artist which are analogous to those that define the functioning of memory. The almost organic relationship between painting and memory in the works of Potworowski has few precedents in European art.

Notes

1 Major publications dealing with the work of this artist in general: Zdzisław Kępiński, *Piotr Potworowski* (Warsaw: Arkady, 1978); *Piotr Potworowski, 1898–1962* [cat.] ed. J. Słodowska (Warsaw: Galeria Sztuki Współczesnej "Zachęta", 1998).
2 Stefania Krzysztofowicz-Kozakowska, ed., *Gry Barwne, Komitet Paryski 1923–1939* [Colour Games: The Paris Committee 1923–1939] [cat.] (Cracow: Muzeum Narodowe w Krakowie, 1996).
3 Volume 1 covers the years 1952–1953; Volume 2, 1953–1954; Volume 3, 1954–1955; Volume 4, 1955–1956; Volume 5, 1960–1961. The set of sketchbooks under consideration here, constituting a deposit of the National Museum in Warsaw, does not cover the entire corpus of Potworowski's sketches and notes. Publication of this material has been very limited to date. Cf. Dorota Jarecka, "Z notatników i szkicowników Piotra Potworowskiego" [From Piotr Potworowski's Notebooks and Sketchbooks], in *Piotr Potworowski 1898–1962*, 90.
4 Cf. Andrzej Turowski, "Co znaczy być malarzem?" [What Does it Mean to be a Painter?] in Marek Szczęsny, *Malarstwo i prace na papierze* [Painting and Works on Paper] [cat.] (Poznań: Muzeum Narodowe w Poznaniu, 2003), 7–10.
5 Sketchbook notes from the years 1950–1951 are in the possession of the artist's family in London. I wish to thank the painter's son Jan Potworowski for making them available.
6 The problem of participatory landscape as opposed to panoramic landscape is discussed by Arnold Berleant, *Art and Engagement* (Philadelphia: Temple University Press, 1991).
7 Volume 6, November 1961.
8 From the letters to Zdzisław Kępiński (15 August 1961), in Kępiński, *Piotr Potworowski*, 41.
9 Hermann Schmitz, *Ciałosfera, przestrzeń i uczucia*, trans. Bolesław Andrzejewski (Poznań: Garmond, 2001); Ger. orig., *Der Leib, der Raum die Gefühle*; Hermann Schmitz, *Nowa Fenomenologia. Krótkie wprowadzenie*, trans. Andrzej Przyłębski (Warsaw: Aletheia, 2015); Ger. orig., *Kurze Einführung in die Neue Phänomenologie* (Freiburg: Alber, 2009).
10 For more on this, see Łukasz Kiepuszewski, "Szyfry miejsca. Proces twórczy Piotra Potworowskiego i Nowa Fenomenologia" [Codes of Place: The Creative Process of Piotr Potworowski and New Phenomenology), *Quart* (Quarterly of the Art History Institute at the University of Wrocław), 47 (2018), 46–57.
11 Quoted after Anna Baranowa, "Prace na papierze" [Works on Paper], in Piotr Potworowski, *Prace na papierze* [Works on Paper] [cat.] (Warsaw: Galeria aTAK, 2015), 9.
12 Artist's note – quoted after Janusz Zagrodzki, "Być artystą" [Being an Artist], in *Piotr Potworowski 1898–1962*, 78.
13 Volume 3, 22 October 1961.

104 *Łukasz Kiepuszewski*

14 Typescript 07.1958, "Kiedy stanąłem przed kasą nie mogłem się zdecydować, gdzie jechać" [When I stood at the ticket window, I couldn't decide where to go], in Katarzyna Jankowska-Cieślik and Agnieszka Zawadowska, eds., *Piotr Potworowski. Człowiek bez granic / Man without Borders* [cat.] (Warsaw: Galeria Studio, 2013), 46.

15 A letter to Teresa Pągowska of 22 October 1959, in Maciej Gutowski, *Teresa Pągowska* (Warsaw: WAiF, 1996), 86.

16 Łukasz Kiepuszewski, *Niewczesne obrazy. Nietzsche i sztuki wizualne* [Untimely Pictures: Nietzsche and the Visual Arts] (Poznań: Wydawnictwo Naukowe UAM, 2013); esp. chapter "Paraliż oka mgnienia. Wokół portretów fotograficznych" (Blink-of-an-eye Paralysis: Around Photographic Portraits], 260–288.

17 On the iconic difference, see Gottfried Boehm, "Die Wiederkehr der Bilder", in *Was ist ein Bild?* (Munich: Fink, 1994), 11–38.

18 Discussed by Gilles Deleuze, *Francis Bacon. Logique de la sensation* (Paris: Editions de la différence, 1984).

19 Volume 5, undated.

20 Similar processes in relation to the work of Pierre Bonnard, above all concerning passivity understood in a phenomenological way, are discussed by Yves-Alain Bois, "Bonnard's 'passivity'", in *The Work of Art: Suspending Time*, ed. Suzanne Pagé (Paris: Musée d'Art Moderne de la Ville de Paris, 2006), 51–63. They are also referred to by Łukasz Kiepuszewski in "Trzy kroki w stronę obrazów. Pierre Bonnard i percepcyjne opóźnienie" [Three Steps towards Pictures: Pierre Bonnard and Perceptive Delay], *Artium Quaestiones,* 27 (2016), 67–92.

21 Maurice Merleau-Ponty, *Fenomenologia percepcji* [Phenomenology of Perception], trans. Małgorzata Kowalska and Jacek Migasiński (Warsaw: Aletheia, 2002); Fr. orig. *Phénoménologie de la perception* (Paris: Gallimard, 1945).

22 Thomas Fuchs, "Pamięć ciała i historia życia" [Body Memory and Life History], trans. Ulrich Schrade, in *Pamięć w filozofii XX wieku*, ed. Zofia Rosińska [Memory in Twentieth-century Philosophy] (Warsaw: Uniwersytet Warszawski. Wydział Filozofii i Socjologii, 2006), 169.

23 Ibid., 168.

24 Sketchbook 1951–53, family archives; 12 April 1952.

9 Smiling in Auschwitz: Instagram selfies and historical representation at the Auschwitz-Birkenau Memorial and Museum

Robbert-Jan Adriaansen

Ever since the summer of 2014, the topic of selfies taken in Auschwitz has recurred regularly in the media. That summer, two cases fuelled debate about the limits of public conduct and the representation thereof at the memorial site. The first was a selfie taken at the Auschwitz-Birkenau Memorial and Museum posted on Twitter by the American teenager Breanna Mitchell, which caused a "twitter storm" that was picked up by numerous media outlets around the globe.[1] The second was an Israeli Facebook page called "With My Besties in Auschwitz", which sarcastically mocked the same "despicable use" of the Holocaust in selfies and posed photos by Israeli teens.[2] The discussion led many to draw broad conclusions about the purported narcissism of "selfie culture" and about the impertinence and lack of understanding of the younger generation.[3]

In 2017, the discussion gained a new dimension as the Israeli–German artist Shahak Shapira created what has been dubbed a "selfie shaming" project. He created a website that juxtaposed cheerful posed pictures of tourists at the Holocaust Memorial in Berlin with versions that showed the same people being photoshopped into authentic photos of Holocaust victims. Intended as a modern-day form of public humiliation, Shapira only took the site down once almost all of the portrayed people had contacted him with apologies and had removed the original photos from their social media – a process Shapira called "undouching".[4]

In 2019, a tweet from the Auschwitz Memorial Twitter account, calling visitors to respect the memory of the over one million victims by behaving appropriately at the site,[5] reinvigorated the debate but also uncovered the difficulties that Holocaust institutions have with the behaviour which visitors display in their desire to snap a picture for their online followers. According to Wulf Kansteiner, the dismissive reaction of the Holocaust institutions to such cases exemplifies the struggle which the gatekeepers of "Shoah memory" have with maintaining the "border between emergent and regimented Holocaust memories".[6] Such reactions comprise not only public shaming, but also the affirmation of established cultural memories and the rise of a "quickly institutionalized Holocaust etiquette".[7]

Observing these diverging attitudes towards self-representation and behaviour at Auschwitz, the suggestion that we are dealing with ways of creating

DOI: 10.4324/9781003264460-11

106 Robbert-Jan Adriaansen

historical meaning on social media which are different from those which Holocaust institutions are accustomed to seems legitimate.[8] Rather than dismissing "selfies" in Auschwitz as disrespectful expressions of a self-centred "selfie generation",[9] this chapter aims to understand the dynamic relationship between self-representation and historical representation on social media, particularly on the image-sharing platform Instagram. It explores the dynamics of Holocaust meaning-making in public Instagram "selfies" taken at the Auschwitz-Birkenau Memorial and Museum. The pivotal question is how meaning is construed in Instagram posts and how this relates to identity and historical representation. This chapter is based on a sample of 498 Instagram selfies. As the selfies will be analysed in the context of Instagram as a social media platform, I will follow the broad definition given by Andja Dinhopl and Ulrike Gretzel which defines selfies as both a photographic object and a practice "characterized by the desire to frame the self in a picture taken to be shared with an online audience".[10] Consequently, not only self-portrait photographs but also pictures of Instagram users taken by others were included, since the fact that these pictures were deliberately posted by Instagram users indicates their intention to frame themselves for an online audience. The sample has been established by applying face recognition to the latest 10,000 Instagram posts with still image content (no video) geotagged with the tag "Auschwitz Memorial/Muzeum Auschwitz", retrieved on 3 August 2017.[11] After a face recognition algorithm filtered out (self-)portrait photos, a manual check removed false positives – such as photos of random people or photos of photographs on display in the exhibition. The posts were analysed using multimodal analysis, focusing on individual semiotic modes – such as image, hashtags, captions and comments – and their interrelations. First, I will expand on the analytical framework. Then I will highlight how two crucial modes – the image and the hashtag – are employed in Instagram selfies at Auschwitz. Finally, I will reflect upon the interplay between the various modes and the relationship between selfies, identity and historical representation.

Historical representation and multimodality

The controversy over selfies at Auschwitz indicates that the meaning of social media posts is essentially ambiguous. Pictures are taken at Auschwitz as direct or indirect references to the Holocaust, and it is in this context that a smile is interpreted as disturbing and irreverent – regardless of the intentions of the poster. Today we know very well that representations do not simply reflect ideas or reality but construct reality. This is a position which poststructuralist semiotics shares with the narrativist tradition in the philosophy of history and hermeneutics. Narrativist theories of historical representation claim that historical representations are not inherently related to past reality (which is unattainable insofar as it even exists beyond language) but are proposals for interpreting the past in a particular way.[12] More specifically, through emplotment in the historical narrative, the historian – or anybody trying to represent the past – narratively orders and connects otherwise unconnected events and thus creates a sequence of historical causality in the totality of the plot.[13] Historical consciousness functions in a quite similar way. In its narrow definition, historical consciousness is defined by Jörn Rüsen as "the mental operations (emotional and cognitive, conscious and unconscious), through which experienced time in the form of memory is used as a means of orientation in everyday life" and relates to the existential human need for temporal orientations.[14] Historical consciousness comprises more than mere factual knowledge about the past, as it links an understanding of the past to temporal orientation in the present and expectations of the future. It is in this temporal nexus that an understanding of the past is constituted in which the past appears as essentially alien to the present, but meaningful through narrative comprehension.[15] Thus identity is treated as a narrative construction. According to Paul Ricœur, historical representation has an analogous function to autobiographical narration, as it creates narrative identity through the emplotment of (narratively prefigured) experience. Ricœur argued that we cannot simply have access to our "selves" through introspection, but we construct mediated images of ourselves that we consequently act upon. It is, according to Ricœur, through narrative emplotment that we grasp a range of actions not intrinsically related to one another and events which are often disharmonious (discordant) in a unified cohesion he calls "concordance".[16]

For two reasons, however, references to the past on social media platforms challenge the dominance and relevance of narrative as the main paradigm of historical understanding. First, social media posts are not static, but interactive representations. According to Ann Rigney, historians are the "chief stakeholders in the production of historical knowledge, they are not its gatekeepers".[17] The Internet has created a space where basically anyone can produce and publish historical knowledge for anyone to consume. In response to the challenges posed by new media, narratologists have broadened the scope of their research to include the analysis of digital representations, arguing, for example, that particularly the *interactivity* that characterises online meaning-making – as exemplified in games, comments, chats, requests, photo tagging and video responses – creates an environment in which the narrativist model of the single autonomous author no longer stands. The Internet should rather be understood as a space of the "dialogical production" of meaning, rather than a marketplace of passive consumers.[18] This implies that we should let go of the (academic) monologue as both the normative model for proper historical representation and the analytical frame of reference for analysis when studying online historical representations.[19]

Second, representations of the past on social media consist of different semiotic modes, of which written text is only one – subordinate, in the case of Instagram. Depending on their intentions, communication platforms can encourage or restrict the use of particular modes and can enable the use of multiple modes at the same time. So within the medium of the mobile phone, the communication form of the SMS is primarily driven by the mode of written

108   *Robbert-Jan Adriaansen*

language, whereas in the same medium, the communication platform Twitter enables users to use the communication form of the tweet, in which various modes – such as written language, hashtags, static and moving images and videos – are available. At the same time, restrictions are placed on the number of characters that can be posted, which creates a significant barrier for narrative emplotment. Although one could argue that these restrictions challenge the creativity of the writer and that even very short accounts can include a plot, the fact that the vast majority of platforms allow and encourage users to configure narratives using various modes at the same time supports the position in semantics that language is no longer *the* main medium of communication and that other modes of communication should not be studied in terms of language.[20] The integrated study of the ways in which multiple modes interact to create meaningful representations is called multimodal analysis. Multimodal analysis does not provide any clues about the extent to which representations are true or not, but – given its background in social semiotics – it does provide a framework in which it is possible to analyse the ways in which and the extent to which "propositions" (whether verbal, visual or otherwise) are represented as true or not.[21]

Modes of representation

In mapping multimodality, numerous taxonomies of available communicative modalities have been proposed. Charles Forceville, for example, included the following: 1) written language, 2) spoken language, 3) static and moving images, (4) music, 5) non-verbal sound and 6) gestures.[22] Although such taxonomies are ideal-typical and always prone to discussion, they are a useful heuristic tool for identifying the various modes at play in a multimodal representation. In its core function, image posts, Instagram employs a limited number of modalities.

The image, or the entanglement of the site and the self

First, there is the image. The image – generally in the mode of a still photograph, although other images can be posted as well – stands at the heart of the platform, as Instagram was originally launched as a photo sharing app and is still mainly used for this purpose. Pictures can be posted on Instagram instantly when taken via the app's camera function, or pre-existing images can be uploaded. To become a broad social media platform, Instagram has implemented other modes, such as moving images (gifs), videos from 3 to 60 seconds, Snapchat-like "stories" that disappear after 24 hours, and livestreams, yet the traditional still photograph remains its core asset. A maximum of ten images or videos can be posted at once, with only the first showing instantly in the post.

It is evident that selfies have the still image as their main mode. The composition of the selfie shows the owner of the Instagram account as the central figure (or one of the central figures) in the picture. Characteristic of the selfie is its self-reflexivity: contrary to the traditional photograph, the selfie "integrates the photographing subject into the picture by making it its actual object".[23] It is an act of self-objectification – one that is never completed, as the viewing subject is captured in the same frame as the object. Moreover, the selfie also captures the act of self-objectification, which adds to its self-reflexive nature.

This self-reflexivity gives selfies taken in the context of Holocaust tourism an interesting dimension that is overlooked by the critics of the "selfie generation". Dinhopl and Gretzel have argued that in the context of tourism, selfie-taking should be regarded as a form of touristic looking. Building on the Foucault-inspired notion of the "tourist gaze", they argue that self-objectification takes place in the selfie. The rise of front-facing cameras enabled the phone to act as something other than a device that one looks through to capture an object of interest: the screen can now act as a mirror which the tourist looks at when taking the selfie. In this way, the camera takes the position of the supposed audience, rather than that of the photographer: "the camera becomes a placeholder for the online audience like a nexus of recursive gazing".[24] This is a crucial remark, as it draws our attention to the specific dynamics of meaning-making in selfies: they do not just represent an objectified self in the context of the Holocaust memorial site, but also represent the act of representing. Selfies constitute a relationship between the self and the site. Although this is not a novel feature in itself, as posed portrait photos can function in similar ways, we must acknowledge that these photos do not serve as private souvenirs but have been either made for the purpose of communicating a message to others or selected for that purpose.

This function of configuring a relationship between the self and the site, and thereby defining both, becomes apparent in our case in facial expressions on posted photos. The smile is not the predominant expression in Auschwitz selfies. Roman_babiichuk, for example, posts a selfie in front of barbed wire with the caption "The impression of this place bad #travel #photo #museum".[25] His facial expression and the caption complement each other, as his haunted expression, with a gaze directed not at the audience but at something unspecified in a remote distance, creates an eerie feeling of a haunted place. The fact that roman_babiichuk's gaze is directed at something behind the camera – that is, behind the viewer – strongly adds to the feeling of being sneaked upon and enhances the darkness of the place. The fact that he used on his photo a filter that highlights the edges adds to this. So even though roman_babiichuk is posting a selfie, his facial expression, gaze and posture configure a specific relationship to the site in which the viewer is immediately engaged.

Instagram users enhance the meaning expressed through facial expressions with captions such as "mucha tristeza" (Sp. "great sadness"), "sombre" or "sad", or more elaborate comments such as "It's cold out? Good! Finally matches the weather in my soul!"[26] Others refrain from comments, or simply comment on the object they are posing in front of or on Auschwitz in general. While generally looking directly in the camera, some, like roman_babiichuk, direct their gaze elsewhere, to show contemplation, introspection or reflection. In some

110 *Robbert-Jan Adriaansen*

cases, the object of reflection, such as the Auschwitz gate, is the main point of focus in the selfie, with the tourist posing in the margin of the picture. Such compositions have an aesthetic function, as they emphasise perspective, as the infinity of the railway or of barbed wire may represent the magnitude of the committed atrocities.

Yet it appears to be a natural impulse to smile when a photo is taken. This sometimes creates uncomfortable situations which posters feel the need to resolve or address in their captions. Under a photo of herself smiling in front of a watchtower, julka_00, for example, comments "nie wiem skąd ten uśmiech" (Pol. "I don't know where that smile came from"), eliciting a response from the girl who presumably took the photo that it may have been her who made her laugh.[27] In this way, the problem of the smile is solved. A translation of the comment even managed to appease a Dutch visitor who took offence at the smile while unaware of the meaning of the Polish caption. Another example shows a man, nishkarshs, posing in front of the main gate, pointing at the "Arbeit macht Frei" sign.[28] Nishkarshs comments on his photo:

> I'm only smiling because I made it here. Next time someone tries to fool you, please remember work doesn't make you free; maybe some cocktail of vocation does. Ok, time to put the wit and the smile aside as I enter #auschwitz #poland #arbeitmachtfrei.

Nishkarshs thus "saves" his smiling self by making a clear distinction between the realm before and beyond the gate, implying a difference between a sacred and a profane realm, in which wittiness about the sacred is sanctioned in the profane as long as the site itself is revered. Thus, any apparent condescension is averted.

The hashtag: configuring metadata

Although the image is the main mode of representation on Instagram, we should acknowledge other modes as well, as it is in their interplay that meaning is generated. Moreover, we should also acknowledge that there is no single audience either. Even though all analysed posts have been published on open profiles that can be viewed by everybody and not only by friends, they all target specific communities which the poster is engaged with on the platform. First and foremost, direct Instagram friends are targeted – these are the ones who will automatically see the post pop up in their Instagram feed. Second, audiences are targeted through the use of hashtags. Hashtags provide one of the main ways in which Instagram is navigable, as one cannot search the captions or comments on search terms, one can only search for persons, hashtags or location tags. Hashtags constitute what is called a "folksonomy": user-generated metadata that provide an index to the content, as opposed to a taxonomy, which would have been created by the platform owners.[29] But hashtags are also a mode of textual representation.[30] This dual function of being an instrument through which to target audiences and a mode of representation creates a specific dynamic.

Because the folksonomy is user-generated, the hashtags used in our sample need not be related to Auschwitz with regard to content. A frequency count of the hashtags used in the sample shows that toponyms are mostly used, followed by general references to the history of the site and history as such ("concentrationcamp", "holocaust" "history"). Both categories comprise direct references to the site and its history. We can, however, discern a third category of hashtags: indirect references. This category's primary task is to attract viewers to the post who browse general or specific hashtags that are only indirectly related to the scene. "Travel" stands out in the top 10, and other hashtags such as "trip", "travelgram", "instatravel" and "travelphotography" frame the post in the context of travel reportage, which speaks to a broader audience (Table 9.1). "Instagood" – the second most popular Instagram hashtag[31] – is used to mark pictures that one is particularly proud of, or which are artistically good. In this sample, photos tagged with this hashtag do not particularly stand out content-wise, and as users use these same hashtags for other posts in their feed, it indicates that the use of hashtags like this mainly serves the purpose of attracting more viewers.

Yet tags are often a combination of direct and indirect references. User 9209.j.b, posing in front of a sign with a wartime aerial photograph of the camp, uses the geometrical pattern of the camp to make his post relevant to an audience that might be interested in Auschwitz from an architectural point of view, using hashtags such as "geometry" and "pattern", but also unrelated hashtags such as "skyscraper" and "urban", as well as general hashtags such as "architectureporn" and "architecturelovers".[32] In another example, _josh2910 is less inclined to use hashtags to reach an audience but consciously uses them to position his post semantically.[33] He positions his picture both topographically and historically using tags such as #auschwitz, #krakow, #hitler, #ww2 and #concentrationcamp but also uses the tagging system to draw attention to aesthetic elements, primarily his sunglasses, in a subtle way.

When a caption text is used on Instagram, hashtags are generally placed after it in the same message. This makes it stand out in relation to other platforms,

Table 9.1 Top 10 used hashtags according to frequency (case insensitive)

1	auschwitz	125
2	poland	96
3	krakow	24
4	concentrationcamp	24
5	travel	23
6	auschwitzbirkenau	22
7	Oswiecim	22
8	Holocaust	22
9	Birkenau	20
10	History	19

112   Robbert-Jan Adriaansen

such as the text-based social platform Twitter, where tags are placed inline, in the sentence itself. This may have to do with the fact that Twitter does enable searching for search terms, or because Instagram, contrary to Twitter, has no immediate limit to the number of characters that can be used. Regardless of the reason, the fact is that this use of tags enables users to position the photo in a semantic network. Moreover, when used in addition to a caption, tags can reflect on the caption or draw implications from it.

Take this caption which 808killawhale posted to a photo of him standing firmly with his arms crossed against a blurred background of grass, railway tracks and a barbed wire fence:

> Today we are visiting #Auschwitz on the anniversary of the day that the 1st prisoners were brought here. Words cannot express the emotions that are running through us as we learn in [sic] extent of the atrocities that took place here that ended the lives of over 1.1 million Jews, Russians, Gypsies, Polish and Christians/Catholics during WW2. #holocaust #europemission #learnfromthepast #hitlerwasthesonofthedevil #concentrationcamp #killingfactory #itreallyhappened #howcouldyoudenythis #satanhatesgodschosenpeople #poland #wakeupcall #jewishlivesmatter #hitlerwasadouche #ireallyjustsaidthat.[34]

In this caption, 808killawhale comments on his visit and the emotions that were involved when learning about the atrocities, and he provides some historical information about these atrocities as well. The hashtags reflect this comment but draw some implications that are not stated in the main comment. #killingfactory refers to the industrial scale of the genocide and the methods involved; #itreallyhappened challenges Holocaust denial and turns 808killawhale into a post-hoc testifier of the atrocities as he witnesses their traces; and #jewishlivesmatter semantically positions the post in the #blacklivesmatter debate, thus creating a reversed historical analogy. This creative, even playful, use of hashtags draws our attention to the topic of narrative representation and its limits on Instagram.

Ludic identity: caption, comments, interaction

Instagram enables users to write captions to their pictures. These are placed directly underneath the picture, and the first lines are immediately visible in an Instagram feed. When the caption consists of multiple lines, the rest are visible when one clicks on the text. Although the number of characters is not directly capped, the possibilities for narrative configuration are limited, due to the subordinate position below the image. Nonetheless, captions enable users to write micro-narratives that convey a message – in direct or indirect reference to the main picture. These narratives make the photo meaningful, as they create a plot around it. These plots configure time in the sense that they tie past events, in this case the Holocaust, to the present of the photo and to the future, as the plot provides an identity in the sense that it creates a meaningful narrative to act upon in the future. One good example is that of stephankeefetravels, who makes a clear identity statement in a caption of a picture of him posing in front of the Auschwitz gate:

> As a Jew, I always felt as though going to Auschwitz was an important thing I had to do and this morning, I got the opportunity to go. It was an obviously humbling experience to walk around a place like this. I'm just proud to be living proof of the fact that this hatred failed.[35]

In his caption – devoid of hashtags – stephankeefetravels narratively connects the experience of walking through Auschwitz to his life narrative. By setting forth his Jewishness, stephankeefetravels turns the visit into a meaningful event with a comic undertone. Comic, not because there is something funny going on, but because its plot resembles the genre of comic emplotment – the trials and tribulations did not result in a tragic demise but testify to the perseverance of humanity in the face of evil. Quite literally, stephankeefetravels configures himself as the embodiment of the ultimate failure of evil. His 'selfie' functions as support to this plot, as his presence in front of the gate underlines Jewish perseverance against all odds.

As Table 9.2 shows, in the vast majority of the sampled posts (79.7%), the caption does not exceed a single line. Moreover, of the one-line captions, 47% consist of three or fewer words, and 21.8% of just one word. With only 4.2% of the posts containing captions with five or more lines, narrative emplotment plays only a minor role in the configuration of meaning in selfies on Instagram. Moreover, even if we consider the posts that do construct meaning through narrative, there is one key element on Instagram that is not covered by narrative theory: the narrative is not finalised in the reader's reconfiguration (as Ricœur

Table 9.2 Frequency distribution of the number of lines per post in the sample of Instagram posts (hashtags excluded)

Number of lines	Frequency	Relative frequency
0	163	32.7
1	234	47.0
2	43	8.6
3	26	5.2
4	11	2.2
5	7	1.4
6	4	0.8
7	5	1.0
8	2	0.4
9	1	0.2
10	1	0.2
12	1	0.2

would put it), but it can open a dialogue with its audience that is also represented in the Instagram post. It is for this reason that Nicholas Mirzoeff calls the selfie a "digital conversation"; it is the interactive nature of digital platforms that turns the visual performance of the self from a long history of static self-portraits into a dialogical one.[36] This can result in many interesting replies and dialogues, but also in unexpected or painful ones. User ivantxi_r34, for example, received a tongue-in-cheek response falsely claiming that his comment – which consisted of the words on the plaques of the International Monument to the Victims of Fascism in Auschwitz Birkenau – was a Wikipedia copy paste (ivantxi_r34, 2016). When user galabuikko called for people to open their eyes to all the cruelty in the world, instead of only feeling bad for the Jews who suffered from the Holocaust, he was met with Holocaust denial and an "RIP Hitler" comment.[37]

Also, the Auschwitz Memorial and Museum and an independent organisation called the Auschwitz Study Group actively engage in social media to convey their message by commenting on well-viewed posts. Their online activities in the comment sections of Instagram can be understood as digital "scripting" of visitor behaviour.[38] The Memorial's strategy, for example, copy pastes the same reaction as a comment to posts that do contain moral lessons or reflections but do not draw any practical conclusions from it. When user sameerhalai closes his reflections with: "Let's recognize our commonalities and let's celebrate our differences", the Memorial's comment adds to these conclusions by calling for reflection on "our individual and collective responsibility". This responsibility entails more than commemoration; it uses memory to "resist new gusts of populism, different slogans of propaganda, various ideologies and attitudes of insensitivity in the future".[39] This comment is more than paratext: the comment changes the plot of sameerhalai's narrative by adding a new conclusion which turns sameerhalai's conclusion into a mere premise of a new deductive argument. The Memorial is enabled to do this by Instagram's layout, which does not visually differentiate between a poster's caption and a viewer's comment – the latter being visible directly underneath the caption or in the place of a caption when there is none.

The fact that the interactive nature of Instagram defies narrative closure and leaves narratives open-ended is perhaps best illustrated by the case of viajabi, who comments on a selfie with his father about the value of going on vacation with your parents as an adult. When the comments turn to the topic of the overwhelming nature of Auschwitz, and a commenter talks about "an incredible experience" and "a mix of emotions", viajabi comments that experiencing this with his dad made it even more moving.[40] By doing so, he tries to restore the narrative closure of the micro-narrative in his caption. He felt forced to do so as the comments drove the meaning of the representation away from the topic he intended to (re)present. This draws our attention to the essential open-endedness of representations on Instagram – an open-endedness that is enabled by the interactive nature of the platform and provided by the platform's design structure.

In his work on identity and narrative in relation to video games, the philosopher Jos de Mul has argued that Paul Ricœur's narrative theory is not fully applicable to digital representations, as they seem to defy narrative linearity, concordant plotlines and closure.[41] Rather, digital representations do not necessarily rely on linguistic text, and another important difference is that where narrative identity rather increases concordance and closure, digital identity formation tends to increase openness. In De Mul's case of video games, this is exemplified by the wide range of possibilities for action that a video game opens for the player, which makes the same openness imaginable in "real" life.[42] This ability to make interactive choices is dominant on social media, as well. In the words of Ana Deumert:

> Every time we log onto Facebook we experience the volitional dimension of who we are: we might receive a comment to which we respond in turn, play a game or fill in a quiz, open the chat window, approve a friend request, post a photo, comment on a photo in which someone we know has been tagged, and so forth.[43]

Interactivity, Deumert argues, encompasses more than interaction, as it also relates to our abilities to change what is represented online and to the fact that we operate in a social context in which we are also responding to others and their representations. For this reason, she agrees with De Mul's statement that online spaces become "a playing field that enables us to (re)configure all kinds of different worlds".[44] It is the concept of play that De Mul uses to substitute narrative. He terms digital identity formation "ludic identity" rather than "narrative identity". The ludic part does not refer to play in the fun sense of the word but to the conceptualisation of play in hermeneutics established by Johan Huizinga and Hans-Georg Gadamer.

It may sound inappropriate to propose using a concept like "play" to study the representation of the past in places like Auschwitz, but it must be added that Gadamer emphasises that play is not the same thing as the behaviour of the player. Whereas the player may behave not seriously, the play itself is a serious, even sacred, matter.[45] The reason for this is that in play (whether it is a formal game or a playful interaction), ordinary sorrows, issues and commitments are suspended. Play creates a realm that fully absorbs those engaged and requires seriousness in the sense that during play, all those involved adhere to the implicit or explicit rules of play.[46] Johan Huizinga spoke of the spatio-temporal framework of play as a "magic circle" that is separated from life routines and has its own rule system to which the "players" consciously or unconsciously adhere.[47] The world of play (such as Instagram) may seem to be dissociated from life, but according to De Mul this is not the case:

> A possible objection could be that life is no game, but we could formulate an analogue answer as Ricœur did in reply to the critique that life is no story. Just because our life is no game, not always joyful and full of

116   *Robbert-Jan Adriaansen*

possibilities, we need games to oppose the continuous threat of closure. And just as in the case of narrative identity, ludic identity is a creation of our imagination that creates real effects in our daily lives.[48]

So even though our social media interactions take place in a ludic sphere that is not "real", at the same time they constitute real effects that can have an impact on our daily life.

When we consider Instagram, we can see that ludic rule systems are also in place. They are limited by the modal structure of Instagram that we have already explored, but they also express what De Mul calls the "ludic prefiguration of life", which can be understood as the "playful way" of relating to the world prior to representation.[49] In this case, it refers to the poster's behaviour at and engagement with the Auschwitz-Birkenau Memorial, which is also governed by explicit and implicit rules. These unwritten rules – both the rules of conduct at Auschwitz and the rules of representation – are sometimes explicitly reflected upon. These reflections are made by the poster in the main post, and by visitors in the comment section as ludic forms of social control. Rarely do they have a scolding tone; often they are ironic tongue-in-cheek comments aimed at other visitors, at oneself, or at the poster. The example of jula_00 that we discussed earlier is not the only case in which the rules of either representation or conduct at Auschwitz are ludically enforced in an interactive way. Posing on the railway tracks in bright blue trainers, gabrielcnobre received a witty comment warning him to be careful not to be barred from the premises with such trainers.[50] This comment, although – or perhaps because – it was jokingly posted, reinforces the sanctity of the site without resulting in the poster's loss of face.

Huizinga makes one very interesting remark about the transgression of the rules of play (this is not the same as the denial of the rules of play, which would disrupt the semiosis, break the magic circle and result in the exclusion of the denier). When rules are transgressed, it ironically does not challenge the rule system: "The spoil-sport is not the same as the false player, the cheat; for the latter pretends to be playing the game and, on the face of it, still acknowledges the magic circle."[51] In a similar way, the rules of conduct and representation are continuously challenged – and prone to change under the sway of those challenges – but never rejected outright. At least, not in this chapter's sample. When user mordyfier posts a selfie in front of a watchtower with the comment "Is it okay to take selfies in Auschwitz?" followed by a thinking face emoji, he embodies Huizinga's false player.[52] He cheats the rules by the very fact that his post is a selfie, but this does not challenge the rule system in any way; it playfully raises a meta question about conduct and representation to which his post is not itself the answer.

Conclusion: historical representation beyond narration?

We can conclude that social media platforms such as Instagram are semiotic systems based on user interaction and that "Holocaust selfies" should not be read as static representations of historical memory, but as expressions of what Jos de Mul calls "ludic identity". As social media platforms are playing fields in which different types of self are mobilised and posited dynamically, conventional maxims of communication and (historical) representation – such as truth and clarity – are often suspended, which may be interpreted as a threat to historical consciousness. However, my analysis confirms Commane and Potton's observation that the majority of "Auschwitz selfies" are used to define the poster's relationship to the act of remembering, rather than to define the individual's relationship to the events or to the contents of a particular memory.[53] It is only by confusing these two relationships that critics such as Shapira dismiss selfie culture altogether.

Critiques on selfies in Auschwitz confuse ludic identity statements for narrative identity statements; that is, they treat selfies as failed forms of intentional, single-authored, concordant representation and think that posters are trying to tell a singular story about the self, wholly disregarding the burdened context of the site. The reality is that no Instagram post can claim concordant emplotment. Although some users are keen to try maintaining one, others do not even bother. If critics challenge the culture of representation on social media platforms, then the interactive nature of social media provides the best platform on which to ironically and playfully convey those critiques. Shutting down the ludic context of digital representation altogether by branding posters "douches" and forcing them to repent by publicly shaming them actually turned Shapira into Huizinga's spoilsport: he used the guise of being a player in an attempt to shut down the ludic system of representing Auschwitz in selfies instead of mobilising the same system for his cause.

In the end, we should not see selfies as direct references to the Holocaust as a historical event, but as entangled references to Auschwitz as a site and to the witnessing and documenting self. Their self-reflexivity gives selfies a quality analogous to what Hayden White, in reference to the comic *Maus*, calls the "middle voice":[54] a mode of discourse that denies the distancing effects of historical realism but gives something more profound in return, namely a mode of relating to the past in which the author inscribes his own act of remembering. The fact that selfies offer these possibilities is something that Holocaust institutions could and should explore further, especially as the temporal distance to the Holocaust increases. When Kate Douglas emphasises that the selfie offers young people a context for "reflecting on the past in light of one's position in the present",[55] she stresses that, with the increasing loss of first-person Holocaust experience, such forms of second-hand witnessing that juxtapose the self and the Auschwitz traumascape are of crucial value to contemporary Holocaust remembrance. It is this juxtaposition, combined with the dialogical nature of social media, that gives selfies immediate value, as they call for reflection and dialogue on the past through its apprehension in the present. In such ways, selfies can open up possibilities for dialogical reflection on the possibilities and limits of representing and understanding the Holocaust.

118   *Robbert-Jan Adriaansen*

Notes

1 Caroline Moss, "This Teenager Is Getting Harassed After Her Smiling Selfie At Auschwitz Goes Viral", *Business Insider*. Retrieved, 13 November 2017, www.businessin sider.com/selfie-at-auschwitz-goes-viral-2014-7, accessed 11 August 2019.

2 Ruth Margalit, "Should Auschwitz Be a Site for Selfies?", *The New Yorker*, 26 June 2014, www.newyorker.com/culture/culture-desk/should-auschwitz-be-a-site-for-selfies, accessed 19 August 2019.

3 For a critique of the "narcissist" interpretation of selfies, see Derek Murray, "Notes to Self: The Visual Culture of Selfies in the Age of Social Media", *Consumption Markets & Culture*, 18/6 (2015), 490–516. https://doi.org/10.1080/10253866.2015.10529 67, accessed 5 August 2019.

4 Shahak Shapira, Yolocaust, 20 January 2017, http://web.archive.org/web/20170120021 311/http://yolocaust.de/, accessed 5 April 2019.

5 "Auschwitz Memorial", Twitter Post, 20 February 2019, https://twitter.com/Ausch witzMuseum/status/1108337507660451841, accessed 5 April 2019.

6 Wulf Kansteiner, "The Holocaust in the 21st Century. Digital Anxiety, Transnational Cosmopolitanism, and Never Again Genocide without Memory", in *Digital Memory Studies. Media Pasts in Transition,* ed. Andrew Hoskins (Abingdon: Routledge, 2017), 110–140, https://www.researchgate.net/publication/333699454_The_Holocaust_in_the_21st_ Century, https://www.taylorfrancis.com/chapters/edit/10.4324/9781315637235-5/ holocaust-21st-century-wulf-kansteiner, accessed 5 February 2019.

7 Ibid., 116.

8 Eva Pfanzelter, "Performing the Holocaust on Social Networks: Digitality, Transcultural Memory and New Forms of Narrating", *Kultura Popularna*, 51/1 (2017), 136–151.

9 Allen Weiner, "Capturing the Horror of the Holocaust for the Selfie Generation", *The Kernel*. 14 December 2014, https://kernelmag.dailydot.com/issue-titles/religion/ 11101/holocaust-selfie-history-education/, accessed 5 April 2019.

10 Anja Dinhopl and Ulrike Gretzel, "Selfie-taking as Touristic Looking", *Annals of Tourism Research*, 57(Supplement C) (2016), 127, https://doi.org/10.1016/j.annals.2015.12.015, accessed 5 May 2019.

11 A percentage of 5% selfies is in line with the 3% to 5% Tifentale and Manovic identified in a study of selfies in urban areas. Note that they only included "actual" self-portraits. Alise Tifentale and Lev Manovich, "Selfiecity: Exploring Photography and Self-Fashioning in Social Media", in *Postdigital Aesthetics: Art, Computation and Design*, ed. David M. Berry (London: Palgrave London: Palgrave Macmillan, 2015), 115.

12 Frank Ankersmit, "Representation as the Representation of Experience", *Metaphilosophy*, 31/1–2 (2000), 148–168.

13 Hayden White, "Historical Emplotment and the Problem of Truth", in *Probing the Limits of Representation: Nazism and the "Final Solution"*, ed. Saul Friedländer (Cambridge, MA: Harvard University Press, 1992), 41.

14 Jörn Rüsen, *Historische Orientierung: Über die Arbeit des Geschichtsbewußtseins, sich in der Zeit zurechtzufinden* (Frankfurt am Mein: Wochenschau-Verlag, 2008), 13.

15 Jörn Rüsen, *Historical Consciousness: Narrative Structure, Moral Function, and Ontogenetic Development*, in *Theorizing Historical Consciousness*, ed. Peter C. Seixas (Toronto: University of Toronto Press, 2004), 63–85.

16 Paul Ricoeur, *Life in Quest of Narrative*, in *On Paul Ricœur: Narrative and Interpretation*, ed. David Wood (Abingdon: Routledge, 1991), 20–33.

17 Ann Rigney, "History as Text: Narrative Theory and History", in *History as Text: Narrative Theory and History*, ed. Nancy Partner and Sarah Foot (London: Sage, 2013), 197.

18 Ana Deumert, "The Performance of a Ludic Self on Social Network(ing) Sites", in *The Language of Social Media*, ed. Philip Seargeant and Caroline Tagg (London: Palgrave Macmillan, 2014), 25–26.

19 Chiel van den Akker, "History as Dialogue: On Online Narrativity", *BMGN – Low Countries Historical Review*, 128/4 (2013), 107, https://doi.org/10.18352/bmgn-lchr.9354, accessed 10 May 2019; Ann Rigney, "When the Monograph Is No Longer the Medium: Historical Narrative in the Online Age", *History and Theory*, 49/4 (2010), 109, https://doi.org/10.1111/j.1468-2303.2010.00562.x, accessed 11 May 2019.

20 Gunther Kress, Regina Leite-García and Theo van Leeuwen, "Discourse Semiotics", in *Discourse as Structure and Process*, ed. Teuna A. van Dijk (London: Sage, 1997), 257.

21 Gunther Kress and Theo Van Leeuwen, *Reading Images: The Grammar of Visual Design* (East Sussex: Psychology Press, 1996), 159.

22 Charles Forceville, "Visual and Multimodal Metaphor in Film: Charting the Field", in *Embodied Metaphors in Film, Television, and Video Games: Cognitive Approaches,* ed. Kathrin Fahlenbrach (Abingdon: Routledge, 2016), 20.

23 Jens Ruchatz, "Selfie Reflexivity: Pictures of People Taking Photographs", in *Exploring the Selfie. Historical, Theoretical, and Analytical Approaches to Digital Self-Photograph*, ed. Jens Ruchatz, Sabine Wirth, and Julia Eckel (London: Palgrave Macmillan, 2018), 62.

24 Dinhopl and Gretzel, "Selfie-taking as Touristic Looking", *Annals of Tourism Research*, 57(Supplement C) (2016), 132.

25 Roman Babiichuk, "The Impression of this Place Bad #Travel #Photo #Museum", Instagram, 15 May 2017.

26 [razwpa], "It's Cold Out? Good! Finally Matches the Weather in My Soul!", Instagram, 6 January 2017.

27 [julka_00], "Nie wiem skąd ten uśmiech", Instagram, 19 April 2017, www.instagram.com/p/BTE6bzkF_zT/, accessed 15 April 2018.

28 [nishkarshs], "I'm Only Smiling because I Made it Here. Next Time Someone Tries to Fool You, Please Remember Work.", Instagram, 29 December 2016.

29 Thomas Vander Wal, "Folksonomy Coinage and Definition", 2 February 2007, www.vanderwal.net/folksonomy.html, accessed 11 April 2019.

30 Michele Zappavigna, "Searchable Talk: The Linguistic Functions of Hashtags", *Social Semiotics*, 25/3 (2015), 288, https://doi.org/10.1080/10350330.2014.996948, accessed 11 April 2018.

31 "9 Instagram Hashtags You Should Know", OxfordWords Blog, 17 March 2015.

32 [9209.j.b], "Ein wenig Geschichte, immer cool #architecture #building #architexture #city #buildings #skyscraper.", Instagram, 21 July 2017.

33 [_josh2910], "#auschwitz #poland #katowice #krakow #germany #hitler #worldwar2 #ww2 #camp #concentrationcamp #birkenau #war #jew #jews #ss.", Instagram.

34 [808killawhale], "Today We are Visiting #Auschwitz on the Anniversary of the Day that the 1st Prisoners Were Brought.", Instagram, 14 June 2017, www.instagram.com/p/BVUYj4NgJuv/, accessed 24 May 2018.

35 [stephankeefetravels], "As a Jew, I Always Felt as Though Going to Auschwitz was an Important Thing I had to do and this.", Instagram, 22 July 2017, www.instagram.com/p/BW3IaE8lGXF/, accessed 17 May 2018.

36 Nicholas Mirzoeff, *How to See the World: An Introduction to Images, from Self-Portraits to Selfies, Maps to Movies, and More* (New York: Basic Books, 2016), 66.

37 [galabuikko], "Auschwitz Sure Didn't Make Me Happy. But Let's Not Forget that Jews Weren't the Only People Who.", Instagram, 20 July 2017.

38 Richard Carter-White, "Death Camp Heritage 'from below'? Instagram and the (Re)mediation of Holocaust Heritage", in *After Heritage: After Heritage: Critical Perspectives on Heritage from below*, ed. Hamzah Muzaini and Claudio Minca (Cheltenham, UK; Northampton, MA, USA: Edward Elgar Publishing, 2018), 86–106, www.elgaronline.com/view/edcoll/9781788110730/9781788110730.00011.xml, accessed 30 May 2018.

39 [sameerhalai], "Yesterday was My Birthday. I Spent All Day at Auschwitz, the Nazi Concentration Camp in Poland", Instagram, 20 July 2017, www.instagram.com/p/BWwrokGBm_u/, accessed 25 April 2019.

120   *Robbert-Jan Adriaansen*

40 [viajabi], "Você já fez uma viagem, depois de adulto, só com seu pai ou sua mãe? Se não fez, programe-se para.", Instagram, 26 March 2017, www.instagram.com/p/BSGsf-NBO8M/, accessed 20 May 2019.
41 Jos de Mul, "The Game of Life: Narrative and Ludic Identity Formation in Computer Games", in *Representations of Internarrative Identity*, ed. Lori Way (London: Palgrave Macmillan, 2015), 159–187, https://doi.org/10.1057/9781137462534_10, accessed 21 April 2017.
42 De Mul, however, is mistaken when he claims that the temporal dimensions of games and narratives are inverted: "Narration, although taking place in the present, aims at an understanding of what has happened in the past; playing, which also takes place in the present, is directed at future possibilities." As stated earlier, configuration necessarily involves the three temporal dimensions, as future possibilities can only be explored in reference to past experience. Mul, "The Game of Life", 178.
43 Ana Deumert, "The Performance of a Ludic Self on Social Network(ing) Sites", in *The Language of Social Media*, 25.
44 Mul, "The Game of Life", 180.
45 Hans-Georg Gadamer, *Truth and Method* (2nd revised edition) (London: Bloomsbury Academic, 2004), 102.
46 Robbert-Jan Adriaansen, "Play", in *The Routledge Handbook of Reenactment Studies. Key Terms in the Field*, ed. Vanessa Agnew, Jonathan Lamb, and Juliane Tomann (Abingdon: Routledge, 2019), 178–186, https://doi.org/10.4324/9780429445637-38, accessed 29 May 2019.
47 Johan Huizinga, *Homo ludens: A Study of the Play-element in Culture* (Abingdon: Routledge & Kegan Paul, 1949), 11.
48 Mul, "The Game of Life", 178.
49 Ibid., 177.
50 [gabrielcnobre], "Inaugurado em maio des 1940, o campo de concentração de Auschwitz, também conhecido como Auschwitz-.", Instagram, 22 February 2017, www.instagram.com/p/BQ0ZihUFzEx/, accessed 11 April 2018.
51 Huizinga, *Homo ludens*, 12.
52 [mordyfier], "Is it Okay to Take Selfies in Auschwitz? 😕", Instagram, 28 March 2017.
53 Gemma Commane and Rebekah Potton, "Instagram and Auschwitz: A Critical Assessment of the Impact Social Media has on Holocaust Representation", *Holocaust Studies*, 25/1–2 (2019), 158–181, https://doi.org/10.1080/17504902.2018.1472879, accessed 12 May 2019.
54 White, "Historical Emplotment and the Problem of Truth", 52.
55 Kate Douglas, "Youth, Trauma and Memorialisation: The Selfie as Witnessing", *Memory Studies* (2017), 13, https://doi.org/10.1177/1750698017714838, accessed 12 April 2018.

10 Image world, memory space

Photographic spectatorship as a mode of remembrance

Robert Hariman

The medium of photography provides an infrastructure for memory. The photograph is a fragment of the past that can serve as aide-mémoire, forensic evidence, educational artifact and mute testimony to catastrophic loss. Photography – which has been in use for almost 200 years – has created an image world of democratic access in which any memorial can be shared on behalf of solidarity and resistance. The discourse on photography – as old as the medium itself – has served as a central place for arguments about representation and whether memory, tradition or history matter within a modernity defined by technological reproduction and political disasters. Nor should any of this be surprising. The medium proved to be both indispensable to exposing history's slaughter pen and as variable as memory itself.

So it is that a reconsideration of photography might be able to contribute to a better understanding of memorial practices, not least as they are mediated practices. I am not claiming that photography contains the most important or full range of the techniques and experiences that constitute public memory. Even when a photograph is relaying another art, the image does not reproduce all of the artwork or its direct encounter on site, and each medium and genre has its distinctive materials, conventions, history and potential. That said, the photographic mediation of the past can expose how history unfolds at the edge of an abyss – the unthinkable, the unimaginable – and it can school spectators in how to make sense of a world that is both shattered and excessive, present and absent, beyond hope and capable of transformation.

Such a reconsideration is underway: as my co-author John Lucaites and I have argued, the dominant discourse on photography of the last 40 years is now a conventional wisdom that is being set aside by photographers, editors, curators, artists and scholars.[1] What might follow is a very open question. One possibility is this paradigm shift might provide specific resources for reworking some of the dilemmas that are shaping the practice of public memory. By breaking out of a discourse of critical misrecognition, we can begin to see the landscape of public memory in the spirit of Andre Malraux, as a "museum without walls." By becoming schooled in what Georges Didi-Huberman has called the "torn imagination" necessary for solidarity with the suffering of others, we can become capable of breaking out of the complacency of the present.

DOI: 10.4324/9781003264460-12

122   *Robert Hariman*

Together, these offer an optic and hermeneutical method for anyone struggling to honour those who were lost to a catastrophic past, confront its recurrence in the present and imagine a better future.

The conventional wisdom

As Susie Linfield has pointed out, one of the oddities of the discourse on photography is that, contrary to thoughtful engagement in all other arts, critical judgement has been weighted heavily towards the negative.[2] That discourse is so ingrained in scholarly, public and professional commentary that it is easily activated each time we are reminded that photographs lack context, don't tell the whole story, are emotional rather than rational, anaesthetise reality or induce compassion fatigue; or that the "deluge of images" is eclipsing any reliable relationship with reality, deifying consumer capitalism, levelling moral values or producing political quiescence; or that spectators are voyeurs, addicts, bystanders, consumers or otherwise morally compromised and unreliable.

The strongest public statement was provided by Susan Sontag's *On Photography*, which began by declaring that "Humankind lingers unregenerately in Plato's cave, still reveling, its age-old habit, in mere images of the truth".[3] Images are on the wrong side of a binary opposition and so inherently suspect. Aesthetic pleasure also is implicated, as delusion and domination come from "reveling" in the dumb show on the walls of the cave. Those caught in the image world forget that they ever were free to walk out into an unmediated world oriented towards reason and justice. No wonder that "the omnipresence of photographs has an incalculable effect on our ethical sensibility".[4]

That negative effect would be "incalculable" because it is comprehensive, affecting all of life. The supposed consequences for history are illustrative. To continue Sontag's critique, "photographs, which turn the past into a consumable object, are a short cut. Any collection of photographs is an exercise in Surrealist montage and the Surrealist abbreviation of history". Photography epitomises the "garbage strewn plenitude" of modernism as it (quoting Baudelaire) is a "cheap method of disseminating a loathing for history". The results are not good: "Photographs turn the past into an object of tender regard, scrambling moral distinctions and disarming historical judgments". Photographs are like quotations, easily taken out of context, and they persuade by displacing reference, analysis or explanation. Photography's natal aesthetic is surrealism (not realism, and hence the boldness of her assertions), and with its taste for found objects, democratic levelling and odd juxtapositions, surrealism "can only deliver a reactionary judgment; can make out of history only an accumulation of oddities, a joke, a death trip".[5]

Thus,

> while traditional arts of historical consciousness attempt to put the past in order, distinguishing the innovative from the retrograde, the central from the marginal, the relevant from the irrelevant or merely interesting,

Image world, memory space   123

the photographer's approach – like that of the collector – is unsystematic, indeed anti-systematic.

Those who hold onto photographs are merely "collectors" drawn to oddities; indeed, "[t]he photographer – and the consumer of photographs – follows in the footsteps of the ragpicker". Photography reflects a profound alienation that leads, not to visions of a better world, but to a kitsch aesthetic twined with a "promiscuous" acceptance of the world as it is. Photographers "suggest the vanity of even trying to understand the world and instead propose that we collect it". Instead of knowledge of a real world, we remain inside the cave, lost to enthrallment: "photographs give people an imaginary possession of a past that is unreal".[6]

And there you have some of the binary distinctions that have dogged the study of collective memory: truth vs imagination; history vs memory; literate judgement vs material fetishism; in place of either authenticity or fine art, the embarrassment of vernacular memorials with their kitschy mashups of teddy bears, flowers, photographs and heart-shaped balloons. Because she is making sweeping generalisations that are far more wrong than they are right, it is tempting to simply reverse Sontag's binaries, but that shortchanges everyone. It might be useful instead to consider how she got close to what are indeed fundamental elements – and problems – of both photography and collective memory. And to realise the value of her insight, one needs to separate it from the value judgements that followed from her conservative mentality. Stated otherwise, her denigration of photography identifies four crucial nodal points for collective representation: the image world, decontextualisation, the spectator and the imagination.

Sontag's image world refers to the totalising envelopment of experience by visual media. That domination operates through material and virtual displacements: we live in an ever more "image-choked world", those images come to "usurp", "consume" or displace the real world, and a negative transvaluation occurs as we become inclined "to attribute to real things the qualities of an image". At that point, enchantment is complete – reality is thought to have the characteristics of the images on the cave wall – and domination becomes easy – capitalism can reproduce itself simply by providing a "culture based on images".[7]

The root cause of this "imprisoning" of reality is the radical decontextualisation produced by technological reproduction. The photograph quickly becomes untethered from its moment and place of origin. It is brought into whatever context the viewer might provide, and, being mute, it can do nothing to correct any misuse. Worse, as the images proliferate widely, they become mixed up with one another, a maelstrom of juxtapositions that annihilates distinctions, hierarchies, tradition, order itself. Everything is shown without telling, nothing is in its proper place. And because "photography makes us feel that the world is more available than it really is", the door is thrown open to desire, fantasy and sloth. Photography's surrealism blurs the lines "between art

124   *Robert Hariman*

and so-called life, between objects and events, between the intended and the unintentional, between pros and amateurs, between the noble and the tawdry, between craftsmanship and lucky blunders". In losing a sense of context, you lose everything that is excellent, disciplined, hard-earned or worthwhile.[8]

For an art to be degraded, its spectators must follow suit. Perhaps Sontag's most vitriolic passages are reserved for the effect photography has on its audience and how quick they are to indulge in experiences that are pathetic, perverse, unseemly or otherwise low. Those who like photographs are "corrupted" across the board: pandered to, morally anaesthetised, indulged in fantasies of violence, pornography or voyeurism. At best, they are described as "tourists" of reality and "people who do not take easily to reading".[9] More darkly, they are compared to "thuggish lumpen-peasants", addicts and predators.[10] At the same time (oddly), they are passive: the medium acts on them, and their use of the medium only strengthens its hold over them. Any action is only in a realm of fantasy and consumption: faux identifications, capricious emotions and "knowledge at bargain prices – a semblance of knowledge".[11]

These several denigrations of the photographic habitus culminate in a radically diminished conception of the imagination. In Sontag's account, photographic meaning is limited to "clouds of fantasy and pellets of information".[12] Both representation and imagination are recast in their most reductive forms: mere information obtained through an industrial process ("pellets") and mere fantasy floating above reality ("clouds"). Unchecked by a stronger sense of reference, this phantasmal quality permeates society, creating "a duplicate world, a reality of the second degree, narrower but more dramatic".[13] Once an imaginary optic is coupled with institutional power, enthrallment and surveillance become the most likely outcomes and critique the necessary response. What is lost, however, is any conception of how the imagination is needed to resist domination and sustain other forms of life.

Re-imagining photography

Let us consider briefly how each of the nodal points can be redefined. Photography has indeed created an "image world," the virtual archive created by the proliferation of images throughout the lifeworld for over a century. Everyone has become accustomed to seeing images that already are somewhat dislocated and reproducible across multiple media. No image is tied resolutely to a single event, while its meaning and significance emerge as one context or another is activated. Stated otherwise, photographic meaning is created as spectators move one way or another through the "museum without walls" that is photography's most comprehensive effect within modern societies.

The phrase "museum without walls" invokes the ghost of André Malraux: the English phrase is the publisher's translation of *Le Musée Imaginaire*. Malraux argued that photography and printing together had created a new capability for experiencing art: one that will "carry infinitely farther that limited revelation of the world of art which the real museums offer us within their walls".[14] Today, photography's giant open-air museum includes not only the art and artifacts of the past but recordings of every visible feature of human existence. Instead of the museum being a refuge from the world, one where politics and other conflicts could be temporarily suspended in aesthetic contemplation, now any part of the world can be framed for reflective reconsideration. And while "the museum was an affirmation, the museum without walls is an interrogation".[15]

Although speaking of specific exhibitions, Ariella Azoulay has put the point succinctly: "Visiting the museum, contemplating visual items, and passing an aesthetic judgment are all necessary actions performed by the modern citizen".[16] Contrary to fears of being trapped within an image world, the museum without walls cultivates opportunities and skills for civic reflection and engagement that can transcend other forms of enclosure. By placing an event within the museum without walls, that event is not stripped of meaning but rather presented for a wider range of judgement. The museum provides the social distance, provisional disinterest, embodied engagement and slow temporality that makes reflection possible, a shift that is summarised by the term "aesthetic judgment", but not limited to that.

The fundamental cause and effect of the image world is a pervasive decontextualisation. Every photograph is a slice of space and time taken elsewhere later; every reproduction and every viewing generate additional meaning.[17] It can be difficult to accept the full force of this idea; it is much easier to fall back on the conventional wisdom that the meaning of the image must be grounded in a verbal description of the specific event being recorded. But if photographic meaning is radically plural, then it cannot be contained by any one interpretation, even one that provides literal fidelity to the immediate social and material context in which the photograph was taken. The choice is not between a surreal image world and the enlightenment provided by critical reason, but between an iconoclastic attitude and another, more capacious understanding based on epistemic pluralism and recombinant capability.

Photography's comprehensive decontextualisation has become the optical unconscious of modern public culture. That culture is defined by a provisional equality of artifacts, plurality of views and comparison across boundaries. These features also are the specific targets of the iconoclastic critique of photography, as when Sontag excoriates the medium for its democratic levelling of the arts and their corresponding taste cultures, and for its mixing of its subject matter to make surrealism the default mentality of mass society.[18] Yet for the same reasons, photography is able to expose how surrealism is the default reality of modern regimes of violence.

Nothing regarding spectatorship has much traction as long as the spectator is thought to be essentially a passive recipient of whatever the media system provides. If so, the only options are to change the system or provide a media literacy grounded in disenchantment and vigilance. Both options have less than stellar track records. Spectatorship is not wholly passive, however. As Jacques Rancière has noted, as it includes reading, listening and thinking, it is the most pervasive modality of education, culture and much more, and it simply is not

126 Robert Hariman

described adequately as being passive or active.[19] Spectatorship is not a series of behavioural reactions (or nonreactions); it is an extended social relationship. Equally important, spectatorship is embedded in a plethora of activities and practices that are additional sources of the deep pluralism of photographic meaning. One can assert, as in a recent book title, that "Photography Changes Everything" because photography is involved in everything, and those involvements carry many different angles and inflections of spectatorship.[20] Because seeing is varied, differential, plural and otherwise overdetermined and underdefined, one also can see the limitations of the allegory of the cave.

So it is that the imagination can be a topic of interest in revitalising the discourse on photography and perhaps memory studies as well. The shift is from information to knowledge, from fantasy to world disclosure, from enthralment to engagement. Imagination is not some fictive alternative to reality but rather a way of extraordinary seeing beyond the horizon of ordinary observation or conventional belief. It can be the only way of seeing effectively when enclosed by walls of domination, trauma or despair. Of course, imagination can fall into fantasy and be colonised by the powers that be, but it also can be the means for solidarity among those who are governed, for sustaining the public sphere and for confronting the most serious problems in the world. What is necessary is not only artistic courage and creativity but also what Didi-Huberman labels the *torn imagination* that allows us to bear witness to radical evil and to the pain of others in many settings present and past.[21]

Method, memory and history

Didi-Huberman's impassioned argument for photographic witnessing provides one answer to what photography can offer to memory studies. Confronting the radical evil of the Shoah and drawing inspiration from Aby Warburg's *Mnemosyne Atlas*, Didi-Huberman provides an optic and a hermeneutic.[22] Both can be read as philosophically intensified articulations of the museum without walls. The optic is that of seeing *"in spite of all"*: an assertion of how photography has become the most important counterforce to the will to obliterate.[23] That death drive has evolved through mechanisation into a world system of ecological destruction that is eliminating species, languages, peoples, forests and other forms of life, while still excreting and recirculating any viciousness they contained. But from mechanisation to system dominance, the will to obliterate has been mirrored by the development of photography and its reproduction of the scenes, gestures, relationships, persistence and value of the life world. This is the deepest level of support for collective memory: the fact that its materials are continually being produced and reproduced, and that everything is likely to be photographed because the images will be taken, preserved and shared in spite of all. Museums, like any site-specific archive, can be destroyed; the museum without walls is endless. It includes sunsets and book burnings, birthday parties and lynchings, life and death, the will to obliterate and the will to live.

The hermeneutic is extensive and can only be outlined selectively here. Most pertinent, I believe, are the following features. First, it is grounded in a critique of the "lazy" aesthetic that places radical evil with an absolute other on the far side of representation. That aesthetic has been dominant in the conventional discourse on photography, not least via Sontag's claim about the extreme suffering and trauma of war: "We don't get it. We truly can't imagine what it was like."[24] This declaration is both true in part and profoundly mistaken. The errors bundled into its pathetic appeal include overvaluing identification, authenticity and knowledge as conditions for communication and community; misunderstanding both witnessing and compassion, denying the role of distance in moral reflection; ceding too much power to the perpetrators of violence; and severing the social bond between the victims and everyone else.

Critique bears the obligation of an alternative, which is provided by a renewed commitment to the imagination as a way of knowing in spite of all. Contrary to both fantasy and a reassertion of proportion and order, Didi-Huberman emphasises crossing the gaps between experience and representation, and between the most distant and different realities, and finding the meeting points between the most opposed things, which can include the "reasons of which reason is unaware".[25] But reason is not the goal: the point is to provide a knowledge of suffering, and one capable of both exposing "the great dismantling of the world" and suturing the wounds of history because it can imagine what really was and what could be otherwise in spite the powers that continue to crush and deny.[26] The knowledge that is offered – say, through Warburg's memory atlas – is necessarily flawed, incomplete, hybrid, neither epistemically nor aesthetically adequate, because it necessarily oscillates dialectically between different modes of representation while staying oriented towards chaos, disaster and suffering.

Another, admittedly simplified way of putting the question is, how is truth to be discerned and communicated after the loss of a grand narrative? (The deep problem has a surface tremor in the question of whether an image can be meaningful without narrative contextualisation.) That loss was felt most deeply after Auschwitz, and yet that is where Didi-Huberman – drawing on Walter Benjamin and Hannah Arendt – stakes his claim. The answer is layered: photographs can provide "instants of truth", as well as the types of images (lacuna images, scratched images, shield images, etc.) that are needed to confront apparatuses of denial, as well as the capacity for montage that is the most fully developed method for the "anxious, gay science" that is Warburg's legacy and unfulfilled project. Images do not do this alone, of course – one must be willing to be changed, and a redemptive hopefulness probably helps – but they can work because of their plural, mixed, troubled character, their refusal to mean one thing alone, their invitations to divination, their reservoirs of emotion, their resolutely dialectical engagement with history. Indeed, they can reveal a world as it is unfolding and self-destructing, precisely because they have those qualities that are misrecognised when labeled fragmentary, perverse, surreal, phantasmal, kitschy and otherwise bathetic.

128 *Robert Hariman*

That critique also ridiculed collecting, and there we find the most explicit reversal in Warburg, Benjamin, Malraux and Didi-Huberman. Collecting, curating and committing above all to the montage, this investment in the recombinant capability of photography is crucial. It also is both intuitive and yet to be realised. Intuitive, because it is the background noise of the image world; yet to be realised, because the Warburg/Didi-Huberman *Memory Atlas* is a perplexing combination of the aspirational and the mundane. Although trying to plumb both the mental heights ("*astra*") and embodied depths ("*monstra*") of human experience, Warburg's montage table has the feel of a ritual practice from a distant culture: what is supposed to be magical, appears exceedingly banal. Note, however, the importance of defining the imagination as "a tool – an apparatus, technically elaborated, philosophically constructed – of an actual critical knowledge of the body and the human mind".[27] By exploring surreal juxtapositions to identify deep contradictions and hidden affinities, one becomes capable of "experiencing *the image in a time of the torn imagination*", a response to the unthinkable that is both impossible and essential.[28]

In this context, the defense of high-mindedness exemplifies establishment denial of the will to obliterate. Far better to acknowledge that history is a junk heap and a joke – on the good days – and more often, as with Benjamin, "one single catastrophe which keeps piling wreckage upon wreckage".[29] But not only that. The deeper meditations on photography contain a hope that Sontag's sophistication could only find embarrassing.

That hope is one of photography's gifts to collective memory. Not the attitude itself, but the means for continually sharing it in spite of all. The will to obliterate is not defeated, but it is checked everywhere by the ongoing disclosure of reality and celebration of life reflected in the abundance of the image world.[30] That celebration includes the moments that shock, the flash of insight and the leap of faith that can crack the complacency of the present and the images of sadness and horror that make public grieving possible. And where there is public grief, there can be prophecy and the seeds of a more just and peaceable community.[31]

In practical terms, the shift underway in the discourse on photography can support artists and advocates as they work to resist obliteration. They can be encouraged to draw on the diverse resources and jumbled logics of the image world, rather than be held back by assumptions of moral and aesthetic asceticism; to embrace the surreal where it represents realities of violence and possibilities of reconciliation; to engage an audience in its flaws and failings as these are signs of diversity and community; and to imagine what was and what could be, not to enthrall but rather to stand with those who suffer and yearn.

The flaws in the image mirror how history itself has been torn asunder: any deep continuity between past and future, and between language and reality, made forever false or bitter by "unimaginable" violence. Which is why

> The question of images is at the heart of the great darkness of our time, the "discontent of our civilization". We must know how to look into images to

see that of which they are survivors. So that history, liberated from the pure past (that absolute, that abstraction), might help us *to open* the present of time.[32]

That time is the time of photography – and the time in which memory is at once the most alien and the most necessary presence.

Notes

1 Robert Hariman and John Louis Lucaites, *The Public Image: Photography and Civic Spectatorship* (Chicago: University of Chicago Press, 2016).
2 Susie Linfield, *The Cruel Radiance: Photography and Political Violence* (Chicago: University of Chicago Press, 2010), 3–31.
3 Susan Sontag, *On Photography* (New York: Picador, 1977), 3.
4 Ibid., 24.
5 Ibid., 68, 68–69, 69, 71, 75.
6 Ibid., 77, 78, 81, 82, 9.
7 Ibid., 15, 154, 179, 158, 178.
8 Ibid., 163, 24, 5. Also: "The traditional fine arts are elitist. . . . The media are democratic" (149); the distinction is not intended to be complimentary.
9 Sontag, *On Photography*, 110 (see also 9, 11, 12, 42, 57), 22. The literacy comment also refers to "a moment in cultural history when everyone is thought to have a right to something called news" – an anti-democratic phrasing if there ever was one.
10 Sontag, *On Photography*, 3, 14.
11 Ibid., 11.
12 Ibid., 69.
13 Ibid., 52.
14 André Malraux, *Museum without Walls*, trans. Stuart Gilbert and Francis Price (New York: Doubleday, 1967), 12.
15 Ibid., 162.
16 Ariella Azoulay, *The Civil Contract of Photography*, trans. Reia Mazali and Ruvik Danieli (New York: Zone Books, 2008), 159.
17 See for example Susan Buck-Morss, "Visual Studies in Global Imagination," in *The Politics of Imagination*, ed. Chiara Bottici and Benoit Challand (Abingdon, Oxon, UK: Birkbeck Law Press, 2011), 228–229; Ariella Azoula, "What is a Photograph? What is Photography?" *Philosophy of Photography*, 1 (2010), 9–13.
18 Sontag, *On Photography*, 51–82.
19 Jacques Rancière, *The Emancipated Spectator* (London: Verso, 2011), 17.
20 Marvin Heiferman, ed., *Photography Changes Everything* (New York: Aperture, 2012).
21 Georges Didi-Huberman, *Images in Spite of All: Four Photographs from Auschwitz*, trans. Shane B. Lillis (Chicago: University of Chicago Press, 2008), 181.
22 Ibidem; Georges Didi-Huberman, *Atlas, or the Anxious Gay Science*, trans. Shane B. Lillis (Chicago: University of Chicago Press, 2018).
23 Didi-Huberman, *Images in Spite of All*, 19–25.
24 Susan Sontag, *Regarding the Pain of Others* (New York: Picador, 2003), 125. On the continuity between *On Photography* and *Regarding the Pain of Others*, see Hariman and Lucaites, *The Public Image*, 7–9.
25 Didi-Huberman, *Atlas*, 161–162, 13, 116, 28.
26 Ibid., 182.
27 Ibid., *Atlas*, 110.
28 Didi-Huberman, *Images in Spite of All*, 181.
29 Walter Benjamin, "Theses on the Philosophy of History," in *Illuminations*, ed. Hannah Arendt, trans. Harry Zohn (New York: Schocken, 1969), 257–258. As Benjamin also

130 *Robert Hariman*

observed, "The tradition of the oppressed teaches us that the 'state of emergency' in which we live is not the exception but the rule" (257).
30 Hariman and Lucaites, *The Public Image*, 227–260.
31 See Walter Brueggemann, *The Prophetic Imagination* (40th anniversary edition) (Minneapolis: Fortress Press, 2018), 11–14, 39–57.
32 Didi-Huberman, *Images in Spite of All*, 182.

Part 2
Memory and identity

11 The memorial topography of the Holodomor between cumulative and cultural trauma

A genealogical approach

Vitalii Ogiienko

The Great Famine of 1932–1933, commonly referred to as the Holodomor (the word "holodomor" literally means "extermination by hunger"), has become a topic of great interest in the last decade to historians and to scholars studying collective memory. This particular attention comes as no surprise, especially considering the features of this memory formation: this famine, which according to Ukrainian demographers took 3.9 million human lives,[1] was almost completely hidden and silenced during the Soviet era, but within just a quarter of a century of Ukrainian independence, it became not only the cornerstone of Ukrainian national memory, but also an important identity marker.

Focusing on this impressive transition, scholars usually consider it the result of nothing more than the pragmatic efforts of post-communist political elites to promote their own legitimisation and advance the process of a national identity building.

As commonly concluded, to construct this kind of memory, the post-communist political elites, supported by intellectuals, public activists and the Ukrainian diaspora in the West, used various tools of politics of memory, such as legislation, historical exhibitions in museums and teaching history in schools. So the focus on the politics of memory is crucial to the studies of memory of the Holodomor.[2]

Such politics-of-memory approach also dominates the studies of the memorial landscapes of the Holodomor, that is studies of memorials and monuments. Derek H. Alderman uses the metaphor "arena" for specifying this method. According to it, the attention is focused on the capacity of memorials and heritage locations to serve as sites for social groups to actively interpret and debate the meaning of the past as a part of larger struggles over recognition and legitimation. Akin to a methodology of politics of memory, examining memorial landscapes as an "arena" recognises the dominant role of actors and groups who through the landscape seek to influence collective decisions or policies, justify their claims to the past and entice others to participate in the public debates.[3]

Therefore, most of the studies on the Holodomor memory landscape implicitly or explicitly consider it to be a result of activities of political and

DOI: 10.4324/9781003264460-14

134 *Vitalii Ogiienko*

cultural actors aimed at legitimising themselves in the post-Soviet situation, constructing the predominant national narrative and promoting a corresponding memory culture in Ukrainian society.[4]

In the present chapter, we will problematise this line of reasoning, suggesting that it rather oversimplifies the explanation of Holodomor memorial visuality. To elaborate a more nuanced way to address this issue, we will avoid analysing Holodomor visuality by examining any particular memorial or monument (the prevailing method for such investigations). Instead, we will concentrate on Holodomor memorial culture in general, conducting our research on the premise that this culture possesses a common unifying meaning. I will call this memorial culture "the memorial topography of the Holodomor".

To begin with, according to our calculations, over the last 30 years, about 7,000 memorials dedicated to the Holodomor victims have been erected in Ukraine. On average, every fourth community has memorial objects in honour of the Holodomor victims. This is a huge number compared, let's say, to the 2,500 monuments to Lenin and other communist leaders that were installed in Ukraine over approximately 70 years of communist rule (although they were largely removed in line with the so-called decommunisation laws).

Moreover, there are several databases of Holodomor places of memory, which provide invaluable sources for studying this memorial landscape as a unique phenomenon.[5]

Even a cursory glance at these databases shows several distinct characteristics of the Holodomor topography. First, the number of memorials seems to be conspicuously large compared to other similar cases. Second, the memorials demonstrate a substantial richness and diversity of design and incorporated symbols: there are huge monuments, especially granite ones, wooden and metal crosses, memorial plaques, various gravestones and sculptures. Most typical, however, are the simple wooden cross and the granite monument (Figure 11.1) [Memorials in the villages of Blahodatne, Amvrosiivs'kyi district, Donetsk oblast and Pereima, Baltskyi district, Odessa oblast]. In addition to crosses in various combinations, other symbols are frequently used in the memorials: candles, ears of wheat, hands stretched to the sky, angels, bells, breadcrumbs and whole pieces of bread and many others. Yet in most cases, the only difference between the Holodomor memorials and those that are usually erected in cemeteries in memory of the deceased is the inscription "To the Holodomor victims".

The memorials are located in different places. Some memorials mark real burial sites, but most of them have nothing to do with actual graves. They were erected in cemeteries, next to village councils, on church or school premises or near memorials in honour of Soviet soldiers killed in the Second World War; that is in the most important or symbolic places, which the local community consider most appropriate.

One easily notes regional specificities to the Holodomor memorial topography. If we examine the memorials in Chernihiv oblast, we can conclude that they mainly take the form of massive oak crosses, which are installed on earth

Figure 11.1 Memorial in the village of Kalanchak, Kalanchatskyi district, Khersonska oblast
Source: photo by Vitalii Ogiienko

embankments. The memorials in Sumy oblast feature compositions comprising three crosses, while Khmelnytskyi oblast has crosses in cemeteries, usually decorated with colourful ribbons. In Luhansk and Donetsk oblasts, metal crosses or stone blocks with a plaque are widely used.

How should one explain the rise of this impressive memorial topography within such a short period? Why is its symbolism diverse and dependent on the region where the memorial is located? These are the two questions that will be addressed in this chapter as well.

It is easiest to apply a politics-of-memory approach and attribute the remarkable spread of the memorial topography to the efforts of government and political elites.

The third President of Ukraine, Viktor Yushchenko, is usually named as the main public actor behind an unprecedented campaign to raise the Holodomor awareness during 2005–2010, in particular the memorialisation of the victims through the erection of memorials.[6]

Also, it is mentioned in this context that on 28 November 2006, the Parliament of Ukraine, the Verkhovna Rada, voted to adopt Bill No. 376 – V "On the Holodomor of 1932–33 in Ukraine", which was soon enacted by President

136   *Vitalii Ogiienko*

Yushchenko. According to this law, the so-called Great Famine was recognised as an act of genocide committed against the Ukrainian people. Pursuant to Article 3 of the 2006 Holodomor Law,

> organs of state government and local authorities of Ukraine shall undertake . . . to take measures to perpetuate the memory of victims of the 1932–1933 Holodomor in Ukraine and of those who suffered from it, in particular through the erection of memorials and obelisks to the victims of the Holodomor.

Article 5 prescribes "resolving . . . the matter of constructing in the city of Kyiv a Memorial to the victims of Holodomors in Ukraine".[7] Thus, local state administrations were commissioned with supervising the construction of memorials, resulting in thousands of them being erected in the years 2008 and 2009 to mark the seventy-fifth anniversary of the Holodomor.

Regarding the regional specificities, it can be explained by the unique circumstances of starvation or local memories preserved in the communities and represented in local narratives.

However, it is important to emphasise that, in Ukrainian conditions, even the excellent implementation of the politics of memory (which is not the case here) could not have provoked such an unprecedented upsurge in Holodomor memorialisation. It is even more telling that the national narrative of the Holodomor is quite homogeneous, implying no particular regional diversity of representations or symbols.

The Holodomor memorial topography, in all its complexity, cannot be comprehended without considering the deep involvement of society in the memorialisation. Many people internalised the Holodomor memory and contributed to the official and unofficial commemorations. In other words, the memorial topography of the Holodomor suggests that the politically driven campaign resonated with the latent but emotionally powerful memory, which is still relevant for modern Ukrainians, making their active and voluntary engagement in the processes of memorialisation possible. We will argue that some sort of traumatic connection was established or revealed (considering the perspective adopted and the research tools applied) between contemporaries and past generations of victims and eyewitnesses. We will designate this connection as "historical trauma". Other terms with close meaning are "transgenerational trauma",[8] "trauma process",[9] "collective trauma"[10] and "chosen trauma".[11]

Historical trauma can be understood as a dynamic process of the transmission and transformation of traumatic memory, which has a certain traumatic event as its starting point. This definition implies an integrated understanding of trauma as a heterogeneous biological, psychological, social and cultural phenomenon that affects not only direct victims but also society as a whole. The concept of historical trauma is essentially a genealogical approach because it aims to illustrate, layer after layer, how trauma originates, progresses and transforms. As historical trauma evolves, traumatic memory reproduces itself,

The memorial topography of the Holodomor   137

is transmitted into cumulative trauma and, eventually, transforms into cultural trauma. That is exactly the case of the Holodomor. It is crucial to our further analysis of the Holodomor memorial topography that we elaborate on the aforementioned triad (traumatic memory–cumulative trauma–cultural trauma), as long as it is helpful in approaching a better understanding of what happened with traumatic memory before the memorials appeared.

The general logic behind the development of historical trauma can be understood as a movement from mental (characterised by a real psychological experience) to cultural representations, from sensorimotor and emotional states to "the construction of meaning" and "the processing of information", or from collective memory to cultural memory in the terms proposed by Jan Assmann.[12]

In our attempt to explain the memorial topography of the Holodomor from the genealogical perspective of historical trauma, the first step will be to define those characteristics of the traumatic memory related to the topic of Holodomor memorialisation. Although the traumatic memory of the Holodomor comprises an extremely complex and multifaceted set of symptoms, emotions and behaviours, we will focus on only one detail, which appears to be the most relevant to the issue.

Methodologically, we will rely on the concept of "deposited images" initially proposed by Turkish Cypriot psychiatrist Vamik Volkan.[13] "Deposited images" form one of the mechanisms that provide a connection between generations of victims and their descendants. "Deposited images" are results of traumatic influence of parents–victims collective psyche. They are inherently collective traumatic mental images which are so strong that like ghosts haunt the victims long after the traumatic event has passed, so the parents are unable to deal with them and deposit their burdens on their children and possibly grandchildren, who therefore have to solve the parents' problem, which now becomes theirs. They must bring the unfinished tasks of their parents to completion and relieve themselves of their burdens.

The eyewitnesses' testimonies extensively demonstrate what kind of "deposited images" were generated during the Holodomor and then transferred to the children of parents-survivors. Maria, a survivor whose testimony was included in the oral history project of the Commission on the Ukraine Famine, confessed that in 1933, when she was an 11-year-old girl, she had a serious quarrel with her mother. Shortly afterwards, her sister died of hunger, which greatly affected Maria, so she could not forgive herself for her bad words and thoughts about her mother and sister. Feeling guilty, she asked God for forgiveness and attempted to visit the place where her sister was buried to bid her a proper farewell, but she could not even find there a cross or a sign of the grave.

> I went weeping for my sister, and there I lost consciousness. I remember that I was lying on my side, and I fainted, and I don't know how long I was there. I woke up and thought: "Where am I? Where am I? I don't know where I am". . . . I was thinking "where am I"? Aha, and I was there, you

138 *Vitalii Ogiienko*

know. I got up, cried and said to myself: "You shouldn't be here, I should be here". I cried so much, I was twelve years old, and I asked her to forgive me.[14]

Another eyewitness, Teodora Trypniak from the khutor of Lozuvatka, Dnipropetrovsk oblast, specified the complicated process of mourning for her deceased sister many years after her death. She remembered her plea for bread on the deathbed and the accusation of intentionally hiding food in an attempt to kill her. In adulthood, Teodora cannot forget her sister's accusation.

There is not one day in my life that I haven't cried. Not a night goes by that I don't think about my family, about what happened to us. All this will stay with me until my death. I will not have peace. What is more, when she died, there was nobody to bury her.[15]

These two fragments from victims' accounts perfectly illustrate the "deposited images" of the Holodomor, especially the feeling of a survivor's guilt. Psychologist Robert Jay Lifton calls this specific kind of guilt, "guilt over survival priority", explaining that it is generated by the belief that a person survived at the expense of those who died.[16] "You shouldn't be here; I should be here" is the typical thought that "feeds" "guilt over survival priority". Survivors always ask themselves: "Why did I survive by letting him, her or them die?" and cannot give an answer. They endlessly return to the image of their loss because they cannot finalise the process of mourning or deal with the mental representations of the deceased.

To free themselves from the burden of guilt, the descendants of survivors have to undertake their primary task, in other words, to "bury" the dead both symbolically and physically, which means finding out the exact places of the burial, erecting memorials in honour of the victims and completing unfinished funeral rites in keeping with the Christian tradition.

It is worth noting that when the starvation was at its peak, it was tremendously difficult to bury the deceased. Relatives often did not know the exact place of burial or simply threw the corpses into common graves. Those who were starving did not have enough physical strength to dig a grave, make a coffin and carry a body to the cemetery. Tetiana Gogol, from the town of Stara Syniava, Khmelnytskyi oblast, said that one woman carried her daughter's body to a cemetery in a sack.[17] Bodies were abandoned at cemeteries or other remote places unburied or slightly covered with earth, making them easy prey for dogs.[18] Those who were too weak to get to a cemetery buried the deceased in their backyard or garden.[19] It was generally impossible to adhere to funeral rites, especially to prepare a meal, sing psalms and hold a ceremony with a priest. Moreover, the general degradation reached such an extent that indifferent people took the wooden crosses from cemeteries to heat their homes.[20]

Later, many people did not place crosses on the burial sites; they were afraid that the authorities would regard these actions as a form of resistance.[21] Political

The memorial topography of the Holodomor 139

pressure made it dangerous to remember the victims of the famine, and common sense dictated that people forget the victims and their graves. So the first generation of Holodomor survivors was completely unable to counteract the "deposited image of guilt over survival priority", which remained unresolved for almost 60 years of Soviet rule in Ukraine. Silence and guilt existed on the individual level for several generations and ultimately passed onto the collective level of cumulative trauma maintained by social practices of amnesia.

The first places of memory to commemorate the Holodomor appeared only 60 years after the famine, in the late 1980s, when the Soviet Union was on the way to collapse. One of the first monuments dedicated to the Holodomor was built in the village of Targan, Kyiv oblast, in 1988. Although the political climate had thawed, at that time such an act still posed a great risk and could have led to negative consequences for both career and personal freedom. The memorial was erected by a group of locals in a cemetery, over the mass grave of the victims of starvation. Many enthusiastic locals contributed to the successful completion of this memorial. For instance, the memorial owes its design to a self-taught architect, a Holodomor eyewitness, while the head of a local collective farm provided organisational and financial support for its construction. A list of the victims was put together, thanks to the eagerness of a local school teacher who conducted several interviews with descendants of the survivors.[22]

In the next decade, the memorial was treated to minor refurbishment. Now the heart of the memorial composition consists of the figure of a sad woman with a cross in her hands. The inscription on the gravestone reads: "To the eternal memory of 367 residents and infants who died of famine in 1933". In front of the monument, there are three black marble stones, on which the names of those who died in the Holodomor are engraved. A wooden cross stands behind the monument, on a raised earth embankment (Figure 11.2).[23]

Erected at a time when no there were no cultural representations of the famine, the memorial in Targan does not look very different from other sites of the Holodomor memorial topography. Like many other memorials, it displays a combination of symbolic forms which seems rather eclectic: in this case, a cross, a burial mound, a sculpture of a woman, tombstones of the persons associated with raising awareness about the Holodomor and memorial stones with a list of those who died of starvation. This is not surprising, because this site appeared voluntarily, thanks to the endeavours of the local community.

In our terms, the monument in Targan corresponds to the level of cumulative trauma: at the time it was erected, there were no cultural representations of the famine or corresponding public discourses. The memorial in Targan and a set of related public commemorations might have been one of the first public attempts undertaken by the children of survivors to deal with the "deposited image of guilt over survival priority".

The point is that the memorial in Targan visually and symbolically does not differ not only from the first wave of the Holodomor memorialisation, which appeared in the late 1980s–the early 1990s, but also from the second wave. The latter is connected with a campaign devoted to marking the seventy-fifth

Figure 11.2 Monument in the village of Targan, Kyiv oblast
Source: photo by Vitalii Ogiienko

anniversary of the Holodomor, which took place 20 years after the construction of the memorial in Targan. This leads us to the conclusion articulated by Wiktoria Kudela-Świątek that shared symbolic content reproduces and processes itself at all "places of memory" of the Holodomor around the world, regardless of their geographical location.[24] In other words, the first and second waves of memorialisation bear some features in common, as they represent a unified image of the famine. Thus, majority of Holodomor monuments, museums and "cemetery sites" look the same, because they are all influenced by the common cumulative memory, "the deposited image of guilt over survival priority" and the process of mourning for victims.

For this reason, when the official campaign to commemorate the seventy-fifth anniversary of the Holodomor commenced, local communities, particularly those of first- and second-generation survivors, repeated the scenario of the community in Targan. Responding positively to the government's call to commemorate the victims of the Holodomor, they began erecting memorials *en masse* and marking the sites of victims' burials. They placed these memorials everywhere: on burial sites, in cemeteries, next to village councils, on church or school grounds, or near memorials in honour of soldiers killed in the Second World War. The erection of memorials and the performance of associated rituals had a therapeutic psychological effect on the still traumatised communities.

From this perspective, however actively these communities may have been involved in the Holodomor commemoration, all of them voluntarily attempted

The memorial topography of the Holodomor   141

to reveal their guilt, adhering to the funeral rites of their regions. Eventually, they had the opportunity to complete the unfinished task of their parents, in other words, to bury symbolically the victims in accordance with tradition. This explains the regional specificity of the Holodomor memorial topography and the richness of its visual forms: local communities utilised for their purposes the forms that were considered customary in their region. That is why people installed massive wooden crosses in Chernihiv oblast, crosses with colourful ribbons in Khmelnytskyi oblast, stone blocks with a plaque in Luhansk and Donetsk oblasts and so on.

This may explain why the Holodomor commemorative rituals explicitly or implicitly draw on Christian motifs, symbols and practices. Indeed, the visuality and symbolism of the Holodomor are directly related to Christian practices because Ukrainian funeral rites are Christian by nature. The elements of the public commemoration of the Holodomor victims, such as funeral services and processions, come from religious funeral ceremonies. Moreover, locals visit the memorials not only on Holodomor Memorial Day (the fourth Saturday in November) but also on other memorial days, especially at Easter. Thus, the Holodomor Memorial Day is widely recognised as an official commemorative day; Easter, by contrast, is perceived as a memorial day for deceased relatives according to an unspoken tradition in society.[25]

And yet we ought to note the differences between the two waves of the Holodomor memorialisation. The second wave demonstrates a certain coalescence of cumulative and cultural trauma of the Holodomor, which appears at once both organic and contradictory. This is mainly because the second wave coincided chronologically with the time when cumulative trauma met cultural trauma, and funeral practices merged with official commemorations.

One can detect this coalescence when considering examples of the Holodomor memorial topography. During the campaign devoted to the seventy-fifth anniversary of the Holodomor, some regional administrations distributed a series of identical memorial plaques to local authorities, which were immediately attached to most memorials in the area. The final result resembles a rather weird and eclectic mix, which does, however, illustrate the previously mentioned coalescence. For instance, in the village of Bohemka, Mykolaiv oblast, a plaque sent by the state authorities was attached to a tree that grows on the place where the victims of the Holodomor were once buried. Thus, the plaque itself identifies cultural trauma, but its placement indicates, in essence, cumulative trauma.

Another case of coalescence concerns the biggest memorial to the Holodomor victims in Ukraine, the name of which was recently altered from National Holodomor Victims Memorial Museum to National Museum of the Holodomor-Genocide (Memorial). It may appear that the Memorial's visual representations support the thesis that it is entirely designed by political and cultural actors seeking, first and foremost, their own legitimisation, attempting to present the Holodomor narrative as an integral part of the national narrative. Moreover, the arguments in favour of that idea are utterly convincing.

142 *Vitalii Ogiienko*

First, President Yushchenko extensively favoured the construction of the Memorial and lobbied it in parliament, and the Holodomor law of 2006 claimed that the Memorial should be built as soon as possible. The Memorial was opened on 22 November 2008, when the financial crisis was at its peak. However, as the project was regarded as highly significant, funds from the stabilisation budget were allocated to complete the construction on schedule. Additionally, the state government and especially President Yushchenko insisted that Pechersk Hills, a sacred space in the ancient heart of Kyiv, be chosen as the site for the construction. Thus, the Memorial was erected not far from the government building and parliament, as well as the most famous Orthodox monastery (Pechersk Lavra), which makes the place special for commemoration. The Memorial now enjoys a very lofty status in the hierarchy of state museums, given the fact that it is the only state museum which foreign delegations are obliged to visit, along with the Grave of the Unknown Soldier, located nearby.[26]

Second, there are many visual signs in the Memorial that largely represent the national narrative (primarily the images of victims and perpetrators). For example, the decorations of the main candle-shaped building within the Memorial complex, known as the Candle of Memory, are made from a collage of archive photos that depict the victims, namely, Ukrainian peasants, and the perpetrators, that is, officers of the State Political Directorate (GPU), the militia and activists. One element of this collage portrays two Red Army soldiers with rifles standing on snow-covered ground blackened with ravens.

Third, the Black Board Alley is located down the slope on which the Candle stands. This is a set of massive stone blocks on which the names of more than six thousand Ukrainian villages afflicted by the Holodomor are engraved. (Figure 11.3). The blacklisted villages were encircled by the GPU forces, making it impossible for the starving to leave the devastated areas. This affected the mortality rate, which was much higher in the blacklisted villages than in other areas. Demonstrating one of the mechanisms that caused mass deaths from starvation, these villages comprise an important part of the Holodomor narrative.

But a closer look reveals that the architectural language of the Memorial echoes the Holodomor memorial topography, which is rather difficult to integrate in the previously mentioned concepts of nationalisation and legitimisation.

First, the Memorial is full of Christian and funeral symbols, although there are no real graves of victims. The central symbol of Christianity, a cross, can be regarded as one of the most popular signs in the Memorial. The Candle also has four massive metal crosses on each side, and it is covered with images of crosses of different sizes (Figure 11.4). "Little crosses are the souls of little children; bigger crosses symbolise the souls of adults", the Memorial guide says. The crosses are engraved on millstones, placed on the ground in the Memorial complex. Even storks are crucified on crosses.

The central hall in the Candle displays 19 volumes of the National Book of Remembrance of the Holodomor victims, which includes, in particular, regional (including small villages) lists of identified victims. Nearby, a visitor

Figure 11.3 The Black Board Alley at National Museum of the Holodomor-Genocide
Source: photo by Vitalii Ogiienko

can find something like a glass altar filled with grain (Figure 11.5). Visitors are allowed to look through the book and can easily find the names of their relatives or other people they may know. You can buy a candle, light it and put it on the altar, and this is strongly reminiscent of rituals commonly performed in Orthodox churches. On leaving the Candle, visitors are invited to ring a bell, the sound of which traditionally informed the community about someone's death.

In other words, the Memorial is full of funeral symbols. It is reminiscent of a functioning church. The funeral symbolism, which dominates the Memorial, manifests itself in the powerful influence of cumulative trauma on the visual representations here. It reflects the inextinguishable longing of second- and third-generation victims, as in the case of Targan, to relieve the burden of their parents, mitigate their guilt and symbolically "bury" the dead, in keeping with the Christian tradition.

From this perspective, all other visual representations can be interpreted differently than before. For example, the projection of the names of the victims on the walls inside the Candle can be regarded as reflecting an intention to remember the victims and symbolically mark their names, which is an indispensable part of the mourning process, and not just an attempt to impress visitors with borrowed technology. At the least, it may be treated ambivalently.

Similarly, numerous traditional Ukrainian folk symbols can be reinterpreted. Storks, grain, traditional ornaments, mascots and home decorations (*pavuk*),

Figure 11.4 The Candle
Source: photo by Vitalii Ogiienko

Figure 11.5 The Altar
Source: photo by Vitalii Ogiienko

as well as the traditional Ukrainian household items in the central hall of the Candle, represent national values, as well as the national narrative, emphasising an underlying assumption that the Holodomor primarily targeted the Ukrainian peasants as the bearers of those values. Yet at the same time, these apparently archetypal Ukrainian symbols correspond quite well with Ukrainian funeral rites, which are deeply vernacular in nature.

The coalescence of cumulative and cultural traumas, although in a different context, can be seen in the Memorial in one of its most emotive and artistic elements: a sculpture of a starving little girl. The official name of this sculpture is *Bitter Childhood Memories*. A little girl with big eyes and a tiny, thin, malnourished body looks in earnest at the visitors; her arms are crossed modestly over her chest. In one hand, she holds a few ears of corn, clearly a reference to the Law of Five Spikelets (*zakon pro pyat' koloskiv*). She is barefoot. Her eyes and the ellipse under her feet are considered to be the most distinctive features of the sculpture. The description on the pedestal reads: "To the dead, the living and the unborn" – words by the most famous Ukrainian poet and national icon Taras Shevchenko (Figure 11.6).

This image has spread virally in Holodomor-related culture and is one of the most well-known symbols of the Holodomor. Needless to say, it has become

Figure 11.6 Bitter Childhood Memories sculpture
Source: photo by Vitalii Ogiienko

a popular icon in the media, reproduced on numerous posters, postage stamps and book covers, which is not surprising considering its memorable appearance and close association with the Holodomor popular discourse and understanding (for instance, it is part of the exhibition at the Canadian Museum for Human Rights).

The sculpture, created by Ukrainian sculptor Petro Drozdovsky in the 2009, appears to belong purely to the sphere of culture. However, a new meaning attached to the sculpture is becoming increasingly vivid: visitors have begun to leave food (especially apples) and coins near the girl's sculpture. This practice relates to the old Orthodox tradition of dropping food onto the graves of deceased relatives in cemeteries, and as such it is associated with the cumulative trauma of the Holodomor.

Another example of this particular coalescence is the idea of placing a lit candle of remembrance in the window of a house. This was proposed by James Mace, an American historian who moved to Ukraine and lived there until his death in 2004. He mentioned the candle as a symbol of the Holodomor in his speech to the Verkhovna Rada (Ukrainian Parliament) in 2003, and since then the idea has found numerous supporters and has been incorporated into almost all public actions and commemorations dedicated to the memory of the Holodomor victims. Thus, candles lit in windows after dark on Holodomor Memorial Day resemble an invented tradition, but at the same time they obviously refer to cumulative trauma, to which the funeral ceremonies of the Orthodox religion are so deeply attached.[27]

Conclusion

As shown previously, this chapter suggests that the focus on public debate and political fighting over the visual memorial landscape associated with trauma cannot be sufficient, let alone comprehensive, in an analysis of this landscape. The location, funding and ideological interpretations, along with the activities of the decision-makers, probably matter more than anything else, but together they illustrate only one side of the issue. I argue that it is important to examine not only the narrative on which the memorial landscape is based, but also the process of the evolution of the historical trauma, its transmission and transformation.

The preliminary findings on the memorial topography of the Holodomor allow us to conclude that the so-called first wave of the Holodomor memorialisation in the early 1990s was primarily affected by cumulative trauma; in particular, the feeling of survivors' guilt, rooted in the belief that the survivors were alive at the expense of those who died.

The first memorials honouring the Holodomor victims were erected strategically to relieve the descendants of survivors from the burden of their ancestors' guilt. The places of memory and related commemorations enable communities to symbolically and physically "bury" their dead, in keeping with the Christian tradition, and so to complete the unfinished task of the previous generation. This explains the presence of anthropomorphic metaphors, the aesthetics of martyrdom and sacrifice and the apparent elements of religious practices in the Holodomor memorial landscape. Thus, the first and second waves of memorialisation appear to have much in common symbolically and visually.

148 *Vitalii Ogiienko*

At the same time, the two waves of the Holodomor memorialisation display some differences. In the second case, through the example of the National Museum of the Holodomor-Genocide in Kyiv, we can observe a kind of coalescence between the cumulative and the cultural trauma of the Holodomor, when funeral practices merge with official commemorations. There are many visual signs in the Memorial, which represent the national narrative and support the conclusion that treats the Memorial as a place of state legitimisation. However, the architectural language of the Memorial contains many Christian and funeral symbols, such as crosses and candles, which imply cumulative trauma. Therefore, I argue that the role of political and cultural actors in attributing any meaning they wish to the memorial visual landscape seems exaggerated. The most interesting example of this coalescence manifests itself in a new ritual attached to the sculpture of a starving little girl, which is derived from funeral ceremonies.

In other words, the visual representations of the National Museum of the Holodomor-Genocide in Kyiv show how cumulative trauma contributed to the construction of cultural trauma and the discovering of a new meaning. At the same time, it is obvious that political and cultural elites do not always consider cumulative trauma and traumatic memory, sometimes acting contrary to them. So these elites do not pay much attention to trauma.

Notes

1 Omelian Rudnytskyi, Nataliia Levchuk, Oleh Wolowyna, Pavlo Shevchuk and Alla Savchuk, "Demography of a Man-Made Human Catastrophe: The Case of Massive Famine in Ukraine 1932–1933", *Canadian Studies in Population*, 42/1–2 (2015), 53–80.

2 Georgiy Kasianov, "How a War for the Past Becomes a War in the Present", *Kritika: Explorations in Russian and Eurasian History*, 16/1 (2015), 149–155; Georgiy Kasianov, "Holodomor and the Politics of Memory in Ukraine after Independence", in *Holodomor and Gorta Mór Histories, Memories and Representations of Famine in Ukraine and Ireland*, ed. Christian Noack, Lindsay Janssen and Vincent Comerford (London: Anthem, 2012), 167–188; Lina Klymenko, "The Holodomor Law and National Trauma Construction in Ukraine", *Canadian Slavonic Papers Revue*, 58 (2016), 341–361; Tatiana Zhurzhenko, "Capital of Despair. Holodomor Memory and Political Conflicts in Kharkiv after the Orange Revolution", *East European Politics & Societies*, 25 (2011), 597–639; Volodymyr Ishchenko, "Fighting Fences vs Fighting Monuments: Politics of Memory and Protest Mobilization in Ukraine", *Debatte: Journal of Contemporary Central and Eastern Europe*, 19/1–2 (2011), 369–395.

3 Derek Alderman and Joshua Inwood, "Landscapes of Memory and Socially Just Futures," in *The Wiley-Blackwell Companion to Cultural Geography*, ed. Nuala C. Johnson, Richard H. Schein and Jamie Winders (Hoboken, NJ: John Wiley & Sons, 2013), 193.

4 Georgiy Kasianov, *Danse Macabre. Holod 1932–1933 Rokiv u Polititsi, Masovii Svidomosti ta Sstoriohrafii (1980-ti – pochatok 2000-kh) [Danse Macabre. The Famine 1932–1933 in Politics, Mass Consciousness, and Historiorgaphy (the 1980s – early 2000s)]* (Kyiv: Nash Chas, 2010), 207–211; Wiktoria Kudela-Świątek, *Miejsca (Nie)pamięci. O Upamiętnianiu Ukraińskiego Wielkiego Głodu z lat 1932–1933 [Places of (non-)memory: on the Commemoration of the Ukrainian Great Famine of 1932–1933]* (Cracow: Księgarnia Akademicka, 2014), 135–140; Tatiana Zhurzhenko, "Commemorating the Famine as

The memorial topography of the Holodomor 149

Genocide: The Contested Meanings of Holodomor Memorials in Ukraine", in *Memorials in Times of Transition*, ed. Susanne Buckley-Zistel and Stefanie Schäfer (Cambridge: Intersentia, 2014), 221–240.

5 "Mistsia Masovoho Pokhovannia Zhertv Holodomoru-Henotsydu" [Mass-grave Burials of the Holodomor-Genocide Victims], National Museum of the Holodomor-Genocide, https://map.memorialholodomor.org.ua, accessed 13 November 2019; Anna Kaminsky, ed., *Erinnerungsorte an den Holodomor 1932/33 in der Ukraine* (Berlin: Leipziger Universitätsverlag, 2008).

6 Olena Veselova, "Memorialni Znaky y Pamiatnyky Zhertvam Holodu-Henotsydu 1932–1933 rr. v Ukraini" [Memorial Signs and Memorials to the Victims of the Holodomor-Genocide 1932–1933 in Ukraine], *Kraieznavstvo*, 1–2 (2009), 169–179.

7 Law of Ukraine No. 376-V, "On Holodomor of 1932–33 in Ukraine" (29 November 2006), https://canada.mfa.gov.ua/en/ukraine-%D1%81%D0%B0/holodomor-remembrance/holodomor-remembrance-ukraine/holodomor-law-ukraine, accessed 30 March 2019.

8 Natan Kellermann, "Transmission of Holocaust Trauma – An Integrative View", *Psychiatry*, 64/3 (2001), 256–267.

9 Jeffrey C. Alexander, "Toward a Theory of Cultural Trauma", in *Cultural Trauma and Collective Identity*, ed. Jeffrey C. Alexander, Ron Eyerman, Bernhard Giesen, Neil J. Smelser and Piotr Sztompka (Berkeley: University of California Press, 2004), 1–30.

10 Hirschberger Gilad, "Collective Trauma and the Social Construction of Meaning", *Frontiers in Psychology*, 9 (2018), 1441, https://doi.org/10.3389/fpsyg.2018.01441, accessed 30 November 2019.

11 Vamik D. Volkan, *Bloodlines: From Ethnic Pride to Ethnic Terrorism* (New York, NY: Farrar, Straus, & Giroux, 1997), 36–49.

12 Jan Assmann, "Communicative and Cultural Memory", in *Cultural Memories. The Geographical Point of View*, vol. iv, ed. Peter Meusburger, Michael Heffernan and Edgar Wunder (Heidelberg: Springer, 2011), 15–27; Jordan Peterson, *Maps of Meaning. The Architecture of Belief* (New York: Routledge, 1999), 59–80.

13 Vamık D. Volkan, "The Next Chapter: Consequences of Societal Trauma", in *Memory, Narrative and Forgiveness: Perspectives on the Unfinished Journeys of the Past*, ed. Pumla Gobodo-Madikizela and Chris Van Der Merwe (Newcastle upon Tyne: Cambridge Scholars Publishing, 2009), 6.

14 Dzheims Meis, ed., *Velykyi Holod v Ukraini 1932–1933 rokiv: Svidchennia Ochevydtsiv dlia Komisii Konhresu USA* [The Great Famine 1932–1933 in Ukraine: Eyewitness testimonies for the US Congress Commission on the Ukraine Famine] (Kyiv: Kyievo-Mohylianska Akademiia, 2008), 107.

15 Ibid., 222.

16 Robert Jay Lifton, *Death in Life: Survivors of Hiroshima* (Chapel Hill: University of North Carolina Press, 1968), 35.

17 Meis, ed., *Velykyi holod*, 730.

18 Ibid., 363.

19 Ibid., 155.

20 Ibid., 121.

21 Ibid., 116.

22 Lefter Serhei, "Holod byl sdelan spetsyalno: chto pomniat o Holodomore te, kto eho perezhyl" [The Famine was Organized Deliberately: What Survivors Remember about the Holodomor], RBC-Ukraine (26 November 2011), https://daily.rbc.ua/rus/show/golod-sdelan-spetsialno-pomnyat-golodomore-1480148878.html, accessed 24 November 2019.

23 Ibid.

24 Kudela-Świątek, *Miejsca (Nie)pamięci*, 217.

25 Serhei, "Holod".

150   *Vitalii Ogiienko*

26 Ukaz Prezydenta Ukrainy № 98/2010 (3 February 2010), "Pro Vnesennia Zmin do Polozhennia pro Derzhavnyi Protokol ta Tseremonial Ukrainy", https://zakon.rada. gov.ua/laws/show/98/2010, accessed 24 November 2019.

27 Stanislav Kulchytskyi, "Slovo pro Dzheimsa Meisa" [The Word about James Mace], *Den* (17 July 2008), http://incognita.day.kyiv.ua/slovo-pro-dzhejmsa-mejsa.html, accessed 24 November 2019.

12 Building the Finnish national mythos: photographs from the Russo-Finnish Winter War of 1939–1940 and their post-war use

Olli Kleemola

On 30 November 1939, Soviet troops attacked Finland to seize the areas that, according to the Molotov–Ribbentrop Pact, belonged to the Soviet Union. Finland, a weak, sparsely populated, and diplomatically isolated nation, succeeded in causing staggering losses for its considerably more potent aggressor. The heavily outnumbered and under-equipped Finnish army put up a skilful and effective defence against the Red Army, waging a war that lasted 105 days. Although the Finns were ultimately forced to sign a peace treaty that meant territorial losses for them, their successful defence spared the land from Soviet occupation. The heroic defensive battle attracted international attention and drew many war reporters to Helsinki. During the war, Finland gained the admiration and sympathy of the entire Western world but still lacked real military support; it was ultimately forced to sign a peace treaty ceding significant areas to the Soviet Union.[1]

Even today, almost 80 years later, the Winter War is something of a sacred battle for the Finns, a part of the country's collective memory and identity.[2] The photographs produced during the war now constitute a significant proportion of Finnish history's pictorial narrative.

In this chapter, I will address two main questions: 1) Which aspects of the war have and have not been included in photobooks, that is which aspects have been considered worth remembering, and which have not? and 2) How has the photographic narrative changed over time? Additionally, in the chapter's concluding section, I will discuss the challenges that must be considered in constructing a photographic narrative of the war as part of a monument.

Source material and theoretical approach

One of the most common uses of historical photographs is for the illustration of photobooks that recount historical events. According to Parr and Badger, a photobook can be defined as a book "where the work's primary message is carried by photographs".[3] Photobooks are often targeted towards the general public, rather than solely for the intellectual class. Because they are considered

DOI: 10.4324/9781003264460-15

152   Olli Kleemola

attractive and accessible, they often play a more important role than anticipated in the historical understanding of people and events. The German social psychologist Harald Welzer has even stated that people's historical memory nowadays mostly relies on images rather than text, meaning that pictures indeed play a key role in constructing our historical understanding.[4]

Photobooks also often play a decisive role in the canonisation process, whereby a specific image becomes increasingly widespread, attracts considerable attention and gradually comes to symbolically represent an entire historical event and acquire iconic status. Here, the impact of permanent photobooks can be considered to be of much greater importance than that of ephemeral publications, such as magazines and newspapers.[5]

The primary source materials considered in this chapter are military history photobooks that include photographs of the Winter War. The first of them, *Kunniamme päivät* ("Our days of honour"), appeared in 1940, just months after the Winter War had ended. It was published by the semi-official propagandist organisation Maan Turva, in collaboration with the WSOY publishing house, and can thus be considered a product of the war's propaganda machine. This book contains many high-quality Winter War images captured by such artists as the American war photographer Carl Mydans, and it has long defined the Winter War's visual narrative. It is also the only book analysed herein that deals exclusively with the Winter War, all others depicting both the Winter War and the Continuation War (1941–1944).

After the Continuation War had ended, ex-officers produced military history photobooks that mainly focused on the battlefront. Examples include *Suomi tahtoi elää* ("Finland wanted to live"), which was edited by Taavi Patoharju, a colonel who had served as head of the military propaganda department, and published by Sanoma in 1955; *Ankarat vuodet. Kuvateos talvi- ja jatkosodastamme* ("Hard years: a photobook of our Winter and Continuation War"), published by Otava in 1957, whose editor-in-chief, Valo Nihtilä, was a colonel and former headquarters officer; and *Viisi sodan vuotta* ("Five years of war"), published by WSOY in 1958.

Viisi sodan vuotta was edited by Arvi Korhonen, a former head of the Finnish army's military history department and headquarters officer who, from 1940 onwards, worked as a professor of Finnish history at the University of Helsinki. The fact that Korhonen's name became well known is most likely among the main reasons why *Viisi sodan vuotta* is one of the most popular and enduring post-war photobooks to narrate the history of the Continuation War: the first edition appeared in 1958 and the last, the fifth edition, was published in 1973. *Viisi sodan vuotta* arguably played a significant role in canonising the photographs taken during the Continuation War. The latest book analysed in this chapter is *Suomi taisteli – Kuvat kertovat* ("Finland fought – pictures tell"), edited by cultural historian Helena Pilke and myself and published by Readme in 2013.

All the books considered here consist of photos taken during the conflict. During the Winter War, the Finnish army had no troops specialised in

Building the Finnish national mythos 153

producing propaganda. Plans had been established for the distribution of propagandist photographs, but the Finnish army leaders had overlooked the fact that someone first had to take the photographs. Thus, the success with which the various fronts were visually documented mostly depended on whether there were eager amateur photographers among the Finnish army's fighting troops and whether the commanders allowed international war correspondents and photographers to access the frontline. Consequently, the photographic record varies significantly from front to front. This has, of course, affected the visual legacy of the war.[6] However, as the photographs were essentially taken to promote the Finnish cause internationally and/or sustain the Finns' morale, the pictures may be regarded as propagandist images that were later reused as material for photobooks.

In terms of theory, this chapter draws on visual history, a field of historical research that has developed in Germany over the last ten years, and which is now one of the country's most active and innovative fields of historical scholarship. Visual history situates pictures as an independent category of sources, capable of transmitting meanings and ideological perspectives. Until recently, photography has been relatively overlooked in historical scholarship. This may be due to the perceived objectivity of photography as a medium: seemingly neutral, it captures moments and images, but in reality, the pictures we take are formed in our heads long before the camera's shutter has closed. Thus, photographs may be considered a product of the information, attitudes and prejudices that the photographer has collected.[7]

Besides its position in the field of visual history, my study can also be located in the field of memory studies, which, in turn, is thriving in many areas of scholarship. My approach is that of a historian: I analyse the photographs of population transfers from one aspect as products of cultural memory but also from another aspect as subjects, material representations that form and alter our cultural memory. The impact of representation on the collective memory and the impact of collective memory on representations of history can thus be understood as a continuous cycle.[8]

Collective/cultural memory may be described as a practice whereby social conceptions regarding a common past are used to create and maintain togetherness and group identity in the present and for the future.[9] Visual images are important modes of communicating and creating conceptions of the past due to their specific characteristics and mechanisms, including persuading through realistic semblance, evoking emotions, creating a sense of identity and their ability to relate narratives in condensed form. Susan Sontag highlights the importance of photographs as follows:

> Photographs that everyone recognizes are now a constituent part of what a society chooses to think about, or declares that it has chosen to think about. It calls these ideas "memories", and that is, over the long run, a fiction. Strictly speaking, there is no such thing as collective memory. . . . All memory is individual, unreproducible – it dies with each person. What

154 *Olli Kleemola*

is collective memory is not remembering but a stipulating: that this is important, and this is the story about how it happened, with the pictures that lock the story in our minds. Ideologies create substantiating archives of images, representative images, which encapsulate common ideas of significance and trigger predictable thoughts, feelings.[10]

The bombings of Finnish cities

Several subjects dominate the photographic narrative of the Winter War, among them the Soviet aerial bombings. At the time of the Winter War, the world had not yet experienced the Blitz in London or the bombing of Dresden. The massive Soviet terror bombings targeting the Finnish civilian population were something new and were thus a popular subject for international war photographers arriving in Helsinki.[11] Another contributing factor was that most photographers were not permitted to go to the front, and, unable to take pictures of actual battles, they were obliged to find alternative subjects.[12]

However, one of the most potent photographs, which, over the years, has become a symbol of the terror bombings during the Winter War, and ultimately also of the war itself, is not a war photograph, but a photograph that depicts one of the very first bombing victims, 7-year-old Armi Hillevi Metsäpelto. The photograph (originally from a family album) of a well-dressed little girl who was later killed while trying to flee Helsinki, was published in the newspapers during the war and soon became a symbol of the cruelty and inhumanity of the Soviet air force.[13]

The cruelty of the Red bombers inspired international war correspondents and photographers to take poignant photographs of civilians hiding in the forests for safety, in the cold, as in Figure 12.1. Some of these images were re-enacted for the photographers who had missed the moment but still wished to get some pictures. (Figure 12.1)[14] This was possible because, during the Winter War, the culture of photojournalism was different. Rather than the authenticity that is of such importance today, it was much more important that the pictures could evoke feelings, such as empathy, and they were mainly used to illustrate the message already conveyed in the text, rather than telling their own story. For this reason, staged pictures were widely accepted.[15]

Another popular image type was of churches that had been bombed, as in Figure 12.2, which shows the bomb-ravaged Lutheran Church in Helsinki. For contemporary viewers, this image was testament to the battle between two different worlds: the deeply Christian Finland and the atheistic Soviet Union. This image has also been published in numerous photobooks since the war.

The Finnish victories and missing weariness

Given the massive resources at the Red Army's disposal, once news of the Soviet attack on Finland had spread, the world expected the Finnish resistance

Figure 12.1 The bomb-ravaged Luther Church in Helsinki (SA-kuva 1547)
Source: Finnish Defence Forces Wartime Photographic Archive

to be overrun within a few days. Instead, the Finns were able to halt the Red Army for more than three months and destroy massive mechanised units using so-called *motti* tactics, whereby the enemy was first encircled and then gradually destroyed.[16] The unexpected victories were considered sensational, and international newspapers sought photographs from the legendary battles of Raate and Suomussalmi. Figure 12.3 depicts some fallen soldiers of the 44th Ukrainian Division of the Red Army at the battle of Raate in early January 1940, as well as equipment that had fallen to the Finns after the division's destruction.[17]

While this picture and many of its kind have been and continue to be published in numerous photobooks depicting the Winter War, almost no pictures convey the weariness of the Finnish army during the latter half of the conflict.

Figure 12.2 A staged picture of a mother with her child hiding in the wintry forest during the bombing (SA-kuva 10825)

Figure 12.3 Remains of the destroyed Soviet 44th Division on Raate Road in January 1940 (SA-kuva 2984)

Building the Finnish national mythos 157

The outnumbered Finns had to fight without reserve units, with insufficient artillery and with practically no tanks or planes.[18] From this aspect, the widely published images, which highlight the Finnish victories and have appeared in numerous photobooks ever since, offer an incomplete perspective on the Winter War. Thus, all analysed photobooks do indeed reinforce the propagandist narrative that was originally created and maintained by the Finnish War Censorship Authority during the conflict.

Exotic winter instead of mass battles

For the international war photographers, Finland, with its snow and cold temperatures, was extraordinary and exotic. Most of them were eager to experience war waged in such extreme conditions. At the same time, the Finnish general in charge of the Lapland front, Kurt M. Wallenius, was one of the few officers who understood the needs of the war reporters and photographers and permitted them to access the front, which, as mentioned earlier, was not usual during the Winter War. Moreover, from Lapland, it was only a short trip to Sweden, where the photographers and reporters could freely send their material to their magazines without needing to disclose them to the Finnish War Censorship Authority.[19] This resulted in considerable quantities of images depicting exotic scenes from Lapland, such as reindeer, snow and skiing soldiers, as shown in Figure 12.4, for example.

Figure 12.4 A Finnish ski troop during the Winter War (SA-kuva 4706)

158 *Olli Kleemola*

While the reality that these pictures depict was certainly part of the Winter War, few pictures exist from the battles that took place on the Karelian Isthmus in the south, where the Red Army's main attack was concentrated. Therefore, with regard to the pictures from the northern front, photobook editors have numerous images from which to choose, but the major decisive battles that took place on the Karelian Isthmus are difficult to illustrate. This has resulted in the Winter War's visual legacy being dominated by images of skiing Finnish patrols. While this, again, is partially accurate, it is far from the reality of the main battles.

The pictorial narrative of the Winter War then, now and in the future

As well as presenting here some of the most iconic photographs from the Winter War, I have discussed both the main image types and pictorial topics that constitute the conflict's pictorial narrative, as presented in numerous photobooks, and also the types of image that are missing.

As shown, the narrative has changed surprisingly little over the years, which may be because only a limited number of good photographs from the Winter War are available. Most of these were published in the first Winter War photobook, and subsequent photobooks have mainly just reprinted these pictures, some of which have thus acquired national iconic status. Of course, there have been minor additions: for example, the books *Ankarat Vuodet* and *Suomi tahtoi elää*, first published during the 1950s, have integrated some Soviet pictures into their narrative.[20] However, later Finnish photobooks reverted to using Finnish photos exclusively. Hitherto, Soviet photographs of the Winter War have only sporadically been presented to wider audiences in Finland; Finnish photographs of the war almost entirely dominate the pictorial narrative.[21] Some images that were used in the book *Kunniamme päivät* have gradually disappeared from the collective memory, as they are no longer used in photobooks. This is mainly because the pictures are now too expensive to use. For example, the photographs of *Life* photographer Carl Mydans are now owned by Getty Images and are very expensive.[22] Here, again, a key difference between textual and visual material emerges: while a text can be cited without any cost, the use of specific pictures can be limited for economic reasons.

In today's world, the importance of visuality is growing daily. Accordingly, the pictorial narrative of the Winter War plays a central role in its legacy, and it has been particularly current since the Finnish national monument of the Winter War was unveiled in Helsinki in early December 2017. The monument includes a pictorial narrative consisting of 105 pictures; that is as many pictures as there were days of conflict.[23] The pictures are exhibited inside the monument's round base and can be viewed through round windows, as seen in Figure 12.5. The narrative can also be viewed online at https://1939-1940.fi.

While I have demonstrated the existence of a relatively consistent visual narrative, the construction of a pictorial narrative as part of a public monument

Figure 12.5 The Finnish National Monument of the Winter War
Source: photo by Tuomas Manninen

presents both similar and different challenges to those encountered when preparing a photobook. First, the photographic narrative in the monument is regularly viewed by numerous foreign visitors, while photobooks about the Winter War are mainly targeted at Finns, who – at least theoretically – should have some basic knowledge about the war, having been taught history at school. Additionally, authors of photobooks can usually use captions to contextualise the images and thus build a narrative, but the pictures in the monument do not have integrated captions. To see the captions, the viewer must use their smartphone to visit the website mentioned earlier, but it is unlikely that every viewer will do so. To further complicate its construction, the narrative exhibited in the monument is not linear, but rather the photographs are presented in groups.[24]

Thus, the narrative of the monument should, to some extent at least, also be intelligible without captions. Moreover, it should also be informative and interesting for both Finns and foreign visitors. To address this, the purely Finnish viewpoint was abandoned, and some pictures not directly connected to the Winter War were incorporated. As a result of their being well known internationally, these images helped viewers to contextualise the other images by providing a time frame.[25] This solution, however, is not without problems: while familiar images may help, they may also confuse the viewer and even mislead them.

160 Olli Kleemola

The construction of a pictorial narrative for a monument also presents challenges that could be described as universal. Chief among them is the question of the "missing pictures", which here may denote the question of how to visualise the mass battles that took place on the Karelian Isthmus when few or no pictures exist. Another issue concerns the use of pictures with explicit content, such as fallen soldiers, or pictures originally created for propagandist purposes. While it is inevitable that these pictures will be used, for example, to illustrate the bloodiness of the war or simply because there are insufficient pictures of some specific topic, it is crucial that the images' potency is acknowledged and appreciated.

Notes

1 On the history of the Winter War, see for example Gordon F. Sander, *The Hundred Day Winter War. Finland's Gallant Stand against the Soviet Army* (Lawrence, KS: University Press of Kansas, 2013).

2 Markku Jokisipilä and Tiina Kinnunen, "Shifting Images of 'Our Wars': Finnish Memory Culture of World War II", in *Finland in World War II. History, Memory, Interpretations* (Leiden: Brill, 2011), 435.

3 Martin Parr and Gerry Badger, *The Photobook. A History. Volume III* (London: Phaidon, 2014), 6.

4 Gerhard Paul, *Jahrhundert der Bilder* (Göttingen: Vandenhoeck & Ruprecht, 2009), 27.

5 Olli Kleemola and Silja Pitkänen, "Photographs and the Construction of Past and Present", in *Photographs and History. Interpreting Past and Present through Photographs*, Vol. 15 of Cultural History, ed. Olli Kleemola and Silja Pitkänen (Turku: K&H, 2018), 9.

6 Olli Kleemola, "Talvisota – Valkoisten lumipukujen muuttumaton kuvakertomus" [The Winter War – an Unchanging Story of White Snow Camouflage Suits], *Ennen ja nyt*, 2015, www.ennenjanyt.net/2015/10/talvisota-valkoisten-lumipukujen-muuttumaton-kuvakertomus/, accessed 2 August 2019.

7 Gerhard Paul, "Visual History, Version 3.0", Docupedia-Zeitgeschichte, 13 March 2014, http://dx.doi.org/10.14765/zzf.dok.2.558.v3, accessed 2 August 2019.

8 Astrid Erll, *Kollektives Gedächtnis und Erinnerungskulturen. Eine Einführung* (Stuttgart: J. B. Metzler, 2017), 11–39.

9 Ibid., 25–26.

10 Susan Sontag, *Regarding the Pain of Others* (New York: Farrar, Straus and Giroux, 2003), 76.

11 On the aerial warfare during the Winter War, see Jari Leskinen, "Pommikuormia Virosta" [Bomb Loads from Estonia], in *Talvisodan pikkujättiläinen* [Handbook of the Winter War], ed. Jari Leskinen and Antti Juutilainen (Helsinki: WSOY, 1999), 668

12 Martti Julkunen, *Talvisodan kuva. Ulkomaisten sotakirjeenvaihtajien kuvaukset Suomesta 1939–40* [The Image of the Winter War: The International Journalists' Reports from Finland 1939–1940] (Helsinki: Weilin & Göös, 1975), 178.

13 See Maan Turva, *Kunniamme päivät* [Our Days of Honour] (Helsinki: WSOY, 1940), [no page numbers].

14 See for example Valo Nihtilä, *Ankarat vuodet* [Hard Years] (Helsinki: Otava, 1957), 39.

15 Kleemola, "Talvisota".

16 On the Finnish tactics, see Vesa Tynkkynen, "Talvisodan taktiikka tentissä" [The Acid Test of the Winter War Tactics], in *Talvisodan pikkujättiläinen* [Handbook of the Winter War], ed. Jari Leskinen and Antti Juutilainen (Helsinki: WSOY, 1999), 590–592.

17 On the legendary battles, see Sander, *The Hundred Day Winter War*, 175–207.

18 Lasse Laaksonen, *Todellisuus ja harhat. Kannaksen taistelut ja suomalaisten joukkojen tila talvisodan lopussa 1940* [Reality and Illusion: The Battles on the Isthmus and the Stand

of the Finnish Troops during the Final Phase of the Winter War, 1940] (Helsinki: Ylio-
pistopaino, 1999).

19 Olli Kleemola, "Lapin maisemia ja tuhottuja kirkkoja – Valokuvapropagandaa Suomesta
ulkomailla 1939–1944" [Views of Lapland and Destroyed Churches: Photographic
Propaganda from Finland 1939–1944], in *Sotapropagandasta brändäämiseen. Miten Suomi-
kuvaa on rakennettu* [From War Propaganda to Nation Branding: How the Image of
Finland Has Been Forged], ed. Virpi Kivioja, Olli Kleemola and Louis Clerc (Jyväskylä:
Docendo, 2015), 107–109.

20 Nihtilä, *Ankarat vuodet*, 39; Taavi Patoharju, *Suomi tahtoi elää* [Finland Wanted to Live]
(Helsinki: Sanoma, 1955), 31–39.

21 For Soviet pictures of the Winter War, see Bair Irincheev, *Talvisodan kadonneet kuvat*
[The Lost Pictures of the Winter War] ([Pori]: Avrora-Design, 2010).

22 Kleemola, "Talvisota".

23 The author of this article worked from 2014 to 2017 as a specialist for the group responsible for choosing the images for the narrative.

24 See https://1939-1940.fi/talvisota/, accessed 20 August 2019.

25 For example, this iconic picture was included in the narrative. Gerhard Paul, "Idylle Met
Schlagbaum", *Die Zeit*, 2014/36, www.zeit.de/2014/36/zweiter-weltkrieg-beginn-foto.

13 Archived and mediated

Trauma and "sense memory" in
Son of Saul, Warsaw Uprising and
Regina

Beja Margitházi

Some recent Eastern European films have engaged directly with the sensual and affective qualities of historical traumas, as we see in László Nemes's *Son of Saul* (2014), which is definitely an outstanding, but not a solitary, example of sensual evocations of individual and collective experiences of WWII trauma.[1] Diána Groó's Hungarian documentary, *Regina* (2013), and Jan Komasa's Polish war documentary, *Warsaw Uprising* (2014), were also inspired by unique visual (and written) war documents created by the victims of German atrocities. *Son of Saul* recalls events documented in *The Scrolls of Auschwitz*[2] and invokes the Sonderkommando photographs taken in August 1944; *Regina*'s initial visual source was the two surviving photographs of Regina Jonas (1902–1944), the world's first woman rabbi, while Komasa used the original newsreel footage filmed during the Warsawian Uprising in 1944. All three movies work with a combination of documentary and fictitious elements and present three different, experimental strategies of engagement with the archival sources.

In the following, I will examine these three movies as typical products of a postmillennial transforming memory culture, conceptualised by Aleida Assmann as a "post memory" era, when new "frames of memory transmission" have emerged.[3] My analysis aims to discover those cinematic, aural and visual techniques by which the three films have framed, adopted, enhanced or animated their archival, analog photographic sources. I will identify these processes as medial "post memory work", and I will argue that, despite their formal, stylistic, generic and thematic differences, these films have a special, phenomenological involvement with a so-called sense memory of the traumatic experiences evoked.[4]

Holocaust, war trauma and post memory culture

As the generation of eyewitnesses and survivors is passing away, new Holocaust cinema is increasingly characterised by the proliferation of different forms of mediated memory. Discourse about the right way and form of Holocaust representation has a long and rich history, since traumatic events and their recall has raised irresolvable epistemological and moral contradictions, seriously

DOI: 10.4324/9781003264460-16

challenging the "limits of representation".[5] In their edited volume on Holocaust cinema in the twenty-first century, Oleksandr Kobrynskyy and Gerd Bayer pointed to the fact that critical discourses on questioning the possibility and the legitimacy of representing the Holocaust (marked by Theodor Adorno's, Elie Wiesel's or Claude Lanzmann's strong disagreements) gave place to an interest in the different modes of representation, the formal and ethical paradigms, particularly the different strategies and techniques by which traumatic memories can be kept alive.[6] Postmillennial Holocaust cinema shows new characteristics: it covers new historical grounds, unfolds hidden and specific aspects (e.g., the Sonderkommando, the responsibility of the civilian population, etc.) and begins to break with old stereotypes (e.g., the "passive Jewish victim"). Kobrynskyy and Bayer also registered the tendency of expressed consciousness about the limits of audio–visual representation, a self-reflexivity on cinematic mediatedness and the growing role of visual archive, especially the insertion of photographs into films, which also reflects explicitly on the mediated nature of commemoration.[7]

Recent Holocaust cinema has also been affected by the new temporal stage of Holocaust remembrance. As any living, communicational connection with the survivors is gradually fading out, the post–witness era brings new "frames of memory transmission".[8] Aleida Assmann identified three of these: near identification mode (characteristic for the children of survivors), ethical mode (appearing typically in the second generation of Germans) and the appearance of "empathy mode",[9] which offers an affective involvement open for everybody without any special personal, familiar or national linkage. This new frame of memory raises sensibility for the suffering, helping the observer to imagine herself or himself in the same pain, but also being able to keep the difference between the self and the other, inasmuch as "empathy mode . . . reconstructs the trauma of the Holocaust from the perspective of the victim".[10] If we have lived lately in an era of "postmemory", defined by Marianne Hirsch as a temporarily and qualitatively different second-generation memory, experienced only through stories and images, the new century for Assmann is the era of "post memory", when all that has been embodied by the survivors as primary witnesses from now on "have to be re-created and re-experienced in a mediated form, in a new media setting" for later generations.[11]

The three East European movies handle photographic, filmic documents like medial "memory anchors". In *Son of Saul*, *Regina* and *Warsaw Uprising*, the original archival materials continue to preserve their status of historical document, while Nemes, Komasa and Groó connect private, personal and public aspects, consciously mixing the analog and digital photographic and filmic media to construct "post memory" products. As a result of these, the past is not only present as a topic or a story but is sensually embodied by the respective photographic or cinematic medium; through these comes the ability to communicate emotional, corporeal experiences and to transmit bodily sensations of past, traumatic events.

164 *Beja Margitházi*

Remediating the "sense memory" of the archival image

Art historian Jill Bennett introduced the idea of "sense memory" to distinguish the ordinary, narrative, representational memory from the affective memory of traumatic events. Quoting psychologist Pierre Janet and trauma researcher Bessel Van der Kolk, Bennett states that while narrative memory expresses thinking processes through language, traumatic memory has a layer that "lies outside verbal-semantic-linguistic representation".[12] Recalling the confessions of Holocaust survivor and poet Charlotte Delbo, Bennett describes this type of memory as "deep" and "affective", which "operates through the body to produce a kind of 'seeing truth' rather than 'thinking truth', registering the pain of memory as it is directly experienced and communicated on a level of bodily affect".[13]

Following this thread, it is highly imaginable how archive images can also preserve "sense memories" of traumatic events in various forms. I argue that this "sense memory" of the archival sources is a main point of reference for the films of Nemes, Komasa and Groó, as they seek for those intimate, sensual details, inner points of view encapsulated in the visual documents of the victims, which can also serve as entry points for a wider audience. This special interest and intense engagement with affective qualities is very close to Assmann's description of the empathy frame of memory transmission, characteristic for the new millennium. According to Assmann, empathy mode "provides . . . more distance than the identification frame and more proximity than the ethical frame".[14] While these two frames of transmission were defined by the collective "we"-group of intergenerational family connections or national origin, empathy mode offers an individual approach, open to all those who do not share any national, diasporic or family connections with the Holocaust.

I argue that *Son of Saul*, *Regina* and *Warsaw Uprising* achieve the affective involvement of spectators by the special treatment of photographic, filmic documents used as sensual "memory anchors". Nemes, Komasa and Groó maintained the historical documentary value of original archival materials, while they succeeded to unwrap the simultaneous public, collective relevance and personal implication of these records. The films address spectator empathy by clinging to the sensual details, bodily sensations and inner points of view, namely the "sense memory" encapsulated in the visual evidence.

Holocaust-related archive documents may reveal many otherwise hidden details but may also exclude important, historical, contextual information, giving way to misunderstandings and misinterpretations.[15] Besides this, any remediation, be it a medially hidden "immediacy", when the medium erases itself, leaving only the strong impression of the represented object, or a transparent "hypermediacy", when the presence of the medium and the process of mediation are made visible, implies alterations in denotation, which adds further complications of meaning when working with archive materials.[16] Michael Zyrd described this ambiguity coded in the archive material as a "spatial and temporal incompleteness", an amount of missing information about what happened "out of frame", before, after and during the recording:

> Into what story is the image inserted and how is that image implicitly and explicitly harnessed for a historical narrative? . . . History does not reside, in a simplistic way, *in* the image; the capacity of the image to serve as historical evidence lies in its contextual framing, what we have been told (or what we recognize) about the image.[17]

While Ebbrecht-Hartmann and Zyrd pointed to the incompleteness enclosed in any type of archive material, which opens the possibility of fabrications, manipulations and misuses, Bennett's concept of sense memory is directly attached to the subtle, affective experience, accidentally and involuntarily registered and documented thematically *in* and stylistically *by* the indexical, archive image. These sensations may be carried by every archival photographic or filmic source; the three movies in discussion use various, explicit and reflective medial strategies to catch and enhance the "sense memory" of their archival sources. Addressing in detail the medial framing of the archive materials and the interplays of immediacy and hypermediacy in the following sections, I will examine the ways in which the three films activate the empathy mode and sense memory.

Son of Saul: the phenomenological trauma and indexical drama of documenting

Clara Royer and László Nemes's script was inspired by *The Scrolls of Auschwitz*, the secretly written and buried diaries of some Sonderkommando members, a special group of Jewish prisoners who were forced to participate in the extermination processes in the crematoria. As Nemes declared, he was also deeply affected by the four Sonderkommando photographs and decided to integrate the moment of picture taking "in the heart of the film".[18] These pictures, called "images in spite of all" by art historian Georges Didi-Huberman were taken before the Sonderkommando rebellion and are recognised by many historians as among "the most astonishing of the various artifacts to have emerged from Auschwitz".[19] "In terms of visual record, they are unquestionably the most important documents that we have".[20] Two of the original shots (nr. 280 and 281) were taken from inside the gas chambers, showing the corpses and some working Sonderkommando members; on the other two (nr. 282 and 283), we can see outside locations, with some naked women in the foreground, who seem to prepare to enter the gas chamber; shot nr. 283 also "documents" the lack of careful targeting, the photographer's unsuccessful attempt to catch the same scene.

Son of Saul follows one day of a Sonderkommando member's life in the Auschwitz concentration camp. While the group secretly plans a rebellion and escape, Saul, the protagonist, seeks to bury the body of his supposed son,

166 *Beja Margitházi*

a young Jewish boy who miraculously survived gasification but was finally killed by an SS officer. At a given moment, risking their lives, Saul and one of his fellow prisoners take some photographs in the camp, documenting the mass extermination of the Jews. Besides dramatising the photo-taking action, Nemes's movie adopts the visual style, namely the strong, affective "sense memory" conveyed by the original Sonderkommando photographs: the "physical imprint of violence", the perspective of "seeing *from*" the witness's point of view, transmitting the tension of horror and trembling, the "attack on the senses", which is documented thematically *in* and medially *by* the original photographs.[21] Nemes's movie looks like a cinematic extension of the phenomenology of these pictures, adapting both what and how it is seen on them: the set, the actions, the hiding attitude, the darkness, the poor targeting, the rush and the emotional confusion become the basic components of *Son of Saul*'s whole audio-visual universe.

The pictures shot in the diegetic situation are certainly not identical to the archival ones, and the scene is totally blurred by smoke; but the specific, incidental focalisation and compositional arrangement of the original Sonderkommando photographs is reproduced and incorporated in some of the scenes' emblematic framings more directly. First, on a more essential level, these photographs' way of looking at things is interiorised by Saul himself, as his way of looking resembles the vision of a photographic camera eye: targeted to focus sharply on the closest foreground, and blurring the background (other people, the environment and corpses, called "Stücke" by the SS officers). This lifeless "technological" gaze was ruled by horror and fear (appearing also on photographs no. 282 and 283) and seems to be closely connected with Saul's mechanic movement and emotionless attitude, enunciating a certain physical closeness, yet constant psychological distance from the events.[22] Beside this, the first two photographs (nr. 280 and nr. 281) have a thick and black inner frame, the "subjective" point of view, which indicates a hidden position in the darkness of the gas chambers, and a view directed outside through a visible door frame (Figure 13.1), is applied in two dramaturgically important scenes of the movie. The inspection of the miraculously surviving boy appears with a very similar composition and framing. Saul is hiding in the background and watching from a distance, while the SS doctor is suffocating the still breathing body (Figure 13.2). Saul's general "seeing" without intention, in this moment turns into "watching", focusing with real attention, although he usually tries not to watch what is going on around him. Later, one of the final scenes repeats this inner framing, and this time it is again associated with death. After their escape, the prisoners take some rest in a shelter in the middle of the woods. Saul suddenly observes a young Polish boy, stepping in the doorway; he reacts with a smile, the first and last one we see on his face, before being executed by the Nazi chasers. These two scenes, together with the re-enactment of the action of taking the pictures, place the Sonderkommando photographs in a narrative filmic situation, in which their cinematic integration is completed through a repeated shot – reverse-shot composition, which reinforces the idea of the

Figure 13.1 Sonderkommando photograph no. 280 framed by the gas chamber's visible door frame (1944)

audience being present then and there. The added reaction shots turn the viewer's attention towards the "other" side, showing the original Sonderkommando photographer's point of view, suturing together the archive photographic and the actual cinematographic apparatuses through this imaginative gesture.

The mental state of fear, panic and extreme tension expressed in the immediate body gestures and documented in every Sonderkommando photograph

Figure 13.2 Watching the inspection of the miraculously surviving boy in Nemes's *Son of Saul*

is remediated in *Son of Saul*'s representation politics, which aims to offer a visceral, intimate and sensually intensive insight into concentration camp life and atrocities. Nemes's script is faithful to historical facts, as through the story of a fictitious character (Saul) it presents Sonderkommando members primarily, not as collaborators, but as witnesses and chroniclers in the extreme conditions of crematoria, where the act of taking a photograph was a collective, advisedly organised protest of a whole community.

Upgrading the archive: immediacy through hypermediacy in the *Warsaw Uprising*

The reconstruction of the archival footage shot during the Warsaw Uprising was one of the many important projects used to commemorate the seventieth anniversary of this tragic episode in modern Poland's national history. Komasa's war documentary was made entirely from archive materials, originally filmed as newsreel, by the Polish Home Army's crew in the 63 days of Warsawian resistance against the Nazi occupation. The surviving, six-hour long footage has been lost, found and re-edited several times in the last 70 years. Being part of a project hosted by the Warsaw Uprising Museum, the original black and white material first was restored and then underwent a careful colorisation and sonorisation process. Historians supervised the restoration of the colors, checking the factual accurateness of every detail (e.g., the dyes used at the time, identified urban sites, buildings, foods, etc.). All the sounds of the city and fighting were carefully reconstructed in the studio, by applying the same types of guns and explosives; while the on-screen characters' dialogues were reproduced by lip-reading specialists and finally dubbed by contemporary Polish actors.

While *Son of Saul's* fictional story was based on some written diaries and photographs, Komasa's movie relies entirely on documentary footage and constructs a fictitious plot, based on a new script dramatising the fight and perseverance of the Polish insurgents. All the action was accompanied by two fictitious cameramen's monologues and comments, namely Karol and his brother, Witek, who interact with and "talk to" insurgents, who seem to react to "answer" them. Komasa's scriptwriters choose to incorporate the originally invisible and unknown cameramen in these two characters, envisioning them as the constantly present persons, who can connect all the filmed events and all persons passing in front of their camera.[23] The emotions, reactions and the phenomenology of the continuous corporeal presence of Karol and Witek are expressed verbally and translated kinetically into unstable camera positions, with shaking and falling movements during the waves of explosions, where detonations pulsate in the sudden twitches of the image, and the filmmaker's hiding position is reflected, in many cases, through the partial views of the streets and buildings (Figure 13.3).

Figure 13.3 Filming the gunfights from the protection of a window in Komasa's *Warsaw Uprising*

170   *Beja Margitházi*

Ebbrecht-Hartmann mentions how music and added comments frequently accompany the use of Holocaust-related archival footage from this period, since originals were "preserved often as mute remnants (that) provoke . . . the use of additional sound or voice over in order to frame and contain the footage".[24] In the case of *Warsaw Uprising*, the reconstructed sounds, the carefully re-created sonic atmosphere, ambient noise and speech sequences undoubtedly accentuate the phenomenological, documentary quality of the archival source; final re-editing seems to work against this authenticity by subordinating the rearranged material to fictive monologues of the imagined, fictional filmmakers.

These two characters have a central role in the creation of the "empathy mode" of memory transmission, as Komasa's documentary seeks to create those entry points, through which anybody can engage from inside with the insurgent's position and the "perspective of the victims".[25] Thus, the cameramen are envisioned as "raisonneurs", classically defined as characters by "whom the author speaks"; the type of narrators who remain part of the action, although they do not have direct effect on it.[26] Komasa's film offers them a vocal embodiment; they remain invisible, but their fictionalised and vocalised agency has a strong interpretative power over the archive material, as their conversation and comments constantly negotiate the meaning of what is seen on the silent footage, whether they are instructing filmed people, or guessing their motivation, in many cases, by giving expression to a contemporary, trauma- and heroism-focused interpretation.

With all the communicated carefulness for historic authenticity and the seriousness of the scientific background research, the archive material appears to be the historically precious, raw source made even more spectacular through audio-visual and technological upgrades, accompanied, at the same time, by a "documentary downgrade". Polish media scholar Wiesław Godzic claimed that *Warsaw Uprising* finally takes the shape of a strange mixture of authentic and inauthentic, fictive elements that cause confusion and create a "metafilm with docu-dramatic elements".[27] He criticises the way real and invented filmmakers interact "in variable dramaturgical structure with the on-screen, actual, insurgents", therefore, the voice-over destined authentic, turns into "authoritative" and presents a desired, revised "supertruth". Although the cameramen's comments, in many cases, are personally or professionally self-reflective, Komasa's film leaves no traces of the potentially polysemous meaning of the original, fragmentary footage, excluding any reflective mark about its own way of (hyper)mediating the archive.

Warsaw Uprising is made up of various episodes of wartime life under constant German attacks, when traumatic events were everyday experiences. The original archive footage documented the flow of the ordinary life, funerals, weddings, gun construction, cooking and flirting but also depicted starvation, hopelessness, horror and death. The archive documentary invites a certain spectatorial engagement, which is particularly challenged by the remediation techniques used in Komasa's film. Jaimie Baron proposed in such cases to take into account the "archive effect" of archive or discovered footage, which is

Archived and mediated   171

the particular effect or consciousness generated by the viewer's perception of the respective material being produced in a different historical moment, thus embodying the phenomenological contrast between "then" and "now".[28] *Warsaw Uprising* challenges this "archive effect" by perplexing the viewer[29] with the simultaneity of a surprisingly colourful, noisy, vivid immediacy unpacked from the original black and white, decaying, silent material and the uncanniness of hidden mediation, the medial inorganic nature of the digitally added tints, hues, voices and sounds. These effects enhance the sense memory encoded in the archive for a contemporary audience, living in a new media environment, marked by speed, never-ending entertainment and hyperstimulation of the senses. *Warsaw Uprising*'s "post memory work" stands in using historical documentary footage to open up past traumatic experiences, even on the price of manipulating the incompleteness of the archive, indicated by Zyrd, in order to display a regular, grand narrative.[30]

Connecting individual biography and transnational archive: *Regina*

Hungarian filmmaker Diána Groó's documentary presents the story of Regina Jonas (1902–1944), the first properly ordained woman rabbi, who finally was allowed to hold services in the Nazi-persecuted Berlin, before being deported to Terezin, and later dying in Auschwitz. Her unique achievements and heritage were collectively forgotten for more than five decades, when the personal documents, papers and letters that she personally handed to the Jewish community center before her deportation were finally discovered.[31] Historian Stefanie Sinclair considered Jonas's story to be a special mnemonic case shaped by the "processes of remembering, forgetting and identity formation".[32] Conducting research on the possible reasons for the total silence around her heritage, Sinclair observed that the extreme and desperate conditions of her ordination in 1935, together with the gender bias, which usually caused women's marginalisation in historiography, and the "forceful forgetting" that followed Shoah as an impact of the trauma, all seemed to work against keeping her memory alive, even by those who were familiar with her and her work.

Apart from Elisa Klapheck's 1999 monograph on Regina Jonas, Groó had a single visual source for her documentary: two, almost identical looking, full figure studio photographs of Jonas,[33] wearing a similar black cap and robe, holding a book in her hand (Figure 13.4). Using authentic written documents revealed by Klapheck, Groó structured her film according to the linear chronology of Jonas's life, negotiating the lack of any other visual recording or survivor testimony by an extended vocal embodiment and various inserted pieces of archival footage. Besides some well-known shots (e.g., Hitler watching Jesse Owens at the Olympic games), Groó compiled photographs and silent footage collected by herself from different German, American, Czech and Polish film archives and private collections, as she was looking for pictures of Jewish girls and women living in Berlin, Warsaw and Kraków between the 1920s and

172 *Beja Margitházi*

Figure 13.4 One of the two surviving photographs of Regina Jonas (1936)

Archived and mediated 173

1940s. The original Jonas portrait serves as a visual memory anchor, strengthening the connection between the archival pieces of different origin; cut out from the original photograph, her figure sometimes shows up as an inserted background or foreground, floating in the streets of Berlin.

Employing a different strategy from Komasa, Groó's hypermediation is transparent, as she does not attempt to hide her documentary's composite nature. She is equally interested in creating a Zeitgeist atmosphere by showing miscellaneous private and public archive footage about the shop windows and passages of Berlin streets, ordinary people and ordinary events. She inserts popular period hits and traditional Jewish songs and, by slowing down and sonorising the silent shots, she also catches the phenomenological, sensual side of such ephemeral, everyday details, such as the arrival of a train, the opening an umbrella or pouring out a bucket of water. These aspects, even if not explicitly traumatic, outline the general mood of the 1930s, sensed in Berlin under the shadow of the growing Nazi party.

The two low-key, laconic, black and white photographs of Jonas at first hardly convey any "sense memory"; affective aspects rather appear as Groó introduces the vocalised layers of various written recollections, letters and articles, and the sensual images of her handwriting and other archive footages. Thus, Regina's thoughtful, camera-shy face and outlook become gradually enriched with intimate nuances of her personality, while Groó mediates and opens up her subjective, intimate perspective for empathic engagement. Jonas's positive and optimistic attitude in the middle of her struggles as the first woman rabbi of the Jewish community hide and cover the deeply interiorised trauma of the gradually strengthening anti-Semitism and later the personal experience of concentration camps.

Collected from different archives, Groó shows numerous shots of young Jewish women in her film (Figure 13.5); thus, we see many different gestures, body postures, moods, clothes, hairstyles, hats and aspects of young girls and women reading and walking, while every word of the voice-over is a

Figure 13.5 Young Jewish woman in *Regina*

174   *Beja Margitházi*

quotation from Jonas's documents, or an idea from Klapheck's monograph. Using this technique, Groó manages to extend the frames of Regina Jonas's identity and personal story into a collective, East-European Jewish intellectual, female fate. Groó maintains a freedom and playfulness in decelerating and freezing the footage, panning, zooming in into photographs and mixing amateur footage with official archive material. In the process of creating a sensual atmosphere of Berlin before and during the Nazi regime, Groó's remediation strategy is open and self-revealing, a total opposite of the one seen is Komasa's war documentary.

Visual techniques are accompanied by a refined sound engineering, with added sound and voices, and this is how Groó builds a different phenomenological authenticity. Black and white photographs and silent footage are supplied with a sonic atmosphere and ambient noises (e.g., the sounds of traffic, noise of rain and wind or carpet dusting, etc.) and vocal embodiment of the different characters evoked in the documents (friends, professors, pupils, parents and journalists). The written testimonies, letters and newspaper articles are read both by actors and non-professionals, including the filmmaker's own Hungarian grandmother, an 86-year-old concentration camp survivor.[34] This authenticity adds a distinct, non-visual indexical layer to the commemoration of Jonas's life, through which Groó can not only connect the individual with the collective, but also redefine her film as not being about Holocaust: "it is about surviving".[35]

Conclusion

Relating to Bennett's sense memory concept, this analysis has explored the medial, photofilmic mnemonic techniques *Son of Saul*, *Warsaw Uprising* and *Regina* used in recalling WWII events and individual and collective traumas. The investigation revealed that "post memory work" in these films was performed on three different, but deeply interdependent levels. *Cinematic integration* 1) of archive photographic and filmic documents was achieved by the audio-visual re-staging or framing of the still, silent photographs (*Son of Saul* and *Regina*) and restoring the raw, mute shots (*Warsaw Uprising*). Each movie practiced a *phenomenological adaptation* 2) of the witness's perspective and sense memory documented *in* and *by* the photographic gaze. Memory work also appears in the *medial/material embodiment of violence, loss, damage and trauma* 3), carried visibly by the film's structure and texture. By these three medial "post memory work" techniques, the films reach the sense memory encapsulated in the silent archival image or footage, while the interplay of immediacy and hypermediacy works against total immersion and helps the viewer keep a reflexive distance. These techniques can work against the often declared "desensitization process" of losing empathy towards the Holocaust and WWII trauma. Geoffrey Hartmann, Susan Sontag and Marianne Hirsch amongst many others, noticed the temporary loss of sympathy and moments of saturation, which often thwart affective remembrance, as decontextualised and overused visual documents may work

Archived and mediated 175

against commemoration, contributing rather to "remembering to forget".[36] It is time to awaken the "sense memory" of the archives.

Notes

1 This paper was supported by the Hungarian National Research, Development and Innovation Office, number of agreement 116708.
2 "Scrolls of Auschwitz" refers to eight stocks of documents written by five known authors, all members of Sonderkommando. These writings were buried in the grounds of crematoria at Auschwitz and were recovered between 1945 and 1980. Historian Ber Mark transcribed and published several of these manuscripts under the title *Megiles Oyshvits*, which later was translated into English as the "Scrolls of Auschwitz". See Ber Mark and Isaiah Avrech, *The Scrolls of Auschwitz* (Tel Aviv: Am 'Oved Publishing House, 1985).
3 Aleida Assmann, "Transformations of Holocaust Memory. Frames of Transmission and Mediation", in *Holocaust Cinema in the Twenty-first Century: Images, Memory, and the Ethics of Representation*, ed. Gerd Bayer and Oleksandr Kobrynsky (New York: Columbia University Press, 2015), 23–40.
4 See Jill Bennett, "The Aesthetics of Sense-memory: Theorizing Trauma through the Visual Arts", in *Memory Cultures: Memory, Subjectivity and Recognition*, ed. Susannah Radstone and Katharine Hodgkin (Piscataway: Transaction Publishers, 2003), 27–39.
5 See Saul Friedländer, ed., *Probing the Limits of Representation: Nazism and the "Final Solution"* (Cambridge: Harvard University Press, 1992).
6 Gerd Bayer and Oleksandr Kobrynskyy, eds., *Holocaust Cinema in the Twenty-first Century: Images, Memory, and the Ethics of Representation* (New York: Columbia University Press, 2015), 2.
7 Ibid., 4–7.
8 Assmann, "Transformations of Holocaust Memory. Frames of Transmission and Mediation", 32.
9 For a critical analysis of empathy and/or identification with the victims in Holocaust and trauma discourses of Walter Benjamin, Dominick LaCapra, Giorgio Agamben and Margarete Mitscherlich, see Allan Meek, *Trauma and Media: Theories, Histories, and Images* (London and New York: Routledge, 2011), 133–170.
10 Aleida Assmann "Transformations of Holocaust Memory. Frames of Transmission and Mediation", 34.
11 Ibid., 37. See also Marianne Hirsch, "Surviving Images: Holocaust Photographs and the Work of Postmemory", *The Yale Journal of Criticism*, 14 (2001), 11.
12 Bennett, "The Aesthetics of Sense-memory: Theorizing Trauma through the Visual Arts", 28.
13 Ibid., 29.
14 Assmann "Transformations of Holocaust Memory. Frames of Transmission and Mediation", 33.
15 Georges Didi-Huberman, *Images in Spite of All: Four Photographs from Auschwitz* (Chicago: University of Chicago Press, 2008), 66–67. Tobias Ebbrecht-Hartmann, "Three Dimensions of Archive Footage: Researching Archive Films from the Holocaust", *Apparatus. Film Media and Digital Cultures in Central and Eastern Europe*, 2–3 (2016), accessed 19 August 2017.
16 Jay David Bolter and Richard Grusin, *Remediation: Understanding New Media* (Cambridge, MA: MIT Press, 1999), 70–71.
17 Michael Zyrd, "Found Footage Film as Discursive Metahistory. Craig Baldwin's *Tribulation 99*", *The Moving Image*, 2 (2003), 47.
18 Antoine de Baeque, "Interview with László Nemes", *Son of Saul*, Paris, *Rendez Vous*, Online Press kit. (2015), http://sonyclassics.com/sonofsaul/sonofsaul_presskit.pdf, accessed 12 July 2017.

176 *Beja Margitházi*

19 László Nemes also declares the influence of Georges Didi-Huberman's book on the Sonderkommando photographs, originally published in France. See Georges Didi-Huberman, *Images malgré tout* (Paris: Minuit, 2015).
20 Dan Stone, "The Sonderkommando Photographs", *Jewish Social Studies*, 7 (2001), 132.
21 Ibid., 135; Bennett, "The Aesthetics of Sense-memory: Theorizing Trauma through the Visual Arts", 33.
22 Stone, "The Sonderkommando Photographs", 132.
23 As Milenia Fiedler, one of the editors of *Warsaw Uprising* explains: "Insurgents appear on the screen too briefly to fully tell their story. This sparked the idea of the film protagonist to be a person who does not appear in the take, but whose presence, emotions and actions are recorded by the camera operator on film. We have edited the material not as an objective recording of reality but *subjective truth about the person who experienced this reality*" (emphasis mine). See in the press book: http://warsawrising-thefilm.com/media.
24 See Ebbrecht-Hartmann, "Three Dimensions of Archive Footage: Researching Archive Films from the Holocaust".
25 Assmann, "Transformations of Holocaust Memory. Frames of Transmission and Mediation", 34.
26 Edward L. Hancock, *Techniques for Understanding Literature: A Handbook for Readers and Writers* (Belmont: Wadsworth, 1974), 124.
27 Wiesław Godzic, "Polish Docudrama: Finding a Balance between Difficult and Easy Pleasures", in *Docudrama on European Television: A Selective Survey*, ed. Tobias Ebbrecht-Hartmann and Derek Paget (London: Palgrave Macmillan, 2016), 68–69.
28 Jaimie Baron, "The Archive Effect: Archival Footage as an Experience of Reception", *Projections*, 2 (2012), 105.
29 The press book reflects on the dissonance of adding colors to the black-and-white archival footage and reveals the desired effect: "Adding color reduces the distance and the historical events acquire a new dimension. They simply become real. The past – as Cyprian Kamil Norwid once postulated – becomes the present, 'only somewhat further away'. . . . Looking at the archival material used in this feature film we experience a cognitive dissonance – while it still represents an important page in Poland's history, the film looks as if it were shot contemporary with the help of film set designers, costume experts, abundance of authentic props and numerous visual effects." http://warsawrising-thefilm.com/media.
30 See Zyrd, "Found Footage Film as Discursive Metahistory. Craig Baldwin's *Tribulation 99*".
31 The main primary source of information about Jonas is the collection of papers (letters, newspaper articles, manuscripts of her talks and a copy of her dissertation) discovered in the early 1990s. Her monographer, Elisa Klapheck "got the impression [that Jonas] designed her legacy. She was very aware of what she wanted to leave for the . . . world. She took into consideration that one day someone will come and find and write about her" (fragment from an oral interview with Klapheck, conducted by Sinclair and quoted in Sinclair 2013, 543).
32 Stephanie Sinclair, "Regina Jonas: Forgetting and Remembering the First Female Rabbi", *Religion,* 43 (2013), 542.
33 The reproductions of the two, almost identically looking photographs (made in 1936 and 1939) were published in Elisa Klapheck, *Fräulein Rabbiner Jonas: kann die Frau das rabbinische Amt bekleiden?* (Teetz: Hentrich and Hentrich, 1999).
34 As Groó confessed: "At the end, when she is speaking about how they could survive in the concentration camps, I was 100% sure I don't want to use actors for the voice-overs. I wanted to use someone who really knows what it is about and my grandmother, although she did not know Regina Jonas, she really knows the meaning of a concentration camp and surviving, and feeling, and talking about this feeling that she also felt at that time at the age of 17". (Dekel 2013) Ayelet Dekel, "Jerusalem Film Festival 2013:

Diana Groó on Making *Regina*", *Midnight East,* July 3 (2013), www.midnighteast.com/mag/?p=26893, accessed 2 August 2017.

35 Dekel, "Jerusalem Film Festival 2013: Diana Groó on Making *Regina*".

36 Geoffrey Hartman, *The Longest Shadow. In the Aftermath of the Holocaust* (Bloomington: Indiana University Press, 1996); Hirsch, "Surviving Images", 5–37; Susan Sontag, *On Photography* (New York: Anchor Doubleday, 1989); Barbie Zelizer, *Remembering to Forget: Holocaust Memory through the Camera's Eye* (Chicago and London: University of Chicago Press, 1998).

14 Memory, history, image, forgetting

Obrona Warszawy (The Defence of Warsaw) by Zygmunt Zaremba and Teresa Żarnower[1]

Stanisław Czekalski

From a reading of *Phaedrus*, Paul Ricœur extrapolated the notion of "memory by default", or "memorisation", based on equating the functions of representation and "standing for" (*représentance*).[2] He stated that the representation of history in the form of texts or images was a paradoxical form of *pharmakon* – a means designed to ensure remembering, which, however, leads to forgetting, as it substitutes for the source of memories. As a result, they are no longer one's own experiences, becoming instead just external signs, detached from the memories and resembling past events only in the way they present them. The past, as the object of memory, is replaced by the forms used to capture and present it and becomes concealed by them. The substitutions which present invisible things of the past become disguised in their own visibility with regard not only to their former shapes and states but also to their replacement by the image produced. And memory recognises its absent object as similar to the one which, vicariously, presents and recalls it.[3]

The emphasis placed on the concealing dimension, *représentance*, brings Ricœur's thoughts close to the considerations of Jacques Rancière regarding the "distribution of visibility" as a common function of politics and art.[4] Rancière stressed that these two realms share the practice of exposing some aspects of the visible reality and including them in the symbolic space and public discourse, and, as a consequence, keeping other aspects unexposed and unarticulated, and thus excluded from the public circulation of knowledge. The setting and resetting of this distribution of visibility is the essence of the aesthetic dimension of politics, on the one hand, and the essence of the political dimension of art, on the other. While politics divides the visible sphere and distributes the visible from the perspective of a certain political interest, art replies by creating its own repartition and redistribution of visibility, and thus it also takes on a political function.

Taken together, Ricœur's concept of memorisation and Rancière's model of politicality enable us to capture clearly the essence of tension and discord between the picture of the Warsaw September of 1939 presented in the recollections of Zygmunt Zaremba and the form of the remembrance of the tragedy of that September depicted in the photomontages of Teresa Żarnower in response to them.[5]

DOI: 10.4324/9781003264460-17

Soon after the capitulation of the city, Zaremba, one of the main activists of the Polish Socialist Party (PPS), a co-organiser of the civil defence of Warsaw during the September campaign and a co-creator of the units known as "Workers' Battalions", was ordered by the party leadership to "present the facts of September, spread knowledge about them and provide an assessment".[6] So he presented the story of the heroic defence of Warsaw from the perspective established by specific political guidelines. He turned the tragedy of the city bombarded by the Germans into a testimony of the heroic stand taken by its defenders mobilised on the initiative of the PPS. He wrote extended accounts of the actions of the workers' units connected with the building of defence installations, as well as with the paramedical services and direct engagement in combat. He presented their concerted resistance as the sacrificial act of a community of one people formed, thanks to the work of PPS activists – an act bearing testimony to the power of the patriotic spirit. In Zaremba's opinion, Warsaw managed to defend its honour, capitulating only after great sacrifice and really "having done all that could be done".[7] The testimony of that heroic and laudable sacrifice conveyed in the book was designed to bolster the spirit of readers during the years of German occupation and give hope for the time of post-war reconstruction. The vision of the future victory of socialism imposed itself upon the September defeat, giving it a historical sense, so that the memory of the destruction of the city and the massacre of its inhabitants would be inseparably linked with that of the unshakeable power of the masses.

If each form of memory representation is inevitably marked with the dialectics of pharmakon, there is nothing to indicate that Żarnower, in her illustrations for Zaremba's recollections, tried to represent and preserve the remembrance of September 1939 conveyed in the text. The photomontages clearly provide a substitute for it, covering it with a distinctly different picture of events. The very choice of the photomontage technique is meaningful in this respect. During the interwar period of the 1920s and 1930s, photomontage earned the reputation of a modern form of documentary evidence based on the veracity of photography and a multifaceted approach to a theme, combining the closeness of looking at specific aspects with a distance allowing the viewer to grasp an entire panorama. While it presents a variety of perspectives, at the same time it allows for a consideration of them all, thus suggesting an impartial and objectified overview. Of course, the visibility of the photomontage, which imposes itself in these categories, conceals meaningful operations in the selective choice of photographs with regard to a desired ideological effect.[8]

Żarnower did not confine her works to an ancillary role, acknowledging the text and concretising its content in the form of a picture. On the contrary, she engaged in a dialogue with Zaremba's recollections, creating a totally different, alternative type of testimony to the events in Warsaw. In her view, photomontage had a substantial advantage as an artistic genre over records of individual memory and, as a form of remembrance, it appeared to be far more sophisticated, credible and convincing.

As noted by Ricœur, individual testimony gives voice to the words "I was there, believe me", requiring that the picture of events preserved in the memory

180   *Stanisław Czekalski*

and clearly linked to the subjective, specific, emotionally involved and limited perspective of the participant be recognised as the truth.[9] The polar opposite is marked by the distance that the historian has to keep, rising above subjectivity and creating a space for the critical juxtaposing of individual memories with documentary evidence – a position implied by the notion of impartial judgement: the ideal historian plays a role analogous to that of a judge, weighing up varying testimonies and assembling them into a reasoned and objective picture of past events abstracted from individual perspectives and representing in its way an impersonal "non-viewpoint".[10] The objectivist model of the work of the historian described by Ricœur is in perfect harmony with the objectivistic myth of the photomontage technique, and Żarnower's illustrations are fully in line with it. Based on this myth, in relation to Zaremba's memories, they took on the appearance of a historical view combining a multitude of documentary evidence in the form of photographs weighed against the subjective recollection of a single witness. Maintaining a distance to Zaremba's testimony, Żarnower confronted it with archive photos which she combined to create a contrary picture.

Much can be seen in Żarnower's photomontages, but not even a shred of that sublime and laudable picture of the heroic defence of Warsaw drawn by Zaremba. They lack not only the emphasis placed on the expression of glory and the mythologised recollections of that tragic September, but also the very elements of its factographic core, that is, the act of the defence of Warsaw itself. This was done in spite of the words in the title, and especially the subtitle added to the New York edition: *Lud polski w obronie stolicy* ("The Polish people in defence of the capital"), in which the photomontages served as illustrations.

Żarnower was well aware of the potential of photomontage as a technique that allows one to take advantage of the persuasive power of photography to authenticate and reinforce the message conveyed in a text. Before the Second World War, she specialised in propaganda photomontages affirming emphatically the power, activities and struggle of the proletariat. If such had been her goal, she would have been able to highlight splendidly the message of Zaremba's book about the tireless and rightful struggle of the working class, but she decided to do the opposite. She did not show the "main hero" of *The Defence of Warsaw*, that is, the Workers' Battalions, and she did not visualise the form of their sacrificial service, such as defence and city protection activities or work on the construction of defensive obstacles in the streets. Contrary to her earlier propaganda works, the layout of photographs does not confirm the verbal message but denies it, and the proud title of the book loses its credibility when confronted with the photomontages. Thus, the key word "defence" loses its meaning.

The title inscribed on the photomontage printed on the cover is highlighted by the motif of a hand pointing at bombers over the city (Figure 14.1). In the photomontages prepared for the canvassing campaign preceding the parliamentary elections in 1928, the same motif of a raised hand was used to highlight, in accordance with the *pars pro toto* principle, the proper action to be taken by the

Figure 14.1 Teresa Żarnower, *Obrona Warszawy. Lud polski w obronie stolicy (The Defence of Warsaw. The Polish people in defence of the capital)*

Source: photomontage, front cover, Polish Labor Group, New York 1942; courtesy of Muzeum Sztuki, Łódź

182 *Stanisław Czekalski*

militant proletariat, that is, the gesture of casting a vote. Here the same motif becomes the synecdoche of defencelessness and helpless terror: a hand pointing at a source of mortal danger appearing from above the faces of children with their eyes raised to the sky and filled with fear. This group of representatives of Warsaw does not present "the Polish people in defence of the capital" mentioned in the subtitle, but only the helplessness of potential victims.

Through such a depiction of the horror of the bombers moving over the heads of the defenceless children exposed to attack, Żarnower departed far from the text of *The Defence of Warsaw* but also made a clear reference to the propaganda from the time of the civil war in Spain. Posters calling people to oppose the fascist rebels and their allies, distributed widely in Europe and the US by the Republican government, perpetuated the image of children falling victim to the bombardment of cities as the essential motif of their iconography.[11] The use of that dramatic image of defencelessness was justified by the need to mobilise international forces to take action in support of the defence of the inhabitants of Madrid or Barcelona in the face of the tragedy, the symbol of which was Guernica. Relating the fate of Warsaw to this Spanish symbol on one hand included it in a wider historical perspective but on the other obscured the heroic act of the defence of the capital undertaken by its people, which was another story, and the remembrance of which was the intention of the author of the book. The result of this was paradoxical: instead of emphasising Zaremba's work written in honour of the heroic defenders of Warsaw, the montage on the cover echoes the rhetoric of Spanish posters alluding to the inappropriate engagement in defence of bombarded cities on the part of those who should have been joining the effort.

Unlike Żarnower's earlier propaganda photomontages, where the documentary references of the source photographs reused to illustrate new content did not matter, the material used for the illustrations for Zaremba's book was largely based on authentic photos documenting September 1939 in Warsaw. However, she took a selective approach to the sources containing the available evidence of the defence of Warsaw that provided the iconography of the subject matter. She turned to sources depicting the annihilation of the besieged city and the tragic fate of the victims, and not those showing the heroic efforts of the defenders.

In one of the photomontages, pictures of men working with spades (among whom two Jews in traditional gabardines stand out) resemble Julien Bryan's well-known shots taken during the digging of anti-tank ditches. The large-scale digging of trenches by large numbers of Varsovians, including Jews, and numerous rows of diggers are one of the motifs in Zaremba's story. They are probably the most typical motif in the photographs of the besieged capital captured for the American media, and among them not only the best known of Julien Bryan's photos and his film *Siege*, but also the press photos taken by Harrison Forman, as well as anonymous agency photographs published in several periodicals, including *Life* magazine.[12] More than anything else, they created the impression of the masses of Warsaw widely cooperating with the

Memory, history, image, forgetting 183

military in their act of defence against invasion. However, in the layout of Żarnower's montage, the group of diggers with two Jews in the foreground is not accompanied by Polish soldiers, as captured by Bryan, but instead by Nazis. In the photographs placed above, we see them tormenting a Jew and a terrified woman with a little girl in tears. Next to them are photographs of civilians being shot dead. In this context, the picture of men digging is distanced from association with the defence of Warsaw and becomes reminiscent on one hand of the Nazi habit of making Jews dig their own graves before execution, and on the other of forcing the Jewish inhabitants of occupied Warsaw to clear the debris – scenes also known from the photographic documentation of German operations in Poland in the autumn of 1939. In this case, Żarnower used a photograph of Jews forced to remove heaps of rubble. Such a misleading reference to a motif characteristic of the iconography of the defence of Warsaw commemorated mainly by Bryan's photos makes one wonder, especially as right next to it Żarnower "quoted" two other photographs from Bryan's cycle entitled *Siege*. So, familiar with these materials where the shots depicting the digging of ditches for the defence of Warsaw held a significant place, Żarnower replaced the picture of the collective effort of the citizens of Warsaw with a similar one depicting Jews ruthlessly enslaved by the occupant.

The only picture showing the citizens of Warsaw in large numbers depicts their mass retreat from the bombarded capital and is given the title *On the Road of Death* (Figure 14.2). Zaremba mentions in his book that such was the name given to the road to Lublin into which "the main wave of refugees poured out" after the call for the inhabitants of Warsaw to leave the city. This road, blocked by thousands of people, was a target for attacks by German aircraft. With these refugees, he counterposed the heroic people who stood tall against all odds and followed the initiative of the PPS for the general defence of the city. However, contrary to Zaremba's heroic narrative, Żarnower's photomontage focused mainly on that "road of death". What for him was a shameful episode preceding the efforts to defend Warsaw, and the antithesis of the heroism of those dedicated to that cause, was presented by Żarnower as one of the main images of the Warsaw September of 1939. Moreover, as the photomontage *On the Road of Death* is the last in the sequence of illustrations in the book, we gain the impression that this road was not the one down which the inhabitants of Warsaw retreated before the defence effort was organised, but the one along which the last survivors of the devastated city tried in vain to escape, unable to find any shelter in the ruins.

Such a message implied by this photomontage results also from its positioning after the previous one entitled *Days of Horror*, depicting only streets of smouldering debris, dead bodies and crosses on provisional graves, and amidst this scenery, the figure of an injured father with his little daughter on his lap (Figure 14.3). This agency photo was taken on 17 September at a first-aid post, where they were both treated by the medical service operating within the system of city defence and provision described in the book.[13] Żarnower, however, decided to cut this context out in order to place the

Figure 14.2 Teresa Żarnower, *On the Road of Death*, photomontage, in *Obrona Warszawy. Lud polski w obronie stolicy (The Defence of Warsaw. The Polish people in defence of the capital)*, Polish Labor Group, New York 1942

Source: courtesy of Muzeum Sztuki, Łódź

lonely figures of a father with his daughter among ruins and corpses, with services no longer in operation. Between the two montages, there appears a hopeless alternative for the survivors: either to hide among the ruins of the destroyed city or to find a way to escape from it, though in vain. There is no place here for any defence or even rescue activities allowing the inhabitants to remain in the besieged city – the affirmative description of which was the subject matter of Zaremba's book. Having rejected his vision of the heroic defence of Warsaw, Żarnower opposed the written testimony with the evidence of documentary photographs from September 1939, assembled in such a way as to demonstrate nothing but the catastrophe of the totally devastated, disorganised and defenceless city, incapable of resistance, and the ordeal of the terrified victims of barbarous attacks aimed at its inhabitants – people who were left on their own and vainly trying to find shelter in order to survive or to escape.

And so, with her photomontages, Żarnower managed to radically redistribute the visibility of the Warsaw events in relation to the way they were presented by Zaremba. By multiplying and accumulating nothing but the images of massacre, she masked all that he displayed first and foremost in his memories:

Figure 14.3 Teresa Żarnower, *Days of Horror*, photomontage, in *Obrona Warszawy (The Defence of Warsaw. The Polish people in defence of the capital)*, Polish Labor Group, New York 1942

Source: courtesy of Muzeum Sztuki, Łódź

organised defence activities supported by the masses, the heroic and supremely stubborn struggle against the German invaders, the important historical meaning and political sense of the unyielding spirit of the people of Warsaw.

As an experienced creator of photomontages, Żarnower also knew the theoretical conceptualisations of this medium as a means of visual communication, broadly discussed in the interwar avant-garde. It was perceived as a new, perfectly communicative and effective form of language enabling verbal messages to be suggestively and even persuasively supported by an appropriate compilation of photographs. It was also seen as an effective substitution of words by an intelligible composition of images. Photomontage was to become a sort of universal language, speaking with all the power of visual obviousness and condensing the sense of the messages within it. It was seen as extremely concrete and precise, directly, immediately and uniformly understandable for everyone on a scale not limited by language barriers. The discourse about this modern and superior equivalent to text revolved around the principle of pharmakon, representation and substitution, while photomontage was to be a remedy for the weakness and limitations of verbal communication, enhancing the power of verbal messages to such an extent as to completely take over and significantly improve the role assigned to them.

186 *Stanisław Czekalski*

However, Żarnower's photomontages became a pharmakon, the whole *représentance* potential of which worked not in favour of an affirmative and reinforcing representation of Zaremba's memories, but exclusively towards their weakening, concealment and substitution. The credibility of the montage of numerous documentary photographs acts against that of the individual testimony of the author of *Defence of Warsaw*. The effectiveness of the substitution and masking of his words with pictures was even stronger, as the photomontages illustrated the Polish text published in the US – in this case, the natural advantage of a montage of photographs over words regarding the possibility of reaching a larger audience was particularly stark. The limitation of the understanding of the text due to the language barrier undoubtedly made the illustrations act as the sole (and independent) transmitters of the content of the book for all those who were not able to read it but could view it. Those who had no command of the Polish language missed the discrepancy between the photomontages and the written testimony and, as a result, the illustrative material became the only representation of the memory of the events of September 1939 in Warsaw.

The effectiveness of the impact of the pharmakon constituted by Żarnower's works in relation to Zaremba's recollections was confirmed by their reception in the context of art history. In this case, the reference to the text – without which it is impossible to understand the pictures created as illustrations – was forgotten.[14] Each exhibition that presented Żarnower's illustrative montages as self-contained works of art, and each discussion about them without reference to the illustrated text, would perpetuate this state of forgetting in which the autonomy gained by the visibility of the photomontages decoded in various external contexts concealed the absent narrative linked to them in the book which provided their original setting. In art history, the illustrations alone represented and eventually replaced – according to the *pars pro toto* principle – the forgotten dichotomous whole.

Notes

1 An abbreviated version of the paper "Jaka obrona Warszawy? O fotomontażach Teresy Żarnower do książki Zygmunta Zaremby" [What defence of Warsaw? On Teresa Żarnower's Photomontages for the Book by Zygmunt Zaremba], presented at the conference *Teresa Żarnower i lewica artystyczna* [Lost avant-garde: Teresa Żarnower and the artistic left], Museum of Art in Lodz, 16 May 2014.

2 Paul Ricœur, *Memory, History, Forgetting,* trans. Kathleen Blamey and David Pellauer (Chicago: University of Chicago Press, 2006), 142.

3 Ibid., 230, 280.

4 See Jacques Rancière, *The Politics of Aesthetics: The Distribution of the Sensible,* trans. Gabriel Rockhill (London: Continuum, 2004).

5 [Zygmunt Zaremba], *Obrona Warszawy. Lud polski w obronie stolicy (wrzesień 1939 roku)* [The Defence of Warsaw: The Polish People in Defence of the Capital (September 1939)] (New York, 1942). On Zaremba's recollections and their subsequent editions, see Andrzej Krzysztof Kunert, "Nota edytorska" [Editor's Note], in Zygmunt Zaremba, *"Żeby chociaż świat wiedział". Obrona Warszawy 1939, Powstanie Sierpniowe*

Memory, history, image, forgetting 187

1944 ["Just So the World Should Know": The Defence of Warsaw 1939, the August Uprising 1944], ed. Olena Blatonowa and Andrzej Krzysztof Kunert (Warsaw: Bellona, 2010), 7–17.

6 Zygmunt Zaremba, *Wojna i konspiracja* [War and Resistance] (London: B. Świderski, 1957), 109. See Kunert, "Nota edytorska", 13.

7 Zaremba, *"Żeby chociaż świat wiedział"*, 93.

8 I have written about this at greater length in *Awangarda i mit racjonalizacji. Fotomontaż polski okresu dwudziestolecia międzywojennego* [The Avant-garde and the Myth of Rationalisation: Polish Photomontage of the Interwar Period] (Poznań: Wydawnictwo Poznańskiego Towarzystwa Przyjaciół Nauk, 2000), esp. 44, 112, 173–174.

9 Ricœur, *Memory*, 163–164.

10 Ibid., 315.

11 The propaganda significance of these posters is discussed in Nigel Glendinning, "Art and the Spanish Civil War", in *"No Pasarán!": Art, Literature and the Spanish Civil War*, ed. Stephen M. Hart (London: Tamesis, 1988), especially 27, Martin Baumeister, "Spain's Multiple Wars: Mobilization, Violence and Experiences of War, 1936–1939", in *"If You Tolerate This. . .": The Spanish Civil War in the Age of Total War*, ed. Martin Baumeister and Stefanie Schüler-Springorum (Chicago: University of Chicago Press, 2008), 9–27, and most broadly in Robert A. Stradling, *Your Children Will Be Next: Bombing and Propaganda in the Spanish Civil War 1936–1939* (Cardiff: University of Wales Press, 2008).

The analogy between one of the Spanish posters and the motif of a woman cuddling a child used by Żarnower was noted by Aleksandra Idzior, *Reaction to a Catastrophe: Cultural Memory in the Photomontages of Teresa Żarnower*, "The Defence of Warsaw", in *Teresa Żarnowerówna (1897–1949). Artystka końca utopii* [Teresa Żarnerówna (1897–1949): An Artist of the End of Utopia], ed. Milada Ślizińska and Andrzej Turowski (Łódź: Muzeum Sztuki w Łodzi, 2014), 131.

12 See Julien Bryan, "Documentary Record of the Last Days of Once Proud Warsaw", *Life*, 7/17 (1939), 73–77; Harrison Forman, "Filming the Blitzkrieg", *Travel*, 74/2 (1939), 18–22; "The German Army Invades Poland", *Life*, 7/11 (1939), 20–21.

13 *Father and Daughter Injured in the Air-Raid on Warsaw, 1939.* The original description/ signature/inscription/ states that the photo was taken at a first-aid post. The photograph comes from the Hulton-Deutsch Collection/ Corbis/ Getty Images and is accessible at the Getty Images website: www.gettyimages.co.uk, accessed 27 August 2018.

14 The long period of the presence of reproductions of Żarnower's photomontages in the field of art history without complete analytical research lasted until Andrzej Turowski broadened the perspective of the history of the Polish interwar avant-garde by adding to it a wartime and post-war epilogue.

In his book *Budowniczowie świata. Z dziejów radykalnego modernizmu w sztuce polskiej* ("Builders of the world: from the history of radical modernism in Polish art") (Cracow, 2000), these works were properly highlighted and discussed for the first time, although without the context of their link to Zaremba's text, as copies of *Defence of Warsaw* were not easily available. Turowski had access to it just once, and only briefly, allowing him to reproduce only the photomontages; later (according to the author), he was unable to find this publication again. Published in a small number of copies, it soon became extremely scarce. There was no other edition after 1942, and only in 2010 was the text reprinted and analysed in the collection of Zaremba's writings *"Żeby chociaż świat wiedział"*.

At the same time, Aleksandra Idzior began studying the photomontages, considering their place between the tradition of "high" art and the iconosphere of contemporary forms of mass communication. In the process, she noticed, among other things, the references to the photographs of Julien Bryan and to the posters from the time of the Spanish Civil War. The broad contextual connections of Żarnower's works, outlined in the paper "Response to a Catastrophe: Mixing 'High' and 'Low' by Teresa Żarnowerówna in 'The Defence of Warsaw'" (High and Low. Second Bi-annual conference of the

188 *Stanisław Czekalski*

European Network for Avant-Garde and Modernism Studies, the Adam Mickiewicz University, Institute of History of Art. in Poznań, 9–11 September 2010), linked those works with the background iconography without any connection to Zaremba's book – a link which so far has not been the subject of analysis. Neither was any such analysis included in the extended and elaborated version of that paper published under the title "Reakcja na katastrofę: pamięć kulturowa w fotomontażach Teresy Żarnower 'Obrona Warszawy'".

15 Pictures and history: art exhibitions as a tool for the validation of communist authority in Poland

Michał Haake

By 1943, it was already clear that after the war, Poland would fall within the Soviet sphere of influence. The Soviet occupation of Poland began when Joseph Stalin established the Union of Polish Patriots and the puppet Polish Committee of National Liberation (PKWN). The appointment of the PKWN created a political structure that was preserved – with only non-essential modifications – until 1989. The regime was based on the Communist Party's monopoly of power and the subordination of Poland to the USSR. The communists held all executive power. Independent political forces were to be dismantled and destroyed and more or less dependent allies allowed only a very limited share in government. In 1947, a rigged election concluded with the appointment of the NKVD agent Bolesław Bierut as president of Poland. In 1948, the political system was turned into a one-party set-up, with the creation of the Polish United Workers' Party, steered from Moscow.

In the years 1944–1953, an armed anti-communist insurrection was pursued in Soviet-occupied Polish lands.[1] The communists set about crushing it, whilst at the same time waging a campaign of propaganda designed to secure society's acceptance of the new regime. In the present paper, I wish to examine the role played by three exhibitions of Polish art in the process of legitimising communist rule in Poland.

In Poland ruled by communists, all areas of social life "were to be subordinated to communist ideology. It was to be a binder enabling the party to lead a passive human mass incapable of independent thinking".[2] Art occupied a prominent place in the construction of the new order. Jakub Berman, one of Bierut's closest associates, said:

> Without the inclusion of literature and art in the fight for socialism, it is impossible to transform human consciousness. We must be aware that art, in all its forms, is an instrument of influence reaching extremely deeply, and that without this instrument, without mobilizing forces in this section, we cannot achieve full victory.[3]

In 1949, socialist realism was proclaimed as the binding doctrine for writers and artists, who were expected to condemn class enemies and glorify prominent

DOI: 10.4324/9781003264460-18

190   *Michał Haake*

leaders, the power of the socialist state and its economic achievements. Socialist realism fought against modernism and the avant-garde, perceived as the degenerate art of the propertied class. Socialist realist art was to be socialist in content and national in form. The notion of national form was merely a smokescreen for a lack of autonomy in the cultural world. Everyone knew that socialist realism, in accordance with the guidelines set out by Maxim Gorky and adopted in 1934 at the Soviet Writers Congress in Moscow, was based on realist form.

Museums have become the main space for creating a new image of art. In 1946, the archaeologist Professor Kazimierz Majewski appealed: "The government must realize, that museums are not only research centers, but also very important institutions of education and ideological education, both for young people and the masses, that next to home and schools, museums must be the third primary educational center".[4] In the museum – Majewski continued– the viewer must understand that "the socialism is an inevitable stage in the development of humanity and revolutions are the correct transition from one economic and social system to another".[5] These appeals soon became official guidelines, which Majewski presented in a paper "Museology at the stage of the struggle for socialist culture" at the 1st National Scientific Conference on Art Research, organised as part of the preparation for the 1st Congress of Polish Science: "Museology – as a Marxist theory of historical and dialectical materialism and acting along the lines of Leninist and Stalinist thesis on nation – is currently beginning to fight for the socialist content of Polish culture", is starting a fight, "in which freedom in the development of museology or randomness in undertaking scientific papers is unacceptable".[6]

Indeed – it was the research on history of art that was to provide justification for the development of socialist realist art. They were quickly included in the process of falsifying history depending on current political needs. It was Professor Juliusz Starzyński who played a leading role in the implementation of the new science model in field of art science. In July 1948, he became a member of the Polish Workers' Party (PPR). At that time, one could no longer have the illusions that the PPR is the advocate for democratic and national values. In the first post-war years, the communists tried to hide their real intention for the Sovietisation of Poland and gain the time to liquidate the independence underground. In 1948, it was after the pacification of the independent Polish People's Party, the people's referendum rigged by the PPR (30 June 1946) and after the rigged election to the Legislative Sejm (19 January 1947). Starzyński's rise came at the height of the communist political omnipotence, and when they joined the "final" trial with the Catholic Church as well.[7] Starzyński's activity "in the model manner depicted 'police' character of post-war Polish history of art as the field, which created the hierarchy of knowledge and occupied a privileged position in social discourse".[8] In February 1949, at the Congress of Artist in Nieborów, it was Starzyński who gave an introductory paper, in which he recognised socialist realism as the binding creative method. He carried out the tasks assigned by the communists in the institutions he managed: International Cultural Cooperation Office at the Ministry of Culture and

Arts (1947–1949) and National Art Institute (from 1949). In 1950, Starzyński's work *Five centuries of Polish Painting* appeared, containing in brief form guidelines for the scientific elaboration of the history of Polish art, understood as the development of realistic element.[9] This book undertook an urgent task, which – in connection with the new doctrine – became the unveiling of roots of realism in the tradition of Polish art. Let's quote one sentence from this book without commenting:

> Through stereotypical threads of the church theme . . . always peeps lively, honest and personally feeling man. . . . It is enough to mention the often encountered figure of "Pensive Christ", in which the Polish people saw not so much the image of the deity, but rather the image of great care in life – a man who was hard-working and over-tired.[10]

First, attention was drawn to Polish artists who had depicted social contrasts. The works of Aleksander Gierymski represented a model of "realist painting" based on "the direct observation of proletarian reality" (Figure 15.1).[11] However, to justify realism as a national form, deeper roots in the history of Polish culture had to be shown than the art of the 19th century. That task was to be met by a number of exhibitions during the 1950s. The most important exhibitions included *Realizm w tradycji malarstwa polskiego od XV do XIX wieku* [Realism in the tradition of Polish painting from the fifteenth to the nineteenth century], held in 1950 at the Society for the Friends of the Fine Arts in Cracow, curated by Professor Tadeusz Dobrowolski.

> The first date (wrote the exhibition commissar) is justified by the fact that it was only around 1450 that realist features became distinctly present in Polish art, and the closing date of around 1900 is explained sufficiently by the fact that from that date on formalist trends began to hold sway, proliferating during the imperialist phase in capitalism, the period of the disintegration of the bourgeoisie, the crisis of culture and the deepening of the moods of scepticism and pessimism, which incline people to flee from real life in both philosophy and art.[12]

In the struggle to establish a new worldview order, based on Marxist doctrine, the exhibition was clearly orientated against the foundations of the European tradition:

> The history of European art in general and of Polish art in particular . . . confirms the illusiveness and powerlessness of the idealism that holds the physical world to be a pure product of the human mind or a pale, imperfect reflection of ideas existing in the fictive sphere of supernatural reality.

In light of this pseudo-scientific propaganda issued by the communist state, its ideology and cultural doctrine guaranteed that the imperialist phase would be overcome: "The political, economic and social watershed of 1944 fundamentally altered the situation of Polish art, opening up before it extensive horizons for development and assigning it weighty social tasks – helping to forge the new reality".[13] It was also pointed out that the realist current in Polish art "never entirely succumbed to the growing formalist tendencies".[14] The victory of communist Poland over imperialist culture paved the way for a return to the centuries-old "national tradition in Polish art". The exhibition was to show the communists in Poland as the heirs to Polish national traditions.

In 1956, the Stalinist period in Poland came to an end. Power was taken by another group of Polish communists, hitherto repressed, led by Władysław Gomułka. However, taking over by him the function of the First Secretary in Polish United Workers' Party (the highest managerial function in the country), contrary to the social expectations, brought an end of the "thaw". Although the system of exercising power was reformed, the essence of a totalitarian state was maintained.[15] The lack of recognition for the new western border of Poland along the Oder-Neisse Line by the administration of the Federal Republic of Germany meant that Gomułka's policies were of an anti-German character. And those policies bore a crucial influence over the character of the celebrations of the Millennium of the Polish State, lasting for several years. In 1960, the communists organised grand celebrations of the five hundred fiftieth

Figure 15.1 Aleksander Gierymski, *Sandblasters*, 1887

Source: oil on canvas, 50x66 cm, Warsaw: National Museum

Pictures and history   193

anniversary of the Battle of Grunwald. During the solemnities held on the battlefield on 17 July, Gomułka warned the thousands of participants in the grand manifestation against the renascent forces of West German imperialism and militarism ("The predatory nature of German imperialism has not altered from the times of Ulrich von Jungingen to the times of Conrad Adenauer"). Across the country, "soil was ceremoniously taken from places stained with the blood of participants in the struggle for national and social liberation, the battles with the German invaders over the course of the Millennium of Polish statehood".[16]

The conflict between the communists and the Polish nation was played out especially in the year 1966, when the Catholic Church celebrated the Millennium of the Baptism of Poland. In 1966, the first ruler of Poland, Mieszko I, was baptised by Bishop Jordan and wed the Christian Bohemian princess Dobrawa. The aim of the state-led commemoration of the Millennium of the Polish State was to "combat the ideological influence of the Polish clergy".[17] The witch hunt against the Polish church intensified in 1965, when Polish bishops sent an address to German bishops calling for mutual forgiveness. The communists regarded the "Address" as an act of betrayal of the Polish *raison d'état* and an expression of acceptance for those political forces in Germany which refused to recognise the current western border of Poland. Hence, the state commemoration in 1966 was largely of an anti-church and anti-German character.

The main ceremonies, those organised by both the state and the church, took place in Gniezno and Poznań, where Mieszko I ruled and the first Polish archbishopric was established. The most important exhibition at that time, titled *Skarby Kultury Polskiej* [*Treasures of Polish culture*], was opened in April 1966 at the Royal Castle, part of the National Museum in Poznań. Forty-six objects linked to rulers of Old Poland were shown. In the catalogue, it was emphasised that the exhibition was being held in a venue that was destroyed by "Nazi barbarianism" and rebuilt by the "Builders of the People's Poland". So the purpose of the exhibition was to demonstrate that the communist authorities contributed not just to defeating the Nazi invaders, but also to maintaining the historical continuity of Poland and its "flourishing culture". Communist Poland was to be shown as the most glorious period in Polish history.[18] The anti-church message of the exhibition was created by the last-minute withdrawal of those objects which attested to the religiosity of Polish rulers (the Prayer Book of Anna Jagiellonka).

Of an equally propaganda character was another exhibition at the National Museum in Poznań, devoted to Polish historical painting,[19] which showed "selected works by various artists who still painted during the last century 'for the fortification of hearts' and continue to fulfil a lofty and important role".[20] As one might expect, attention was focused above all on the history of fighting with Germany.[21] So the struggle against the Nazi invaders was also indirectly inscribed in the narrative of historical battles, recalled to the memory of visitors in an obvious way.

Not by accident were Wojciech Gerson's *Opłakane apostolstwo, (1147)* [*The Capture of the Wends*] and Aleksander Lesser's *Śmierć Wandy* [*The Death of Wanda*] chosen among the paintings linked to the legendary beginnings of Polish history, as they showed Germanic aggression against Slavic tribes (Figures 15.2– 15.3). According to numerous accounts, the legendary princess Wanda did not wish to become the wife of a German ruler and transfer rule over her lands into German hands. This figure also symbolised the times when the Slavs' power extended beyond the River Oder. During the 14th century, those lands fell into the hands of the Bohemians and the Germans. In 1966, *The Death of Wanda* was to remind viewers of the historical claims to western lands and to the borderlands on the Oder and the Neisse. It became a pretext for building an ideological parallel: just as Wanda did not wish to give up her lands to the Germans, so communist Poland stood in their defence, opposing the revisionist forces in the Federal Republic of Germany that were questioning the Oder-Neisse border. At the same time, this narrative enabled the communists to mask the fact that the Western Territories were awarded to Poland not on account of the historical truth and the desire to satisfy historical justice, but as compensation for the Soviet Union taking far greater eastern areas away from Poland after 1945.

The paintings by Gerson and Lesser were also perfectly suited to the vision of Slavonic history propagated by the communist authorities as independent of the adoption of Christianity. Wanda was a ruler of the pre-Christian era.

Figure 15.2 Wojciech Gerson, *The Capture of the Wends, (1147)*, 1866

Source: oil on canvas, 290x460, Cracow: National Museum

Figure 15.3 Aleksander Lesser, *The Death of Wanda*, 1855
Source: woodcut, engraved by Edward Gorazdowski, "Kłosy" 1884, vol. XXXIX, nr 1006, p. 233/234

Her legendary grave near Cracow became part of the ideal communist town of Nowa Huta, which the communists began creating in 1949. The town was built for workers at the planned metallurgical plant: the Vladimir Lenin Steelworks. Nowa Huta was originally conceived as an atheist, godless town, and none of the official designs included a site for a church. The communist authorities declared Wanda patroness of this model communist town, and her name was given to one of the estates.

At the exhibition of Polish historical painting, viewers were reminded of German aggression against the Polish state by Gerson's *Śmierć Przemysława I w Rogoźnie* [*The Death of Przemysław I in Rogoźno*] and Jan Matejko's *Konrad Wallenrod* (sketch) and *Bitwa pod Grunwaldem* [*The Battle of Grunwald*] (Figure 15.4). Each of these paintings depicted events that supposedly showed that the strengthening of Polish statehood – first after the period of fragmentation during the 12th century, then in alliance with Lithuania – always triggered counteractions from the Germans. According to the propaganda,

Figure 15.4 Jan Matejko, *The Battle of Grunwald*, 1882
Source: oil on canvas, 426x987, Warsaw: National Museum

communist Poland found itself in a similar situation, threatened by the "renascent forces of West German imperialism and militarism". *The Battle of Grunwald* was described in the exhibition catalogue as "a mighty vision of the noble struggle of nations, embodied in that historical moment, for the independence of their lands, the struggle of the united forces of Poland, Lithuania and Rus against the common enemy: the Teutonic Order". Mention was made of the "nameless figures of the populace" to which the artist "assigned the role of capturing the Teutonic commander".

The authors of the exhibition were inspired by the book *Jan Matejko's The Battle of Grunwald*, written by art historian Mieczysław Porębski (1953). Porębski was a PhD student and collaborator of the previously mentioned Juliusz Starzyński. In 1953, he was introduced by Starzyński to the Academy of Fine Arts in Warsaw as part of the ideological mastery of Polish humanities. At that time, he was also a teacher at the "party school": "Graduates of these schools then often worked in the state administration, eventually they were to be sent to PZPR apparatus".[22] Porębski used Matejko figures to fuel class struggle. He made Matejko's monograph written in 1897 by Count Stanisław Tarnowski the subject of criticism. He claimed that this representative of the possessing classes did not consider both "nameless figures of the populace" as an important element of the picture. He counted him among "the leading ideologists of Galician obscurantism" and accused of identifying "the people" with "barbarism" done under the guise of "defending civilisation". According to Porębski, a "significant ideological sense" of Matejko's work consists in "revealing those barbaric forces that shape and change the order of history".[23] The decisive role of Polish king did not matter to Porębski.

In showing Matejko's painting, the communist authorities set themselves up as the heirs to those representatives of the populace in the work of "changing the order of history". The catalogue also informed readers that *The Battle of Grunwald* had such a powerful effect on society that over the last half a century, "it has become a national symbol of the struggle several more times".[24] In connection with the anti-German character of the celebrations of the Millennium of the Polish State, that remark may be regarded as tantamount to suggesting that in 1966, this painting might once again fulfil that role. The exhibition was to show that the role of "fortifying hearts" once played by the assembled paintings remained current in light of the threat from German revisionism. It also enabled the communist authorities to be represented as guardians of the Polish patriotic and independence tradition. It goes without saying that the figure of St Stanisław, patron of the Polish-Lithuanian armies, was not mentioned once in the description of *The Battle of Grunwald*.

This context allows us to offer a judicious appraisal of the millennial exhibitions abroad which communist Poland prepared during the 1960s. These were exhibitions presenting the achievements of Polish culture through the ages, shown at the Musée des Beaux-Arts in Bordeaux (1961), under the title *Trésors d'art polonaise*; at the Art Institute of Chicago (1966), the Philadelphia Museum of Art and the National Gallery of Canada in Ottawa (1967), under the title *Treasures from Poland*; in Paris (1969), as *1000 ans d'art en Pologne*; and in London (1970), under the title *1000 Years of Art in Poland*. Yet those exhibitions, devised as part of the state celebrations of the Millennium of the Polish State, were of a different character to the exhibitions in Poznań, not only due to the much greater number of exhibits (e.g. 127 in Chicago and Ottawa, 320 in Paris and 590 in London).[25]

In negotiations with the Americans, it was agreed that objects from the 11th to the 19th centuries would be displayed in the Chicago exhibition. The aim was to show that "Poland has contributed to the development of European culture for a thousand years". On the cover of the exhibition catalogue and on the portico of the Art Institute in Chicago, the current emblem of Poland was placed: an eagle without a crown.[26] So the exhibition *Treasures from Poland* was intended to clearly define communist Poland as the heir and steward of that centuries-old heritage. Unlike the exhibitions at home, however, the shows abroad included many treasures of sacred culture and art, including a cross with diadems from Wawel Cathedral, the Madonna of Krużlowa and the Herma of St Sigismund (Figure 15.5). The religious tradition was evidently covered because the exhibitions were addressed largely to Poles who had settled abroad after the Second World War and were unwilling – or, more often, unable – to return to a communist Poland. For all those efforts, the Chicago exhibition did not attain the anticipated visitor numbers.[27] In the opinion of the organisers, this was due partly to the American Poles' aversion to the communist propaganda symbolised by the new version of the Polish emblem. That mistake was rectified for the next exhibition in Philadelphia, which – like the shows in Paris and in London – was successful, largely thanks to the presence of early sacred art, which was regarded as its strongest point.

Figure 15.5 1000 Years of Art in Poland, exhibition poster, 1970
Source: London, Royal Academy of Arts (with *Virgin and Child from Krużlowa*)

Pictures and history   199

To conclude, one may infer from the art exhibitions patronised by the communist state of Poland that their aim was the same regardless of the time they were organised. They were designed to present the communists as the rightful heirs to the national heritage. They were to create a picture of Polish history that was not at odds with the atheist, Soviet-dependent Poland of the communists.

Notes

1 Adam Dziurok, Marek Gałęzowski, Łukasz Kamiński and Filip Musiał, *Od niepodległości do niepodległości. Historia Polski 1918–1989* [From Independence to Independence: The History of Poland 1918–1989] (2nd edition) (Warsaw: IPN, 2011); Dawid Golik, *Żołnierze wyklęci. Antykomunistyczne podziemie zbrojne po 1944 roku* [The Cursed Soldiers: The Armed Anti-communist underground after 1944] (3rd edition) (Warsaw: Volumen, 2013); Marta Markowska, *Wyklęci. Podziemie zbrojne 1944–1963* [The Cursed: The Armed Underground 1944–1963] (Warsaw: Ośrodek Karta, 2013).

2 Filip Musiał, *Triumf i pierwszy kryzys "ludowej" Polski (1948–1956)* [Triumph and the First crisis of "people's" Poland], in *Od niepodległości do niepodległości*, ibid., 289.

3 Quoted in Włodzimierz Sokorski, *O sztukę realizmu socjalistycznego* [For the Art of Socialist Realism], in *Sztuka w walce o socjalizm* [Art in the Fight for Socialism] (Warsaw: PIW, 1950), 142.

4 Kazimierz Majewski, "Muzea historyczne jako instytucje badawczo-oświatowe" [Museums as Research and Education Institutions], *Życie Naukowe*, 11–12 (1946), 388.

5 Ibid.

6 Kazimierz Malinowski, *Muzealnictwo na etapie walki o socjalistyczną kulturę* [Museology at the Stage of the Struggle for Socialist Culture] (Warsaw: MdSiD, 1950), 179–180.

7 Musiał, *Triumf i pierwszy kryzys "ludowej" Polski*, 252–273.

8 Marta Leśniakowska, "Władza spojrzenia–władza języka. Juliusza Starzyńskiego obraz sztuki i jej historii" [Look Power – Language Power: Juliusz Starzyński's Picture of Art and its History], *Modus. Prace z historii sztuki*, 12–13 (2013), 30.

9 Juliusz Starzyński, *500 lat malarstwa polskiego* [Five Centuries of Polish Painting] (Warsaw: PIW, 1950).

10 Ibid., XI.

11 Tadeusz Adamowicz, "Przewodnik" [Guide], in *Realizm w tradycji malarstwa polskiego od XV do XIX wieku, urządzonej przez Komitet Organizacyjny I.ej Ogólnopolskiej Konferencji w sprawie Badań nad Sztuką, listopad-grudzień 1950, Kraków, Towarzystwo Przyjaciół Sztuk Pięknych* [Realism in the Tradition of Polish Art from the Fifteenth to the Nineteenth Century, Organised by the Steering Committee of the First All-Poland Conference on Art Research, November-December 1950, Society for the Friends of the Fine Arts, Cracow], ed. Adamowicz (Cracow: TPSP, 1950), 25–26.

12 Tadeusz Dobrowolski, "Wstęp" [Introduction], in ibid., 3.

13 Adamowicz, "Przewodnik", 27–28.

14 Ibid.

15 Musiał, *Triumf i pierwszy kryzys "ludowej" Polski*, 298.

16 Cf. Władysław Gomułka, "Przemówienie na uroczystości 550 rocznicy zwycięstwa pod Grunwaldem wygłoszone na Polach Grunwaldzkich 17 VII 1960 r." [Speech on the 550th Anniversary of the Victory in the Battle of Grunwald Given on the Battlefield on 17 July 1960], in *Przemówienia 1960* [Speeches 1960] (Warsaw, 1961), 279–285; "Wielkie uroczystości na Polach Grunwaldu" [The Grand Commemoration on the Fields of Grunwald], *Trybuna Ludu*, 18 July 1960, 1; Bartłomiej Noszczak, *"Sacrum" czy "profanum"? – spór o istotę obchodów Milenium polskiego (1949–1966)* ["Sacrum" or "Profane"? – a

200 *Michał Haake*

Dispute about the Essence of the Celebrations of the Polish Millennium] (Warsaw: TNW, 2002), 134–137.

17 APP, KW PZPR, 1312, 77–78. *Projekt Programu obchodów Tysiąclecia Państwa Polskiego w Wielkopolsce w 1966* [Project for the Programme of the Celebrations of the Millennium of the Polish State in Greater Poland in 1966]. Quoted in Krzysztof Stryjkowski, *Koncepcja i przebieg Tysiąclecia Państwa Polskiego w województwie poznańskim w aktach Archiwum Państwowego w Poznaniu*, in *Milenium kontra Tysiąclecie – 1966*, ed. Konrad Białecki, Stanisław Jankowiak, Jan Miłosz, (Poznań: Instytut Pamięci Narodowej 2007), 154.

18 *Wystawa Skarbów Kultury Narodowej* [Exhibition of Treasures of National Culture], catalogue of an exhibition held at the National Museum in Poznań. Przemysł's Castle, 20 April to 10 May 1966 (Poznań: Muzeum Narodowe w Poznaniu, 1966).

19 The other exhibitions organised at the National Museum in Poznań as part of the celebrations of the Millennium of the Polish State were *1000 lat muzyki polskiej* [1000 Years of Polish Music] (October–November), *Tysiąc lat monety polskiej* [A Thousand Years of Polish Coins] (October–December) and *1000 lat Poznania* [1000 Years of Poznań].

20 Piotr Michałowski and Janusz Lehmann, *Polskie malarstwo historyczne* [Polish Historical Painting], exhibition catalogue (Poznań: MNP, 1966), 2.

21 The Turkish Wars: Józef Brandt, *Bitwa pod Chocimiem* [The Battle of Chocim] and *Husaria* [The Hussars]; Jan Matejko, *Sobieski pod Wiedniem* [Sobieski at Vienna] (oil sketch); Henryk Rodakowski: *Posłowie austriaccy u Jana III* [Austrian Envoys with John III]; Fabian Sarnecki, *Wjazd Jana III do Wiednia* [John III enters Vienna]. The Danish and Swedish Wars: Józef Brandt, *Czarniecki pod Koldyngą* [Czerniecki at Kolding]; Leon Kapliński, *Portret Stefana Czarnieckiego* [Portrait of Stefan Czarniecki]; January Suchodolski, *Śmierć Stefana Czarnieckiego* [Death of Stefan Czarniecki]. The Russian Wars: Jan Matejko, *Stańczyk, Batory pod Pskowem* [Báthory at Pskov] (oil sketch).

22 Anna Olszewska, "Obecność prac humanisty. O Mieczysławie Porębskim w 2013" [The Presence of Humanist Works: About Mieczysław Porębski in 2013], *Rocznik Historii Sztuki*, XXXVIII (2013), 7; Bartosz Cichocki and Krzysztof Jóźwiak, *Najważniejsze są kadry. Centralna Szkoła Partyjna PPR/PZPR* [Staff is the Most Important: PPR/PZPR Central Party School] (Warsaw: Trio, 2006), 105, 117.

23 Mieczysław Porębski, *Jana Matejki "Bitwa Pod Grunwaldem"* [Jan Matejko's *The Battle of Grunwald*] (Warsaw: PIW, 1953), 14–15.

24 Michałowski and Lehmann, *Polskie malarstwo historyczne*, 4–6.

25 *1000 Years of Art. in Poland*, ed. Anna Różycka-Bryzek, exhibition cataloque, London, Royal Academy of Arts, 3 January–1 March 1970 (Uxbridge: The Hillington Press, 1970); Stanisław Lorentz, "Wystawy millenialne", *Muzealnictwo*, 19 (1970), 26–28; Jerzy Banach, "1000 lat sztuki w Polsce. Wystawy w Paryżu i Londynie w latach 1969 i 1970", *Muzealnictwo*, 19 (1970), 29–39; Zdzisław Żygulski (jun.), "Wystawy 'Skarbów z Polski' (Treasures from Poland) w Chicago, Filadelfii i Ottawie (1966–1967)", *Muzealnictwo*, 19 (1970), 40–48.

26 Żygulski, "Wystawy 'Skarbów z Polski", 42.

27 Ibid., 44; Robert Jarocki, *Rozmowy z Lorentzem* [Talks with Lorenz] (Warszawa: PIW, 1981), 452–454.

16 *Hungary in Flames*: photographic, cinematic and literary memories of the Hungarian Revolution of 1956, and their impact on the history of ideas

Tamás Gergely Kucsera

> It would indeed be difficult for us to be worthy of such sacrifices. But we can try to be so.[1]
>
> Albert Camus

The present study discusses the Hungarian Revolution of 1956 within a historical framework[2] and examines its artistic and cultural relevance through the contemporary work and careers of renowned Hungarian-American cinematographers László Kovács and Vilmos Zsigmond, the visual elements and imagery used by poet Gáspár Nagy, and the childhood photography turned art career of photographer László Haris.

Ungarn in Flammen – Hungary in Flames

The study takes its title from a documentary made in 1957 in West Germany; the original German-language version was translated into several languages, with the Hungarian version receiving the subtitle, *Egy nép harca a szabadságért* [*A Nation's Fight for Freedom*].[3] This film was the first documentary made of the Hungarian Revolution of 1956 and was intended as a means of informing Western public opinion of the Hungarian events of October and November.

The film is 83 minutes long and was shot on 33 mm film. The makers attempted to simultaneously appeal to the emotions as well as the rational minds of their audience. The documentary begins with text shown briefly on screen, followed by one of the most popular European actresses of the 1950s, Maria Schell, addressing the audience; the film then spends over 20 minutes providing an overview of the history of the Hungarian nation from its arrival in the Carpathian Basin and 1,100 years of statehood to 1956, followed by almost an hour of detailed accounts of the events of the Hungarian Revolution of 1956.[4]

DOI: 10.4324/9781003264460-19

202 *Tamás Gergely Kucsera*

The documentary was intended as a call for help, and begins with the following text:

> In eternal memory of the heroes and martyrs of the Hungarian Revolution. Produced by anonymous Hungarian cinematographers living as stateless citizens, with the enthusiastic support of their German, Austrian, French, and U.S. colleagues. Their goal: to use a Great Power, this Film, to turn the Hungarian nation's unquenchable thirst for freedom and exemplary heroic struggle into an unforgettable experience and rouse the world's conscience: It cannot be that all in vain so many hearts have bled. . . . [5] To spread it to every free country, to spread it to those who preside over the fate of the people, to bring them to their senses! To make them reflect upon themselves! To never forget: There is no peace without Hungary's freedom![6]

The documentary records the events of the Hungarian Revolution in Budapest, where the protesting masses removed the symbols of the Stalinist dictatorship. The revolutionaries knocked down the red stars from public buildings, tore up the red flags, burned portraits of Stalin and photographs of Hungarian dictator Mátyás Rákosi, toppled statues (including the statue of Stalin) and smashed them, and where symbols or other works of socialist realism commissioned by Hungarian communist leadership could not be removed, these were covered up with the Hungarian national flag, as shown from 00:46:00 to 00:50:15. In the same segment, the ending shot shows the center of the daily newspaper of the Hungarian Communist Party, *Szabad Nép* [*Free People*], with the embossed lettering on the building still intact – I shall discuss the fate of this embossed lettering later.

During the revolutionary events and struggles in the Hungarian capital, a total of six different film crews were continuously filming in Budapest. Within 13 days, they shot approximately 10,000 metres of film, and according to the memoirs of the participants, on the morning of 4 November, they were going to transport the film to Vienna to the International Red Cross and the organisations of the United Nations in order to objectively inform global public opinion on the events of the Hungarian Revolution. However, the panic that ensued in the wake of cannon fire at dawn and the tragic announcements on the radio caused someone to turn on the lights and thus destroy part of the material still in development; in the end, only a few boxes worth of shots could make it to Austria, tucked away in the backpacks of cinematography students László Kovács and Vilmos Zsigmond. This fragmentary material ultimately became the backbone of the documentary *Ungarn in Flammen*, which was produced in Munich, West Germany by Hungarian director István Erdélyi in cooperation with the company Karpat Film,[7] which operated in West Germany in the 1950s and 1960s.

The young Hungarian film-makers who had emigrated to Western Europe and thus rescued recordings of the Hungarian Revolution of 1956 that would later be used in the documentary eventually became world famous: László Kovács is renowned to this day for his cinematography in *Easy Rider* and *New York, New York*,[8] while Vilmos Zsigmond's name is most associated with *Close Encounters of the Third Kind* and *The Deer Hunter*, which received BAFTA, Emmy and Oscar awards. In 2003, the International Cinematographers Guild nominated Zsigmond as one of the ten most influential cinematographers in history.[9]

Fifty years after *Ungarn in Flammen*, Vilmos Zsigmond and László Kovács produced the film *Torn from the Flag*,[10] which can be considered a sequel or conclusion to the documentary from 1957. The two Hungarian cinematographers, now internationally renowned masters of their craft, had remained friends for the rest of their lives, and their last joint project before the death of Kovács was thematically tied to the Hungarian Revolution of 1956:[11] both were listed as executive producers, and Kovács was also listed as a cinematographer. *Torn from the Flag* focuses on the era of the bipolar world order from 1945 to 1991, where the Hungarian Revolution of 1956 is presented as the beginning of the eventual fall of the Communist Bloc and the road leading towards democracy. The documentary was presented to audiences in 2007 after nine years of hard work and community effort: in North America, approximately 2,000 persons and their families rendered their support alongside the local Hungarian community, Hungarian foundation and Hungarian churches. The documentary features, among others, former United States Secretary of State Henry Kissinger (1923-), and Otto von Habsburg (1912-2011), the contemporary heir to the Hungarian throne and honorary president of the International Paneuropean Union.

1956 – personal history and a life of art: part one

Photographer László Haris[12] recounts his childhood memories of the Hungarian Revolution of 1956 and the story of the photographs he had taken in the days of the revolution as follows:

> November 2 was an absolutely gorgeous day, because we learned from the radio that the Soviet troops had left Budapest. It seemed that the revolution had won. The city was quiet, the sun was shining. That's when I received permission from my parents to go out and take photographs.
>
> The crowd wanted to break off the huge [embossed] lettering spelling "SZABAD NÉP" ['FREE PEOPLE'] (by that time, they had knocked down a ton of red stars across the city), and when they started, they did not demolish the lettering completely: what they left behind spelled "A NÉP" ['THE PEOPLE']! So the slogan "Free People" turned into: "The People!" This photo is fantastic! Even as a child, I obviously realized the splendor of "the people as a force capable of punishment!" And so I photographed it. And this photo brings out the human nature, the very soul of the entire event: that we were about to demolish what the lying communists had put

204 *Tamás Gergely Kucsera*

there when they spelled out "Free People," and we had already started, and managed half way, when some people from the crowd interjected with, wait, don't destroy the whole thing! Let's leave just enough to spell "THE PEOPLE."[13]

Haris was interviewed by Lajos Szakolczay[14] (marked with "L. Sz." in the next excerpts) on the events following the repression of the Hungarian Revolution of 1956. The artist's answers (marked with "L. H." in the excerpts) offer insight into the psychology of the dictatorship:

L. Sz.   *"It was probably only after [the repression of the Hungarian Revolution] that you developed the pictures."*
L. H.   "Definitely after! Yes".
L. Sz.   *"Were you scared that perhaps you had seen something with your camera that you weren't supposed to see? Especially after November 4!"*
L. H.   "I certainly wasn't so afraid as to not consider it important to have them developed! Since I was a child, and children aren't so aware of their situation, I was less afraid than a more experienced adult would have been – at the same time, I wouldn't claim that I possessed courage enough to laugh in the face of death. . . . I simply considered it important that these photographs be developed. We didn't go to school for a long time: there was a coal break, school probably started sometime at the end of January, so I had plenty of time to develop the photographs and make magnified copies. I probably wasn't that afraid, because once school had started again, I took these pictures with me to school, and as I was wont to do after school excursions, I showed them off in class and gave some copies to my friends".[15]

Haris later recounts destroying the negatives of the photographs he had taken in the days of the Hungarian Revolution of 1956 for fear of political persecution:

L. Sz.   *"Let's talk about your photographs. . . . When and how did you destroy the photographs taken in 1956? Also, where did you hear that you would be in grave danger should these documents be found?"*
L. H.   "My parents knew about the photographs, but they said nothing, they were preoccupied with other things. I entered high school in the fall of 1957. . . and the house searches continued . . . at least they shouldn't find the pictures from 1956. I was still a child back then, but having matured a little during the resistance, I thought it could lead to trouble. . . . So I went – this happened in the fall of 1960 – and took every negative (which I had kept in relatively good condition) and copy I could find – and burned them!"
L. Sz.   *"You were seventeen years old?"*

L. H.	"Yes, seventeen. I graduated in 1961; I was in the fourth grade [of high school]."
L. Sz.	*"And you burned every negative, every copy."*
L. H.	"Yes. More precisely, I thought I had burned all of them. I threw them into the fire, and I saw them burn up with my own eyes! The negatives and the copies, too, to leave no trace of anything. . . . They probably knew everything about me. A bunch of our friends had already gone through the interrogation process, and they instructed us, boys, the way you do it is, you don't try to hide what they already know! If we tell them what they already know, then they will at least believe that we're honest. That is how you have to behave!"[16]

In the 1960s, Haris graduated from the Faculty of Mechanical Engineering at Budapest University of Technology and Engineering, but from the 1970s, he had become a participant of the sometimes "prohibited" and sometimes "tolerated" movements of Hungarian photographers and artists. His repertoire later included animated cinematographic experiments as well.

L. Sz.	*"Let us return to the fact that you later became an artist, and in a sense carried out resistance activities with your photographs. But how did these lost photographs – the photographs you thought had been lost – return to you?"*
L. H.	"This is a very exciting and incredible story comprised of two chapters. The first chapter is basically that sometime in 2000, at home . . . while searching among some old things . . . I discovered two of my pictures from 1956. . . completely by accident!"
L. Sz.	*"The positives?"*
L. H.	"These were not the slides, but the six by nine [centimeter] magnified images, since I did burn the negatives! So there is no hope of finding any of those. But these two copies I found a good forty years after the fact. By that time, I had become a well-known photographer, and the story even inspired an article in *Népszabadság* ['Freedom of the People'] by my friend Zoli [Zoltán] Trencsényi, published around October 23, 2000, maybe exactly on the 23rd! Here I spoke of my experiences from 1956, and how these two copies were discovered by accident, well after the 'burning.' One of the pictures was even published in the newspaper, the photo titled 'THE PEOPLE.' Well, that's when the second 'miracle' occurred. In 2005, I held an exhibition in Kolta Gallery, I was the opening exhibit of the gallery. The miracle took place at the opening. I have mentioned . . . Laci [László] Varga . . . he was a very good friend of mine from high school. I usually send him invitations to my exhibitions, and most of the time he doesn't have time to come, though he does attend occasionally. Well, he did come to attend my exhibition in 2005. . . . Not long after, he called me and said he had heard what

206 *Tamás Gergely Kucsera*

> I said at the opening about the burning of the negatives, and how he had fifteen of my pictures. Madness! First, that he had attended the exhibition at all, and second, that I had forgotten what he remembered perfectly: in 1958 or 1959, he visited us in Szigetvári Street, and together we magnified some of my photographs from 1956 for him. And he had kept them for over fifty years. It was so moving and beautiful, how we were both children, and how much this meant to us! . . . And so the pictures I thought had been lost were found, these are the six by nine [centimeter] paper copies we made with contemporary technology, and which I had reprocessed and fixed the tones."[17]

Regarding his photographs of the events of 1956, Haris said of his artistic self-image, "It is undeniable that I was seriously lacking in terms of technique. But of the fifteen pictures, there are four or five that I wouldn't do any different, even today."[18]

In the past 25 years, the photographs discussed previously have become an integral part of the iconography of the Hungarian Revolution of 1956[19] for depicting human acts of the desire for freedom and demonstrating the art, technique and ability of photography to capture the moment and preserve it in time.

1956 – personal history and a life of art: part two

The Hungarian Revolution of 1956 determined the lives and careers of many artists, including György Szemadám, an artist who lived near one of the centers of the resistance on Széna Square in Budapest. He was an adolescent at the time of the Hungarian Revolution, and in 2012, he composed a free verse titled "Nagy Gáspár emlékének" ["In Memory of Gáspár Nagy"], which is primarily based on the rhythm of thought: while it reads like prose, it is structured like a lyrical composition.

An excerpt from the poem reads as follows:

> But by then we knew:
> we mustn't stop remembering!
> But what?
> Perhaps that during the struggles
> approximately two thousand and five hundred people
> had fallen.
> Item: the number of registered casualties
> was twenty thousand.
> Item: two hundred thousand was the number of those
> who had fled from this country.
> Item: that the prosecutions began,
> and thirteen thousand people were interned.

Item: that more than twenty thousand people were imprisoned.
Item: that of the four hundred death sentences,
approximately two thirds
were executed.
Item: that based on the verdict of hanging judge Ferenc Vida
Imre Nagy, Pál Maléter, and Miklós Gyimes
were murdered on the sixteenth of June in Nineteen Fifty Eight,
and József Szilágyi and Géza Losonczy
were murdered earlier in prison.
Item: that in Nineteen Fifty Nine
they executed eighteen-year-old Péter Mansfeld,
who for thirteen minutes
thrashed in agony on the gallows.
Today he would be seventy-two years old.
Item: that the last execution
was in Nineteen Sixty One.
As Kölcsey had once predicted:
Though in caves pursued he lie,
Even then he fears attacks.
Coming forth the land to spy,
Even a home he finds he lacks . . . [20]

The title of the poem invokes the memory of poet Gáspár Nagy, as does the second line of the excerpt quoted previously: "we mustn't stop remembering!" This line is followed by a literally itemised list of the revolutionary losses of the Hungarian nation and the crimes of dictatorial terror, followed by lines quoted from Ferenc Kölcsey's poem "Himnusz" ["Hymn"] (the national anthem of Hungary today), which refers to national disunity and treason: "Though in caves pursued he lie,/Even then he fears attacks./Coming forth the land to spy,/Even a home he finds he lacks."[21]

In the poem discussed previously, Szemadám used his personal experiences to commemorate a fellow artist as well as his life work. But who was Gáspár Nagy,[22] and which of his poems did Szemadám reference in his own poem?

Gáspár Nagy graduated from the Benedictine High School in Pannonhalma, one of the few religious high schools that managed to remain operational during the communist dictatorship. From 1969, he was placed under observation by the political police, which inspected his mail and intercepted his phone calls. After graduating from higher education, Gáspár Nagy worked as a book editor.

Today, several of Gáspár Nagy's poems are lauded as the spiritual and artistic harbingers of the political system change of 1989 and 1990, such as his 1981 poem "A Fiú naplójából" ["From the Diary of the Boy"], and the 1983 concrete poem "Öröknyár: elmúltam 9 éves" ["Endless Summer: I Turned Nine"]. The English literary translation by American poet Len Roberts reads as follows:

208 *Tamás Gergely Kucsera*

Endless Summer: I Turned Nine
the tomb

       Is Nowhere

the tomb   the murderers

the body   neither HERE

       Is Nowhere

the body   nor THERE

the skeleton   the murderers

       Is Nowhere

the skeleton

       (p. s.)

       sometime he'll need buryINg

       and we mustn't stop rememberINg

       to name those who did the murderINg![23]

From its emergence in ancient history, concrete poetry has been character-ised by the interaction of the subversive spatial arrangement of writing and its contents; in other words, form and content play off each other to create layers of meaning. The capitalised "IN" ("NI" in the Hungarian original) stands for the initials of Prime Minister Imre Nagy, and the title references the date of the execution of Imre Nagy on 16 June 1958, the year the poet had turned 9 years old. According to his memoirs, Gáspár Nagy saw his father and uncle mourn the executed prime minister and his associates, and this experience preserved the memory of that summer day forever: hence, the expression "Endless Sum-mer" in the first half of the title, while the other half, "I Turned Nine," sug-gests the realisation that the child is entering adulthood.[24] Finally, regarding the arrangement or form of the words, this concrete poem is structured around the presence of a gap or lack: neither the remains nor the perpetrators can be found.

The original poem was written in 1983 and published in the October 1984 edition of the literary journal *Új Forrás* ["New Source" or "New Spring", which drew the ire of the Kádár regime upon those involved. The copies of the journal were destroyed, the chief editor was forced to retire, and editor József Sárándi (who maintained even after 1990 that the poem had been published not deliberately, but due to mistaking the poet's meaning) was dismissed from the editorial. As for Gáspár Nagy, he was forced to resign from his position as Secretary of the Hungarian Writers' Association, and after several published volumes, his contract with the publishing company Magvető was terminated. It was only three years later in 1987 that Gáspár Nagy was allowed to publish his volume, with the poem quoted earlier omitted.[25]

Another poem of Gáspár Nagy worth mentioning is "From the Diary of the Boy", which was published in the June 1986 issue of the literary journal *Tiszatáj* ["Tisza Region"], and met the same fate as "Endless Summer". The journal, first published in 1947, was shut down several times in the course of history: between October 1956 and September 1957, publication was halted on account of the Hungarian Revolution of 1956, and in 1986, the journal was banned for six months for the publication of the poem mentioned earlier. The relevant copies of the journal were destroyed, and the editors of the journal were dismissed.

Three more years and the communist regime would collapse, but back in 1986, one would not have guessed it from the reprisals carried out by communist leadership – banning journals, destroying physical copies and dismissing those involved. Although society had shown support for the editors of the journal, many others felt that resistance was futile.

At the beginning of September 1986, the board of the Hungarian Writers' Association issued a carefully scripted letter addressed to the Ministry of Culture, and over two months later, on 12 November, a total of 114 writers issued a more critical letter to the Central Committee and the Hungarian government, which was signed by party members and unaffiliated persons, residents from the regional areas and the capital and younger and older people alike.[26]

The Hungarian Writers' Association held its quinquennial assembly meeting on 29-30 November 1986, in the presence of the representatives of communist leadership, where Gáspár Nagy, who had been punished for the publication of "Endless Summer: I Turned Nine" two years ago, quoted the Second Letter of St Paul to Timothy:[27]

> Preach the word; be instant in season, out of season; reprove, rebuke, exhort with all longsuffering and doctrine. For the time will come when they will not endure sound doctrine; but after their own lusts shall they heap to themselves teachers, having itching ears; and they shall turn away their ears from the truth, and shall be turned unto fables. But watch thou in all things, endure afflictions, do the work of an evangelist, make full proof of thy ministry.
>
> (2 Timothy 4:1–5)

Without the approval of the Ministry of Culture, or rather, the approval of Minister of Culture Béla Köpeczi, the leadership of the Hungarian Writers' Association was not allowed to publish the minutes of the assembly meeting, and journalists could only give heavily censored accounts of these events, but Gáspár Nagy and his fellow writers were right: like the evangelists before them, they "endured afflictions", and their persecutors were eventually punished for their hubris.

In conclusion

The present study aimed to show that from a history of ideas perspective, the Hungarian Revolution of 1956 was considered of extraordinary significance compared to other protests of the 1950s. It is also important to note that in subsequent decades, the only anti-dictatorial movements comparable to the

210   *Tamás Gergely Kucsera*

Hungarian Revolution were the Prague Spring of 1968 and the Polish Solidarity Movement of the 1980s.

We may argue that in 1956, the European left did not exercise self-reflection, at least not on a broad scale, as any attempts to do so were easily marginalised; however, the cracks appearing in the wake of 1956 ultimately shattered the Marxising identity of the left. In the intellectual sense, Aleksandr Solzhenitsyn's 1973 publication of *The Gulag Archipelago* could be considered the final blow.

As discussed earlier, in the communist satellite states neighbouring Hungary, the events of 1956 served as an *apropos* for the marginalisation, provocation and criminalisation of the members and leaders of the local Hungarian minority. Meanwhile, the Hungarian socialist dictatorship, which lasted for over three decades until its collapse in 1989 and 1990, had also been based on the repressed Hungarian Revolution of 1956.

To conclude, let us quote Réka Földváryné Kiss, according to whom the Hungarian Revolution of 1956 was "more than a shared historical experience: it became a universal cultural code on both sides of the Iron Curtain".[28] This explains why on 16 June 1988, on the thirtieth anniversary of the execution of Prime Minister Imre Nagy and at the initiative of the Hungarian emigration, French leadership agreed to dedicate a monument in honour of the former prime minister and his fellow martyrs in Père Lachaise Cemetery, Paris, where the designated plot was donated by the Mayor of Paris, Jacques Chirac. This motion was also supported by a sponsorship composed of 27 Nobel Prize winners and dozens of European parliamentary representatives, including the president of the French Senate, two former French heads of government and renowned writers, scholars and artists such as Eugene Ionesco, Danilo Kiš, Yves Montand and Paul Ricœur. Meanwhile, the commemoration held simultaneously in the center of Budapest was violently broken up by the police.

Under the communist regime, the Hungarian Revolution of 1956 was first labeled as a "counterrevolution" and afterwards treated as taboo until 1988 and 1989, when it was recognised first as a popular insurrection and later as a revolution. On 16 June 1989, the thirty-first anniversary of the execution of Imre Nagy and associates and one year after the unveiling of the monument in Père Lachaise Cemetery, over 100,000 people gathered in Heroes' Square in Budapest to attend the commemoration celebrating the re-burial of the former prime minister and his fellow martyrs. The traumatisation of the Hungarian nation finally came to an end on 23 October 1989, the thirty-third anniversary of the Hungarian Revolution of 1956, when the Hungarian National Assembly convened as a constitutional body to change the form of government from "people's republic" to "republic".

Today, the new world once brought about by the Hungarian Revolution of 1956 and existing for less than two weeks at the time has long become a reality. The year 1956 has given us everything, and now we are the ones who owe it to the glorious past to have a happier future.

Notes

1 Albert Camus, "The Blood of the Hungarians", Letter to the World, 23 October 1957, www.americanhungarianfederation.org/news_coldwarmuseum.htm, accessed 12 March 2020.

2 For more details on the historical and history of ideas aspects of the Hungarian Revolution of 1956, see Tamás Gergely Kucsera, "Nem könnyű méltónak lennünk ennyi áldozathoz. De meg kell kísérelnünk." ["It Would Indeed be Difficult for Us to be Worthy of Such Sacrifices. But We Can Try to be so."], *Magyar Művészet*, 4/4 (2016), 145-152.

3 The original film is available online at the following link: *Ungarn in Flammen* [Hungary in Flames], *YouTube*, 16 January 2011, www.youtube.com/watch?v=uk2mrL2K-xU, accessed 12 March 2020.

4 At 00:24:00, the documentary features changes in the Soviet Union following the death of Stalin; from 00:25:00, it shows the destalinisation processes of Hungarian internal affairs; from 00:26:34, it recounts the return of Gomułka and the changes and revolutionary antecedents in Poland; from 00:27:12, it shows the meeting held at the statue of József Zachariasz Bem, a legendary Polish general of the Hungarian Revolution of 1848 and 1849 (there is a close-up of the statue of Bem at 00:28:05); at 00:27:44, a sign carried by protesters features Bem's name on top; at 00:28:20, we can see the Polish flag carried by protesters in Budapest in support and sympathy of the events in Poland; finally, at 00:40:10, in the section on international support and aid, it features an aid shipment sent from Poland.

5 The original lines, "Az nem lehet hogy annyi szív hiába onta vért." are quoted from "Szózat" [Appeal], a poem written in the 19th century by renowned Hungarian poet Mihály Vörösmarty, which is considered one of the most important poems on Hungarian national unity aside from "Himnusz" [Hymn] by Ferenc Kölcsey. The lyrical translation of "Szózat" by Canadian scholar Watson Kirkconnell can be found here: https://en.wikipedia.org/wiki/Sz%C3%B3zat, accessed 12 March 2020.

6 Literal translation of the Hungarian version quoted in the original article.

7 Stefan Erdélyi, *Ungarn in Flammen* [Hungary in Flames]. Documentary produced by BR Deutschland, 1957, www.filmportal.de/film/ungarn-in-flammen_e82da7ac-d98545798ec856a88c7a61a8, accessed 12 March 2020.

8 In 2018, László Kovács was posthumously elected an honorary member of the Hungarian Academy of Arts. On his life and career, see IMDb, *László Kovács*, www.imdb.com/name/nm0004088/, accessed 12 March 2020.

9 Vilmos Zsigmond passed away in 2016 as a member of the Hungarian Academy of Arts. On his life and career, see IMDb, *Vilmos Zsigmond*, www.imdb.com/name/nm0005936/, accessed 12 March 2020.

10 On *Torn from the Flag*, see the following link: "TORN FROM THE FLAG." Clip from the documentary Torn from the Flag produced by George Adams. *YouTube*, 1 October 2007, www.youtube.com/watch?v=d1o0ZeSzoxk, accessed 12 March 2020.

11 Stephen Farber, "Torn From the Flag", *The Hollywood Reporter*, 1 November 2007, www.hollywoodreporter.com/review/torn-flag-159408, accessed 12 March 2020.

12 László Haris (1943-) is a photographer and a member of the Hungarian Academy of Arts and its Supervisory Board.

13 Lajos Szakolczay, "Jövőkép – gyerekszemmel – Beszélgetés Haris László fotóművésszel" [Vision of the Future - In the Eyes of a Child - An Interview with Photographer László Haris], *Magyar Napló*, XVIII/ 10 (2006), https://sites.google.com/site/mitcsinaltam-56ban/home/03-irodalmi-szakasz/szakolczay-lajos-joevokep-gyerekszemmel, accessed 12 March 2020. The lettering mentioned in the excerpt is the lettering referenced in the present study's analysis of *Ungarn in Flammen*.

14 Lajos Szakolczay (1941-) is a literary historian, literary and art critic, editor and a member of the Hungarian Academy of Arts.

15 Szakolczai, "Jövőkép – gyerekszemmel – Beszélgetés Haris László fotóművésszel".

212 Tamás Gergely Kucsera

16 Ibid.

17 Ibid.

18 Attila Medveczky, "Az értékes fénykép nem ég el" [Valuable Photographs Do Not Burn], *Magyar Fórum*, 19 July 2012, 10.

19 Ernő P. Szabó, *Haris László* [László Haris] (Debrecen: HUNGART, 2013), 12.

20 György Szemadám (1947-) is a painter, arts writer, film director and a member of the Presidium of the Hungarian Academy of Arts. He presented us with a manuscript of his poem "Nagy Gáspár emlékének" [In Memory of Gáspár Nagy], the 2013 version of which was used in the present study, here translated by Éva Misits.

21 The original version and literary translation of Kölcsey's poem can be found here: Ferenc Kölcsey, "Himnusz / Hymn", Babel Web Anthology, www.babelmatrix.org/works/hu/K%C3%B6lcsey_Ferenc-1790/Himnusz/en/21666-Hymn, accessed 12 March 2020.

22 Gáspár Nagy (1949-2007) was a poet, prose writer and editor. He is a posthumous honorary member of the Hungarian Academy of Arts.

23 Gáspár Nagy, "Öröknyár: elmúltam 9 éves" [Endless Summer: I Turned Nine], Poem, 1983, http://nagygaspar.hu/honlap/versek/oroknyar-elmultam-9-eves/?vk=1185, accessed 12 March 2020

24 András Görömbei, "Két rendszerváltó vers" [Two Poems of the System Change], *Új Forrás*, 35/9 (2003), www.jamk.hu/ujforras/030909.htm, accessed 12 March 2020

25 It is interesting to note that at the time of the original publication of the poem, the publishing company was directed by György Kardos (1918-1985). As early as the 1930s, Kardos joined the illegal communist movement, and at the end of World War II, he was liberated as a prisoner of the Theresienstadt Ghetto in Terezín, Protectorate of Bohemia and Moravia, where he had been deported for his Jewish ancestry. Following the end of World War II, he was transferred to military counterintelligence: during the Stalinist Hungarian dictatorship of the 1950s, he was a lieutenant-colonel of the Military Political Department and later the State Protection Authority (the political police). Kardos was responsible for countless political trials and the deaths of countless innocent people, though he himself was later indicted in a trial. He was rehabilitated in 1954, and in 1956, he returned to the armed forces of the Ministry of the Interior to fight against the revolutionaries. Following the communists' rise to power in 1956, he served at Hungarian foreign military intelligence under the Ministry of Defense in the rank of colonel. From 1961, he worked as the director of Magvető Kiadó until his death in 1985.

26 "Közgyűlésen és közgyűlés után" [At and after the Assembly Meeting], *Beszélő*, 19 (1987/1), http://beszelo.c3.hu/cikkek/kozgyulesen-es-kozgyules-utan, accessed 12 March 2020.

27 Géza Vasy, "Júdásfa és maszkabál" [Judas Tree and Masquerade], *Napóra*, 10 (1990), 9-13, http://nagygaspar.hu/honlap/irasok/judasfa-es-maszkabal/, accessed 12 March 2020.

28 Réka Földváryné Kiss, "1956 - Approaches, Interpretations and Unresolved Questions" [1956: Symbolism, Emphasis, Interpretations], in *European Remembrance: Lectures, Discussions, Commentaries, 2012-16* (Symposium of European Institutions Dealing with 20th-century History.) (Warsaw: European Network Remembrance and Solidarity, 2012), 195-203, https://enrs.eu/uploads/media/5c24d0cfe97c6-european-remembrance-2012-16.pdf, accessed 12 March 2020.

17 Pictures for the Fathers: Baselitz's *Heldenbilder* as anti-images of the socialist and fascist body

Justyna Balisz-Schmelz

This chapter focuses on Georg Baselitz's celebrated series of pictures titled *Hero Paintings* (*Heldenbilder*), from 1965 to 1966. *Heldenbilder*'s exceptional quality and enduring relevance would appear to reside in the sharp contrast between the simple, almost classical compositions, each with a centrally placed, grotesquely deformed male figure, painted with traditional (even "regressive", according to some critics[1]) formal means, and the enormous interpretative potential. The multiplicity of formal and thematic references inherent in these pictures creates an extensive semantic layer where autobiographical motifs are carefully interwoven with social, political and cultural threads.

Moreover, all these aspects converge within the image of the body, which testifies to the artist's truly ingenious intuition, since his visual arguments found theoretical confirmation only a decade later, in the aftermath of 1968 and its events, when critical reflection on the body and its various determinants gained new formulations.[2]

At the same time, the body is also the most immediate medium of memory. The corporeality of memory reveals itself both on the level of the individual, psychological context of remembering and forgetting, as well as within social and cultural processes.[3] It was Friedrich Nietzsche who first transferred the memory of the body from an individual to a collective level. He described the mechanisms of the oppressive cultural practices that sought to implant socially approved normative principles in citizens' minds.[4] The Foucauldian conception of the embodiment of power structures derives directly from the Nietzschean project of genealogy. Following Nietzsche's arguments, Foucault claimed that it was the body that most fully reflected history. The body is inherently marked by the individual's personal past, as well as – and this is the groundbreaking aspect of this concept – by the past of his or her ancestors.

Foucault believed that the individual's ancestry was manifested in the minutest aspects of their physical existence – in their *habitus*, external appearance and physiology. The body is, then, a historically formed being and cannot be construed without reference to memory, both individual and collective.[5]

The ongoing relevance of the *Heldenbilder* series for both dimensions of memory seems confirmed by Georg Baselitz's recent dialogue with Alexander Kluge.[6] Significantly, Kluge and Baselitz represent the same generation,

DOI: 10.4324/9781003264460-20

214 *Justyna Balisz-Schmelz*

which Aleida Assmann defined as the "generation of children of war". Assmann claims that "every generation carries its own history in its bones, emanates it, confronts it, goes through a lifetime of challenging it in a variety of ways".[7] The "generation of the children of war" shares a difficult, often traumatic childhood, during which its representatives witnessed bombings, displacements and mass migrations. According to Assmann, it is a generation that would constitute the avant-garde of new forms of the commemoration of war. She calls them the older brothers and sisters of the 1968 generation. In spite of increasing politicisation, many of them remained unadjusted intellectuals – a phenomenon which seems to be borne out in the figure of Baselitz.[8]

Baselitz was born in 1938 as Hans Georg Kern, in the village of Deutschbaselitz (Němske Pazlicy), located in Upper Lusatia. In the early 1990s, he recalled the events from the end of the war when the school building where his family lived was completely ruined, while thousands of refugees from Poland moved through the village. Soon they were joined by Baselitz's family as well.[9] This personal experience shaped Baselitz's extreme individualism and his distinct ideological attitude, manifested in his distrust of all comprehensive political programmes. This nonconformist approach had an impact on his subsequent life choices and on developments in his painting: his decision to leave East Germany and then – when he was living in the West – his opposition to the modernist paradigm that dominated in West Germany at the time.[10]

In Kluge's reading, Baselitz's *Heroes* are epitomes of the *signum temporis*, a *pars pro toto* of the period between 1945 and 1965. Even though Baselitz does not depict any specific individuals, Kluge finds his figures rather familiar, yet impossible to identify. They are familiar merely in evocative terms, as – to apply the crucial term – embodiments of a certain "rule", as Kluge puts it, which determines their existential grounding.[11]

Taking Kluge's remark as a hint, I would like to consider how the pictorial convention used by Baselitz could be read as an attempt to position himself and his whole generation in reference to history. What kind of effect does Baselitz achieve by making his *Heroes* conceptual vehicles of post-war reality, an embodied meaning that links retrospection with prospection?[12]

Let me cite at this point, somewhat surprisingly, the Polish artist Tadeusz Kantor. After his return from Paris in 1947, he wrote as follows:

> The image of man previously considered the only truthful image is gone. . . . This act of the deformation of classic beauty did not take place in aesthetics. It was the war and the time of the "lords of the world" that made me and many others lose our faith in this old image. . . . I remember how reluctant and coldly indifferent I was looking at all those images of the human body that cover museum walls, glancing at me innocently, as if nothing had ever happened.[13]

Kantor was writing around the time when Germany, plagued by the postwar crisis of representation, was witnessing the "debate about human images", sparked partly by the controversial Austrian art historian Hans Sedlmayr's 1948 publication *Verlust der Mitte*.[14]

That discussion peaked with the public debate that took place at the Darmstädter Stadthalle on 15–17 September 1950. It brought together major intellectuals and artists (e.g. Johannes Itten, Theodor W. Adorno, Willi Baumeister, Hans Sedlmayr, Alexander Mitscherlich). The frontline ran between the small camp of the advocates of Sedlmayr's restorative ambitions and the propagators of abstract internationalism. Moreover, the debate was accompanied by an art exhibition showcased under the telling title *Das Menschenbild in unserer Zeit* (*The Image of Man in Our Times*).[15] Hans Belting suggests that this "debate about the human image" was merely a pretext for a new discussion about the urgent problems concerning the definition of culture: "Is culture in any sense capable of reinvigorating the annihilated image of man?" asks Belting, leaving the question open.[16]

The Darmstadt debate marks the final moment in the Manichean clash of different visions of art in post-war Germany. In the West, figurative painting would soon disappear almost completely, and the human figure was disembodied and reduced to the spiritual dimension, while in the East, ideologically driven realism served to illustrate party slogans, including the production of model representations of the prototype of the "new man". Several paintings from the *Heldenbilder* series are titled *The New Type* (*Der Neue Typ*), which seem to echo the debates that engaged the party leaders of East Germany in the mid-1950s.[17]

On 15 November 1952, *Neues Deutschland* published a keynote article by Walter Besenbruch in which he specified the party's guidelines regarding the "typicality of art". This text defines the notion of realism and the characteristics of the new "positive hero".

According to these formulations, realism means not so much the faithful representation of the superficial image of things, but the "actual" representation, that is such that provides a reflection of the ideology of the party. It is not the facts that matter, since the party hierarchy of values dismisses facts in favour of a monopolised higher "truth" to which one should aspire. This "truth" should be reflected in art in a canonised form, manifested in the rule of "typicality":

> Typical is not what is most common, typical is not something ordinary, but a prefiguration of the normative shaping of the "being"; a positive hero is not an embodiment of an actual person but represents the catalogue of his perfect qualities.[18]

The year 1957, in which Baselitz left East Germany after he was dismissed from the Academy for "socio-political immaturity",[19] was marked by the uprising in Hungary and the echoes of the so-called *Picasso Debatte*.[20] It was also a year of repressions against the advocates of cultural reform. A year later, the relatively liberal Minister of Culture Johannes Becher was removed from the political scene, supplanted by an apostle of ideological orthodoxy – Alfred

216 *Justyna Balisz-Schmelz*

Kurella. In July 1957, Kurella stated: "Among some East German art theorists and artists it has become fashionable to deny that decadence is a tendency that destroys culture. . . . Numerous theorists only confirm this decline, annihilating the classic image of man".[21]

Kurella's arguments drew extensively on the theories of *Entartung*. It is possible, therefore, that his intellectual development was heavily influenced by the writings of his father – the psychologist Hans Kurella, who wrote under the sway of Cesare Lambroso, whose concepts were adopted by Max Nordau.[22] As a young man, Alfred Kurella wrote articles in which he addressed the issues of body and soul: "We should not practise the propaganda of souls but create bodies where the soul can find a home".[23] It was only a body fit to host a socialist soul that could become a building block of the desired collective. Representation of the body in public discourse was based on unification and designed to express the idea of the "new man" as an embodiment of the idea of a perfect, classless society.

The project of the "new man" seems to fully manifest the totalitarian nature of the two systems – communism and Nazism.[24] Both regimes strove to represent not so much a real body, but its constructed image, which suggested the way it was to be perceived. Both made a distinction between reality and "truth", where art was meant to serve "truth" rather than reality, defined by the party and its forcefully implemented ideology.[25]

Much like the communist propaganda, the Nazi propaganda sought to represent "types", exemplary figures of Germans, rather than images of particular individuals. In the Third Reich, the model of the "perfect body" became universalised and developed into a required model for all Germans, with its general aspects defined by the category of race. Individual bodies served to create the collective body, the *Volkskörper*, which, as Boaz Naumann persuasively shows, should be understood in terms of an actual being, rather than a metaphor.[26] The ontology of the *Volkskörper* was based on the construction of opposite identities, where the Other, the Jew, was the vehicle of the *Fremdskörper*. In those binary terms, *Fremdskörper* was a hotbed of dirt, disease and corruption, which posed a threat to the health and integrity of the *Volkskörper* and therefore should be destroyed. The racial difference was embodied, while the obsessive investment in the body served to highlight the difference and make it evident.[27]

Moreover, for Hitler, the Arian body was the carrier of culture,[28] which required its biological and sexual aspect to be set aside and made invisible. Subversively, exactly these features are monstrously exaggerated in Baselitz's pictures: the bodies of the *Heroes* with ostentatiously displayed phalluses appear as pure carnality that has got out of control.

Sexuality and perversion were qualities ascribed to the Other (communists, Jews). Their bodies were carnal, lecherous, and even animal-like, while the Arian body was construed as a disciplined body, with its enemy and antithesis in the form of a discordant body driven by needs and desires. The *Soldatischer Mann* (man-soldier) continuously trained his body, to prevent it falling under the sway of base instincts: carnality, physical drives and pain.

Figure 17.1 Georg Baselitz, *The Modern Painter*, 1965
Source: oil on canvas, 162 × 130 cm, Städel Museum, Frankfurt. © Georg Baselitz 2020

All that effort was taken to conceal one fundamental, cruel truth, that, in fact: "The major objective and effect of war is that it leaves wounds" – literally, "The transformation (by burning, destruction, chopping, cutting) of human tissue".[29] It is not the ecstatic elation experienced when the enemy is defeated, but the bitter and painful reality of the suffering, lethally wounded, torn or

Figure 17.2 Georg Baselitz, *The Shepherd*, 1966

Source: photo by Jochen Littkemann, Berlin; oil on canvas, 162 x 130 cm, Museum Frieder Burda, Baden-Baden. © Georg Baselitz 2020

handicapped, but always deformed, body which is the fundamental experience of the participants of armed conflicts.

The wound is also one of the most striking themes in *Heldenbilder*. Not only the hands of the figures are bleeding, but also the broken tree branches (*Der Baum*, 1966); some of the men are one-legged invalids, dressed in torn rags that

Picture for the Fathers 219

Figure 17.3 Georg Baselitz, *Economy*, 1965

Source: photo by Jochen Littkemann, Berlin; oil on canvas, 162 x 130 cm, private collection. © Georg Baselitz 2020

used to be an army uniform (*Versperrter Maler*, 1965). After the war, the misshapen bodies of veterans posed a serious social problem, as well as constituting a permanent cultural phenomenon of the post-war landscape, epitomised by the figure of the *Heimkehrer*, returning from the front in rags, often physically handicapped.[30]

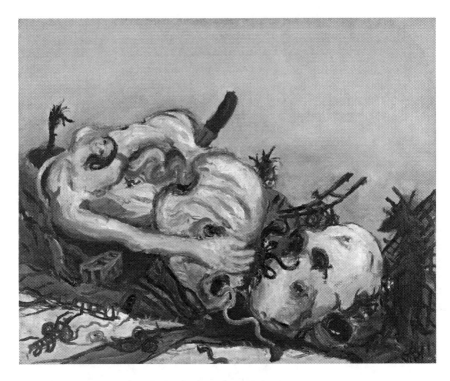

Figure 17.4 Georg Baselitz, *Picture for the Fathers*, 1965
Source: oil on canvas, 50 x 65 cm, Moderna Museet, Stockholm. © Georg Baselitz 2020

The image of the *Heimkehrer* was soon replaced with its positive pendant in the form of the iconic *Trümmerfrau* (woman of ruins). The experience of the war differed according to gender; women, in contrast to men, who carried the burden of their military past, fought mainly on the home front, so they were not blamed and could be made to work as symbols of the positive renewal. A deeper goal of this new symbol was to fill in the representational void that remained after the dismissal of "military images of National Socialism".[31] From this perspective, the "male-centrism" of Baselitz's pictures, as it was defined by some feminist critics,[32] suddenly gains a much more nuanced meaning.

As I attempted to show earlier, both Nazi and communist propaganda sought not so much to depict actual people, but to construct images of the model "new man". Both "political religions" drew these ideas from the Bible (*kainòs anthropos* in Greek, *homo novus* in Latin), secularising their meaning, so that the "new man" was now not born after death through salvation, but shaped here, on earth, by the new society.[33] Their images were not faithful portraits but vehicles of the one and only rightful ideological "truth", which was the foundation of both the Nazi and the Soviet doctrine of renewal. As Boaz Naumann argued in reference to the *Volkskörper*, in the fascist view, the metaphor was never merely a metaphor, but an actual existence, which formed certain rules that had their tangible, often tragic consequences, which could be observed and felt in real life.

It seems, then, that with his apparently random remark that although figures in Baselitz's paintings are not portraits of particular people, they still exist as a "rule", which finds its equivalent in reality, Kluge identified their crucial aspect. Baselitz appropriates the mode of representation of totalitarian states (as suggested by titles such as *Der Neue Typ*), at the same time denouncing it. By investing his "heroes" with all the features associated with "otherness", he constructs them as perfect antitheses of the fascist and socialist bodies, their tragicomic caricatures, embodied commentaries on the regime's phantasm of the "new man". His anti-hero is somehow alien to himself, his body is out of control, becoming its own "other" (undisciplined, monstrous, grotesque, sexual, disarmed, alienated from the unity of the collective), which cannot be simply rejected with a race- or class-based sense of superiority but needs to be considered.

The German sociologist Bernhard Giesen distinguished the debatable category of the trauma of perpetrators (*Tätertrauma*).[34] He claimed that trauma comes not only from the experience of war, but also from the sudden, enforced confrontation with one's own conscience, which, in turn, requires the restructuring of the previous normative system.[35] The trauma of perpetrators brings emotions such as shame, a sense of failure or a loss of self-esteem.[36] In such cases, psychological hygiene necessitates integrating the guilt with identity,[37] which is itself a long-term project, sometimes stretching into future generations.

As Klaus Theweleit argues: "When I observed my father and his circle, I saw that they were not Nazis 'ideologically', they were not 'intellectually' capable of repeating the Nazi nonsense or defending it. They were Nazis corporeally".[38] Therefore, it is not surprising that as soon as the ideological corset imposed on the body bursts, all the mental and psychological structures crumble.

What also collapses is the shaky balance of the outside world, with the "new man" as its measure and lawmaker. The body, previously treated as a unified, coherent, total and integrated armour for the self, suddenly becomes dismembered and shattered, as in Baselitz's paintings. This violates its superficial nature, baring, in this process of quasi-therapeutic gutting, the social taboo, and doing so in the wake of the events of 1968.[39]

Insistent in its monstrosity, the intensely corporeal presence of the protagonists of these paintings reveals the body in its biological, biographical, political and cultural dimension, as an expression of the bankrupt idea of humanism, which calls for revision. The pictures from the *Heldenbilder* series are thus both reflections on the *condition humana* and complex meditations on the *condition humanitas*. Thus, in Baselitz's paintings, the bodies of his protagonists work – as Sigrid Weigel would put it – as "the space of displacement and symbolization" and therefore as a vehicle of collective memory.[40]

222 Justyna Balisz-Schmelz

Notes

1 See Benjamin H. D. Buchloh, "Figures of Authority, Ciphers of Regression: Notes on the Return of Representation in European Painting", *October*, 16 (1981), 39–68.
2 Michel Foucault, *Discipline and Punish. The Birth of the Prison*, trans. Alan Sheridan (New York: Pantheon Books, 1977); Klaus Theweleit, *Male Fantasies: Psychoanalysing the White Terror*, trans. Erica Carter and Chris Turner (Minneapolis: University of Minnesota, 1989). See also Jacek Kaczmarek and Marek Krajewski, "Wcielona rewolucja" [The Embodied Revolution], in *Rewolucje 1968* [Revolutions 1968], ed. Hanna Wróblewska (Warsaw: Zachęta, 2008), 43–47.
3 See Justyna Balisz, "Ciało" [The Body], in *Modi memorandi. Leksykon kultury pamięci* [*Modi memorandi*: A Lexicon of the Culture of Memory], ed. Magdalena Saryusz-Wolska and Robert Traba (Warsaw: Scholar, 2014), 73–79.
4 Friedrich Nietzsche, *On the Genealogy of Morality*, trans. Carol Diethe (Cambridge: Cambridge University Press, 2007).
5 Michel Foucault, "Nietzsche, Genealogy, History", in *The Foucault Reader*, ed. Paul Rabinow (New York: Pantheon, 1984), 76–100.
6 Georg Baselitz and Alexander Kluge, *Weltverändernder Zorn: Nachricht von den Gegenfüßlern* (Frankfurt am Main: Suhrkamp, 2017).
7 Aleida Assmann, "Verkörperte Geschichte – zur Dynamik der Generationen", in *Geschichte im Gedächtnis: von der individuellen Erfahrung zur Öffentlichen Inszenierung* (Munich: Beck, 2007), 55.
8 Ibid., 31–67.
9 Georg Baselitz, "Reden über Deutschland. Derneburg. Oktober 1992", in *Bilder denkt man sich aus, man holt sie nicht von draußen. Manifeste und Texte zur Kunst 1966–2001* (Bern: Gachnang & Springer, 2001), 53.
10 Götz Adriani, "Unterwegs zum Gegen-Stand", in *Baselitz. 50 Jahre Malerei*, ed. Götz Adriani (Ostfildern: Hatje Cantz, 2009), 25.
11 "Diskussion mit Georg Baselitz und Alexander Kluge", Haus der Kunst, Munich [video], *YouTube* (recorded 8 December 2016, uploaded 31 January 2017), www.youtube.com/watch?v=jS5TnADQ_ic., accessed 12 July 2019.
12 Baselitz's paintings can be also read as visually anticipating the debate on the advent of the era of post-heroism which has been ongoing in Germany since the mid 2000s. See Herfried Münkler, "Heroische und postheroische Gesellschaften", *Merkur. Zeitschrift für europäisches Denken*, 61 (2007), 742–752.
13 Cited in Piotr Piotrowski, *Znaczenia modernizmu. W stronę historii sztuki polskiej po 1945 roku* [Meanings of Modernism: Towards a History of Polish art after 1945] (Poznań: Rebis, 2011), 27–28.
14 Hans Sedlmayr, *Verlust der Mitte: die Bildende Kunst des 19. und 20. Jahrhunderts als Symptom und Symbol der Zeit* (Salzburg: Otto Müller, 1948).
15 Clea Catharina Laade, *Die Ausstellung Das Menschenbild in unserer Zeit und das erste Darmstädter Gespräch* (Berlin: Logos, 2016).
16 Hans Belting, *Identität im Zweifel. Ansichten der deutschen Kunst* (Cologne: Dumont, 1999), 185.
17 Moreover, the fourth issue of the East German art magazine *Bildende Kunst*, from 1957, was dedicated to the problem of typicality in art.
18 Cited in Eckhart Gillen, *Das Kunstkombinat DDR. Zäsuren einer gescheiterten Kunstpolitik* (Cologne: Dumont Verlag, 2005), 65.
19 "Georg Baselitz im Gespräch mit Heinz Peter Schwerfel", in *Ausgebürgert. Künstler aus der DDR und aus dem Sowjetischen Sektor Berlins 1949–1989*, ed. Werner Schmidt (Berlin: Argon, 1991), 21.
20 See Piotr Bernatowicz, "Picasso behind the Iron Curtain: From the History of the Postwar Reception of Pablo Picasso in East-Central Europe", in *Art beyond Borders: Artistic*

Picture for the Fathers   223

Exchange in Communist Europe (1945–1989), ed. Jérôme Bazin, Piotr Piotrowski and Pascal Dubourg Glatigny (Budapest: Central European University Press, 2016)

21 In Gillen, *Das Kunstkombinat*, 82.

22 In his 1892 book *Entartung* ("Degeneration"), Max Nordau attacked what he believed to be degenerate art and commented on the effects of rapid urbanisation and its negative impact on the human body.

23 Cited in Gillen, *Das Kunstkombinat*, 81–82.

24 See Gerd Koenen, *Utopie der Säuberung. Was war der Kommunismus?* (Berlin: Alexander Fest, 2000).

25 See Boris Groys, *The Total Art of Stalinism. Avant-Garde, Aesthetic Dictatorship, and Beyond*, trans. Charles Rougle (Princeton: Princeton University Press, 1992).

26 Boaz Neumann, "The Phenomenology of the German People's Body (*Volkskörper*) and the Extermination of the Jewish Body", *New German Critique*, 106 (2009), 149–181.

27 Ibid.

28 Rosa Sala Rose, *Krytyczny słownik mitów i symboli nazizmu* [Critical Dictionary of the Myths and Symbols of Nazism] (Warsaw: Sic!, 2006), 41.

29 Elaine Scarry, *The Body in Pain: The Making and Unmaking of the World* (Oxford: Oxford University Press, 1985), 64.

30 Elena Agazzi and Erhard H. Schütz, eds., *Heimkehr: Eine zentrale Kategorie der Nachkriegszeit. Geschichte, Literatur und Medien* (Berlin: Duncker & Humboldt, 2010).

31 Elisabeth D. Heinemann, "The Hour of the Woman: Memories of Germany's 'Crisis Years' and the West German National Identity", *The American Historical Review*, 2 (1996), 356.

32 See Lisa Saltzman, "Our Fathers, Ourselves: Icarus, Kiefer and the Burdens of History", in *Anselm Kiefer and the Art after Auschwitz* (Cambridge: Cambridge University Press, 2000), 38–54.

33 Sabine A. Haring, "Der Neue Mensch im Nationalsozialismus und Sowjetkommunismus", www.bpb.de/apuz/233462/der-neue-mensch-im-nationalsozialismus-und-sowjetkommunismus?p=all, accessed 20 November 2017.

34 Bernhard Giesen and Christoph Schneider, eds., *Tätertrauma. Nationale Erinnerungen im öffentlichen Diskurs* (Konstanz: UVK Verlagsgesellschaft, 2004), 22.

35 Cf. Margarete and Alexander Mitscherlich, *Die Unfähigkeit zu trauern. Grundlagen kollektiven Verhaltens* (Munich: R. Piper & Co., 1967).

36 Aleida Assmann, *Der lange Schatten der Vergangenheit: Erinnerungskultur und Geschichtspolitik* (Munich: Beck, 2006), 97.

37 Ibid., 112.

38 Klaus Theweleit, "Posłowie" [Afterword], in Littell, *Suche i wilgotne* [Dry and damp], 128.

39 Notably, in 1965, at the same time as the *Heldenbilder* series, Baselitz painted a prophetic picture titled *Painting for the Fathers* (*Bild für die Väter*).

40 Sigrid Weigel, *Bilder des kulturellen Gedächtnisses. Beiträge zur Gegenwartsliteratur* (Tende: Dülmen-Hiddingsel, 1994), 50.

18 The everyday life in the GDR in individual, cultural and political memory

Maria Khorolskaya

After the reunification of Germany, the united country faced the question of assessing the past of the GDR. The government and part of the public tried not to repeat the mistake which was made with the history of the Third Reich, whose crimes and criminals were ignored for a very long time. However, an attempt to transfer experience in rethinking the past of the Reich to work on rethinking the history of the GDR led to contradictions and to dissatisfaction among the citizens. To better understand the strong disagreements over the past of East Germany, we refer to the methodology of Aleida Assmann, who identifies several types of memory: individual, social and collective. The dividing line between individual and social memory is blurred. A person combines private experience with the memory of previous generations. At the same time, every person is influenced by historical events, and individual memory is formed within the framework of generational and social memory. Collective memory, according to Assmann, is not memory in the universally recognised sense of the word. It is a convention of what and how to remember, backed by visual images.

Assmann divides collective memory into political and cultural memory. Both are important ways of constructing national identity. However, the former is of a unified nature; it seeks to endorse a single interpretation, which is reinforced by political institutions. Political memory is realised on the political level. Methods for establishing an official understanding of history are called the "politics of memory". Cultural memory receives a new interpretation with every individual appeal to it.[1]

In the first decade after reunification (during the process of disputes between political parties), mechanisms of the politics of memory in relation to the history of the GDR on the scientific level were formed.[2] In particular, two commissions (*Enquete-Kommissionen*) were convened, and the Federal Foundation for the Study of Communist Dictatorship in East Germany was founded. The main result of this period was the official definition of the political regime of the GDR as a dictatorship.[3]

On the recommendation of the second commission, in 1999, the Concept of Future Federal Support for Memory Places was launched. This guaranteed 50% state funding for memorials of federal significance.[4]

DOI: 10.4324/9781003264460-21

The everyday life in the GDR in memory   225

In 1999, 11 memorials received state support: four of them were dedicated to the Nazi past, three had dual significance, two addressed the division of Germany (the Bernauer Strasse memorial and the Medlar Museum) and two were devoted to persecution by the SED regime (the Stasi prison Berlin-Hohenschönhausen and places of memory devoted to the camps in Bautzen and Torgau).[5] So memorials reflecting the history of the GDR were devoted to the problem of repression and crimes on the border between the two German states (especially at the Berlin Wall).

This interpretation of the history of the GDR caused dissatisfaction among East Germans, due to both the essential causes and the subjective mistakes of the politics of memory.

Political memory, striving for an unambiguous conception, came into conflict with the diverse memory of witnesses, including robust critics of the SED regime, people seeking to reform the GDR, those who believed that not everything was bad, others who longed for stability, etc. The picture constructed by politics of memory will never be complete enough to reflect the experience of all witnesses.[6]

At the same time, mistakes were also made. The East Germans were dissatisfied with the fact that West Germans, who often showed considerable arrogance, were engaged in rethinking the history of the GDR. Native East Germans had the impression that West Germans considered them incapable of evaluating their lives in the GDR.[7] Former citizens of the GDR heard that they lived in a lawless state and it was nearly their own fault.[8] Of course, this brought them together in a community of solidarity, which was previously inconceivable. At the same time, even former East German oppositionists could not criticise the past and present of West Germany on equal terms.[9]

Because the themes of repression and Stasi supervision came to dominate political memory, the fate of ordinary citizens, who were neither functionaries of the regime nor oppositionists, was passed over in the history of East Germany.

According to sociological surveys, the majority of the population of the new federal states did not agree with the presentation of certain aspects of life in East Germany. In particular, most respondents claimed that work, kindergartens and nurseries, health care, social security, relations between people and education in the GDR were actually better than reported in the media. Fifty-seven per cent of East Germans and only 25% of West Germans said that the GDR was far better than bad.[10]

Differences in perceptions of the GDR persist even among generations born after reunification, because they can enrich their personal experience through the experience of others.[11] The perceptions of the generation born after the fall of the Berlin Wall are formed both through information transmitted by the media and educational institutions, and also through social memory – the accounts of their older relatives. According to sociological surveys, the fact that the GDR was a dictatorship was confirmed by two-thirds of western and fewer than half of eastern pupils.[12]

226 *Maria Khorolskaya*

Thus, while historical politics in the 1990s formed a negative image of the GDR, shared by the majority of West Germans, many East Germans (81.3%) associated East Germany with positive memories.[13] The memories of former citizens of the GDR, not reflected in the official picture of East Germany, were expressed in culture.

Interest in the culture of the GDR was dubbed "ostalgie". This notion, formed from the words "ost" (East) and "nostalgie", in the broad sense means longing, nostalgia for the GDR, and narrowly means the desire to preserve in one's memory the elements of a socialist past that are important for an individual person, first and foremost memories of everyday life. This phenomenon began to take shape after reunification, peaked in the early 2000s, then began to decline, but it still persists today.

In the arts, this phenomenon was manifested most strongly in literature. Various illustrations of the GDR theme, some of them critical, are present in the works of such writers as Jens Sparschuh, Ingo Schulze, Christa Wolf, Thomas Brussig, Jana Henzel and Uwe Tellkamp. The significant influence of the topic of the GDR on literature is demonstrated by the results of the yearly German Book Prize, whose prize-winners have often highlighted this aspect in their books.

In cinema, many films are devoted to the past of East Germany. The most popular and significant of them are Leander Haussman's *Sonnenallee* (1999), which was accused of idealising the past, and Wolfgang Becker's *Good Bye Lenin!* (2003), which analysed "ostalgie".

There is a trade in everyday objects from the GDR, above all in tourist shops (Rotkäppchen sparkling wine, Ampelmännchen, Trabant cars (Trabi), etc.).

The historical gap that arose from the one-sided reflection on the GDR past has been filled by private museums. The most famous is the interactive Museum of the GDR in Berlin. Lesser-known museums include the GDR Time Travel Museum in Dresden, Museum of GDR Products in Erfurt and Trabi Museum in Berlin.[14] The displays in such museums are chronologically arranged and have few explanatory texts. The exhibits are meant to create a nostalgic atmosphere.

"Ostalgia" is criticised by West German politicians, as well as former East German dissidents, who claim that the regime's dictatorial essence may be lost behind the facade of everyday joys. However, it seems that "ostalgia" is a more complex phenomenon than an attempt to "whiten the dictatorship".

In this regard, it seems useful to analyse one example of an "ostalgia" store-museum in Berlin: VEB-Orange. Its owner, Mario S., kindly agreed to a brief interview.

At first sight, the store-museum looks like a very impressive cornucopia of objects. They are grouped according to form, purpose or even colour. There are items from the past of various countries – GDR, FRG and USSR – so Mario S. does not consider his store-museum to be a "museum of ostalgia". At present, however, the bulk of goods and exhibits are from East Germany.

The everyday life in the GDR in memory   227

Most objects can be bought, although rarer exhibits are not for sale. There are no explanatory texts.

The owner of the store-museum was born in 1974 in GDR (Karl-Marx-Stadt, now Chemnitz, in Saxony). He opened VEB-Orange in 2005. The products are in demand among foreign tourists and Germans alike. Most visitors give a positive assessment of his store-museum, but a couple of times a year he is criticised for displaying items bearing the symbols of the GDR.

Mario S. himself does not think that the presentation of everyday life in East Germany is "whitewashing a dictatorship". He is critical of the official interpretation of the history of the GDR in modern Germany. In his opinion, the media are reducing the past of the GDR to the Stasi and the Berlin Wall, while "it was something more – a different system, a different society". Mario believes that life in East Germany was simpler – "there was no need to choose from a variety of sorts or between different health insurances". Regarding reunification, Mario S. considers: "I would not want to reverse the reunification, but I don't feel good in a united Germany".[15]

This interview does not claim to be universal; however, in conjunction with published analysis and interviews,[16] some conclusions can be drawn. "Ostalgia" is not connected with a desire to return to the GDR. Moreover, as in the example of VEB-Orange, it allows people to make a profit in the capitalist system. In this regard, it is useful to turn to the concept of researchers Thomas Ahbe and Dominic Boyer, which argues that "ostalgia" helps East Germans to find their identity and shed the status of "second-class" citizens.[17] Nostalgia for the GDR is explained by the disappointment of some East Germans in the united Germany; it is an indirect criticism of the present through comparison with an idealised past. Another factor is the desire to reflect the entire complexity of the history of the GDR, and the "defensive reaction" of some East Germans to "belittling personal achievements in their lives".[18] "Ostalgia" is associated with each individual desire to prevent the past from falling into oblivion. Finally, for many, memories of the GDR are memories of youth and childhood.

Thus, political memory and the reflection of the GDR in cultural memory began to develop in two different directions. The former developed the themes of Stasi persecution and the German-German border and represents the history of the "culprits-victims"; the latter focused on everyday life. This discrepancy may have contributed to the revision of the politics of memory.

A milestone in the development of the politics of memory was the work undertaken in 2005–2006 by the Sabrow Commission, named after its chair, the historian Martin Sabrow, comprising scholars, historians and former members of the civil resistance of the GDR. In 2006, the commission issued a report, which criticised, on the one hand, the tendency in the mass media and society to trivialise and whitewash the SED regime, and, on the other hand, the predominance of the theme of repression in political memory, while the themes of opposition, society and everyday life remained underrepresented.[19] The committee's proposals aroused widespread criticism.

228   *Maria Khorolskaya*

But in 2008, after a proposal from Bernd Neumann (CDU), the Federal Government's Commissioner for Culture and the Media, a new memorial concept was developed: "Take responsibility. Strengthen research. Enhance memory". In this concept, memorials were grouped into four main categories, along the lines of the Sabrow Commission's recommendations: "division and borders", "surveillance and persecution", "everyday life in the GDR" and "opposition to the dictatorship of the SED".[20]

The development of the first two topics did not display any significant changes in comparison with the document from 1999. The topic of resistance received more attention.

The main difference was the thematic block of everyday life in the GDR. However, in this context, "everyday life" was not a reflection of another aspect of reality but an expansion of the research field of the theme of repression and dictatorship. The main aim of this theme was "to resist the whitewashing and trivialisation of the dictatorship of the SED and 'ostalgie'".[21]

The new theoretical positions were realised in the displays of the German Historical Museum and the Centre for the Documentation of Everyday Culture in the GDR. The Forum of Contemporary History in Leipzig added such aspects as everyday life and biographical materials of normal citizens to its permanent displays devoted to "dictatorship, resistance and civil courage". In 2010, the permanent display of the DDR Museum in Berlin was supplemented with information on the dictatorship of the SED and the Stasi and reconstructions of the Ministry of State Security's interrogation room and a prison cell. Also the "Palace of Tears" (Tränenpalast) memorial devoted to the separation of relatives from East and West Germany at the station and a long-term exhibition on everyday life in the GDR at the Berlin Kulturbrauerei cultural centre were created by the Haus der Geschichte der Bundesrepublik Deutschland Foundation. Here I will focus in particular on this last exhibition.

In contrast to most private museums, the Kulturbrauerei gives plenty of texts (explanatory notes, audio guide), to minimise the possibility of ambiguous interpretation of the exhibits. The main objective of the display is to show how the SED dictatorship influenced everyday life in the GDR; consequently, all manifestations of everyday life are shown through the prism of dictatorship. On the theoretical level, we can single out several key topics that contribute to the development of this idea.

First, the display shows the SED's direct forms of control over society: the brutal suppression of the 1953 uprising, the fight against dissidents, the activities of the Stasi, which included wiretapping, searches and arrests.

Second, the section on "The Rhythm of the Collective" explores the indirect influence of the party on citizens through collective practices. The role of the explanatory texts is heightened in this section, because (unlike the stories of Stasi victims) these objects are more open to interpretation. One of the stands is dedicated to the organising of leisure activities at public enterprises, which might be positively assessed by visitors. However, the explanatory text and the audio guide explain that the organisation of leisure was aimed at exerting

The everyday life in the GDR in memory   229

control over the free time of citizens, their thoughts and conversations, and also to form a sense of the collective. Stands dedicated to kindergartens and nurseries inform visitors about the public education system. Theoretically, this phenomenon could be assessed in various ways (from a positive assessment, as the emancipation of women, to criticism from conservatives for the destruction of the traditional family). In this case, the audio guide evaluates kindergartens and nurseries as a means to satisfy the economy's need for female labour and to raise children in the spirit of collectivism and socialism. The baby-stroller for six children, according the audio guide, prepared children to "live as part of a group".[22]

Another approach is to reflect the shortages of everyday life in the East: the lag in comparison to living standards in West Germany, the differences between propaganda and reality and the "dispelling of myths about the GDR"; for example, stands devoted to food shortages and the functioning of the state-owned Intershop chain. The infographics show the shortfall in the provision of goods in the GDR (TV, telephone, car, etc.). "The dispelling of myths" includes criticism of the notion that gender equality was achieved in the GDR.

The most interesting approach is a reflection of happy everyday life. It is displayed as a kind of "niche" into which a person could go. The term "niche society" (*Nischengesellschaft*) was first used by German publicist Günter Gaus to describe the life of the GDR. Accordingly, the daily routine of the GDR is displayed only as a way to escape from the intolerable political reality. Perhaps this is the best illustration of the redesignation of the symbols of "ostalgie". A dacha, a nudist beach and a Trabant with a tent are in themselves neutral signifiers, but in "ostalgie" they can receive nostalgic connotations, and in state-financed museums, they are inscribed in the semantic framework of the dictatorship. In particular, one of the central objects of the long-term exhibition at the Berlin Kulturbrauerei is a Trabant with a tent. The Trabant, despite its poor technical qualities, has become a symbol of "ostalgie", with a museum, a monument and motor rallies all dedicated to it. In this exhibition, it is designated as "freedom in a tent", so as a means of escape, the freedom to choose one's form of relaxation. And accordingly, as a sign of escape from party supervision, the Trabant also signifies the dictatorship of the GDR.

Thus, in the first decade after reunification, two irreducible pictures of the history of the GDR were formed. In response to the growth of "ostalgia", historical politics integrated the theme of everyday life in the GDR, but the "ostalgic" symbols and achievements of the GDR (kindergartens, women's equality, etc.) received a new meaning; they were re-signified.

This type of politics evokes mixed feelings. On the one hand, there is a justifiable fear that the absence of democratic freedoms and violations of human rights in the GDR may be hidden behind the facade of everyday life and that the experience of the victims of the regime may be devalued. On the other hand, an attempt to show the whole history through dictatorship seems questionable, since history thereby loses its variety and richness, and the voice of the interpreter (more than usually) deforms the voice of the witness and the historical source.

It seems unlikely that the display of various memories (both nostalgic and tragic) about life in East Germany will lead to the "whitening of the dictatorship". Information about the crimes of the Stasi and the fate of political prisoners has a stronger emotional connotation and a greater impact on visitors.

Notes

1 Алейда Ассман [Aleida Assmann], Длинная тень прошлого: Мемориальная культура и историческая политика [The Long Shadow of the Past: Memorial Culture and Historical Politics] (Москва: Новое литературное обозрение, 2014), 35.
2 Carola S. Rudnick, *Die andere Hälfte der Erinnerung. Die DDR in der deutschen Geschichtspolitik nach 1989* (Bielefeld: Transcript, 2011), 37.
3 "Bericht der Enquete-Kommission 'Aufarbeitung von Geschichte und Folgen der SED-Diktatur in Deutschland' gemäß Beschluß des Deutschen Bundestages vom 12. März 1992 und vom 20. Mai 1992", Deutscher Bundestag, http://dipbt.bundestag. de/doc/btd/12/078/1207820.pdf, accessed 30 July 2019; "Schlußbericht der Enquete-Kommission Überwindung der Folgen der SED-Diktatur im Prozeß der deutschen Einheit", Deutscher Bundestag, http://dip21.bundestag.de/dip21/btd/13/110/1311000. pdf, accessed 28 July 2019
4 "Konzeption der künftigen Gedenkstättenförderung des Bundes und Bericht der Bundesregierung über die Beteiligung des Bundes an Gedenkstätten in der Bundesrepublik Deutschland", Deutscher Bundestag, http://dip21.bundestag.de/dip21/ btd/14/015/1401569.pdf, accessed 8 August 2019.
5 Ibid.
6 Saskia Handro and Thomas Schaarschmidt, *Einleitung in Aufarbeitung der Aufarbeitung. Die DDR im geschichtskulturellen Diskurs* (Schwalbach: Wochenschau, 2011), 5.
7 Hester Vaizey, *Born in the GDR: Living in the Shadow of the Wall* (Oxford: Oxford University Press, 2014), 130.
8 Йоахим Вальтер [Joahim Walther], "Певчие вороны, каркающие соловьи" [Singing Crows, croaking nightingales], в *Госбезопасность и литература на опыте России и Германии (СССР и ГДР)* (Москва: Рудомино, 1994), 124.
9 Ibid., 125.
10 Jacek Kucharczyk, Agnieszka Łada, Gabriele Schöler, and Łukasz Wenerski, *Partnerschaft unter Spannung. Wie die Deutschen über Russland denken* (Warsaw: Bertelsmann Stiftung, Gütersloh: Institut für öffentliche Angelegenheiten, 2016), 7.
11 Ассман [Assman], *Длинная тень прошлого* [The Long Shadow of the Past ...]; Морис, Хальбвакс [Maurice Halbwachs], "Коллективная и историческая память" [Collective and historical memory], *Неприкосновенный запас*, 2–3 (2005).
12 Monika Duetz-Schroeder and Klaus Schroeder, *Oh, wie schön ist die DDR* (Schwalbach: Wochenschau Verlag, 2009), 47.
13 "Wie beurteilen Sie rückblickend das Leben in der DDR?, Statista", https://de.statista. com/statistik/daten/studie/13027/umfrage/beurteilung-des-lebens-in-der-ddr/, accessed 15 August 2019,
14 Irmgard Zündorf, "DDR-Museen als Teil der Gedenkkultur in der Bundesrepublik Deutschland", *Jahrbuch für Kulturpolitik*, 9 (2009), 142–143.
15 Interview with Mario S., 19 October 2018. It is worth noting that the respondent has fulfilled himself in the united Germany.
16 Vaizey, *Born in the GDR*; Хайнц Каллабис [Heinz Kallabis], "Германия: единое отечество – расколотая нация" [Germany: a single Fatherland - a divided Nation], *Полис. Политические исследования*, 5 (1991).

17 Thomas Ahbe, *Ostalgie. Zu ostdeutschen Erfahrungen und Reaktion nach dem Umbruch* (Thüringen: Landeszentrale für politische Bildung Thüringen, 2016); Dominic Boyer, "Ostalgie – oder die Politik der Zukunft in Ostdetschland", *Deutschlands Archiv*, 9 (2006).

18 Ансельма Галлинат, Забине Киттель, "О современном подходе к гэдээровскому прошлому", в ГДР: миролюбивое государство, читающая страна, спортивная нация? (Москва: Мысль, 2017), 311.

19 "Empfehlungen der Expertenkommission zur Schaffung eines Geschichtsverbundes 'Aufarbeitung der SED-Diktatur'", Bundesstiftung Aufarbeitung, www.bundesstiftung-aufarbeitung.de/uploads/pdf/sabrow-bericht.pdf, accessed 20 August 2019.

20 "Fortschreibung der Gedenkstättenkonzeption des Bundes 'Verantwortung wahrnehmen, Aufarbeitung verstärken, Gedenken vertiefen'", Deutscher Bundestag, http://dip21.bundestag.de/dip21/btd/16/098/1609875.pdf, accessed 30 July 2019.

21 Ibid.

22 "Alltag in der DDR", Audioguide, https://audio.hdg.de/kulturbrauerei/de/7.html, accessed 2 September 2019.

19 Between memory and myth

The images of Joseph Stalin in
new Russian media[1]

Andrei Linchenko

The mythology of the images of Joseph Stalin in many ways reflects the transformations in historical awareness. The collapse of the Soviet Union and disappointment with the democratic changes in the 1990s became a source of
growing pessimism, disillusionment and nostalgia in modern Russia. At the
same time, the mythologised images of the Soviet leader are also a product of
the construction of the media, which in the 2000s lost its autonomy from the
political power. The mythologised images of Stalin have already been considered in religious and public discourses,[2] in the context of politics of memory.[3]
There have also been studies on the myth of Stalin as a great commander and
the specificities of the Stalinist myth in Soviet cinema.[4] However, the specific
ways in which the mythology of the images of Joseph Stalin is constructed in
modern Russian media have not yet received a comprehensive study.

In this chapter, based on a comparative analysis of the mythology of Stalin's
images in cinema and television journalism, an attempt will be made to identify
and correlate the underlying myths about Stalin in the 2000s. Our interest in
the 2000s is associated with the coming to power of Vladimir Putin and the
creation of a new arrangement between official politics and the media.

Methodological foundations

The mythology of the images of Stalin is a combination of social mythology
and elements of the traditional myth of the hero, which retains its significance
in the cultural memory of Russia. Out of all the heritage of mythology, we
will rely on the conclusions made by Roland Barthes. The reason for using
Barthes's myth model in our research is that it is not only orientated towards
the study of contemporary forms of social mythology in general but is also
devoted to the myth of Stalin in particular.[5] Barthes writes that "myth is a system of communication, . . . a message. This allows one to perceive that myth
cannot possibly be an object, a concept, or an idea; it is a mode of signification,
a form".[6] Myth does not hide anything, nor does it demonstrate anything – it
just creates a form; its strategy is neither true nor false – it is a deviation (related
to deformation). A contemporary myth is discrete: it is rendered only as a discourse rather than a long fable.

DOI: 10.4324/9781003264460-22

Between memory and myth   233

To begin with, we should distinguish mythological narratives about Joseph Stalin from Stalin's panegyric narrative. Aleksandr Prilutsky emphasises that

> the Stalinist panegyric narrative is not yet a "Stalin myth"; in order to become one, it needs to acquire a plot. Therefore, the discourses of the "Stalin myth" do not include arguments about Stalin's holiness, his prescience, since they do not contain any elements of the eventfulness of a plot, confining themselves to a statement.[7]

We will consider mythological narratives about Joseph Stalin in the context of accounts of events which reveal the sacred qualities of Stalin and affirm their influence on the present. Such narratives, regardless of modality and historical authenticity, allow us to see the features of mythologisation today. In this regard, we turned to mythologies about Stalin. It is the mythologeme that acts as the basic unit of our comparative analysis. In Yuri Lotman's opinion, a mythologeme is something that follows the words "myth about . . .", that is a word or phrase that can appear in a text as a proper noun:

> Mythologemes – collective and singular – are proper nouns, or words which function as proper nouns. It is senseless to speak at all about the content of proper nouns, let alone try to break down such content into component parts. However, every word, especially a mythologeme – apart from its referential meaning and regardless of whether it has or has not a significant meaning – is included in the range of associations of a speaker or a listener, which are comprehensible only to the medium of a particular culture.[8]

In our case, such mythologemes are directly connected with the life of Stalin as a politician and as a person, which actualises the myth of the hero. The heroic myth occupies a special place in Russian culture. Modern research points out that "a hero is always a leader of a rebellion against the heartless state machine, which he is called to conquer and subordinate to his will for the sake of the common good".[9] Paradoxically, the latter has always been applied in Russian culture not only to well-known bandits, such as Yermak, and the leaders of peasant uprisings (Stepan Razin, Yemelyan Pugachev), but also to the representatives of supreme power. While a huge faceless mass of local officials has traditionally been perceived as something evil or alien in the Russian folk culture, the "Tsar" or "Emperor" in Russia has always been "God's anointed one", who wishes his people no evil and is unaware of the theft and injustice of his officials. Another equally important feature of any heroic myth in Russia is always the hero's opposition to external forces that threaten Russia and its people. The third key aspect of the heroic myth in Russia is the hero's selflessness. In Russian culture, the feat of the hero is a military feat, first of all, or a feat in the service of God, the Church, the people, the poor and the oppressed.[10] It is significant that the traditional hero of Russian epics or fairy tales is a peasant, a monk or a warrior.

234 *Andrei Linchenko*

The mythology of the images of Joseph Stalin correspond to all three fundamental features of the heroic myth in Russia. The image of Joseph Stalin in the historical memory of Russians is associated less with repression and more with the fight against dissent and the establishment of order in the country.[11] In this case, the myth of the "strong hand" covers up the unattractive aspects of Stalin's policy. As a result, we obtain several, mostly interconnected, mythologemes: "Stalin is a strong personality and a strict but fair ruler", "Stalin the pragmatist", "Stalin the effective manager". The mythology of the images of Joseph Stalin also corresponds to the second most important feature of the Russian heroic myth. The most important episode in the epoch of Joseph Stalin's rule was the victory of the USSR in the war against Germany, the liberation of Eastern Europe from Nazism and the creation of the world socialist system. The absolute majority of respondents in modern Russia associate the name of Stalin with victory in the Great Patriotic War of 1941–1945. This manifests itself in such mythologemes as "Stalin the defender of the people" and "Stalin the saviour and protector of Russia". In this regard, the conclusions of the All-Russian "The Name of Russia" Competition, held in 2008, are important. Three most significant names for Russia were identified during the all-Russian vote. The names of Alexander Nevsky, Joseph Stalin and Peter Stolypin came first, second and third, respectively.[12] Finally, one quite widespread personal characteristic of Stalin is his lack of covetousness. There is a well-known legend about how, after Stalin's death, his personal property amounted to only a few pairs of shoes, a greatcoat, several pipes and a small sum of money in his safe. In this case, we are dealing with such mythologemes as "Stalin the saint" and "Stalin the selfless". From the perspective of the traditional heroic myth, the mythology of the images of Joseph Stalin can be described within the framework of several thematic blocks: the origin of Joseph Stalin, the qualities of Joseph Stalin, the destiny of Joseph Stalin, the life of Joseph Stalin, the interaction of Joseph Stalin with supernatural forces, the struggle of Joseph Stalin with enemies, the trials and martyrdom of Joseph Stalin.

The mythology of the images of Joseph Stalin in modern Russian cinema and fictional television

While presenting the results of our analysis of Russian films and fictional television series devoted to Joseph Stalin in the 2000s, we should note that their quantity has increased significantly since the 1990s. While in the 1990s, there was only one film about Stalin made in Russia (*Stalin*, 1992), in the 2000s, we can observe a surge of interest in the figure of Stalin in Russian cinema and television, with such works as *Stalin's Wife* (2004), *Stalin Live* (2006), *The Gift to Stalin* (2008) and *Comrade Stalin* (2011). The films and series about Stalin made in the 2000s mostly represent the leader's daily life and his relations with his relatives and closest associates. Many of those films are devoted to the post-war time and tend to present Stalin as an ordinary ageing person. At the same time, everything that surrounds Stalin in the films is immersed in an atmosphere of fear, suspicion and lack of freedom. Notably, this atmosphere is generated by the main character himself. The mythological narrative of Stalin is woven into the plotline of the era of terror and generalised fear, where Stalin is the source of this system of evil. Compared with Soviet films about Stalin, modern Russian cinema is not so dependent on ideological clichés. However, certain mythological narratives or mythological images of the leader remain significant. Among them, the most notable individual mythologemes are as follows: "Stalin as the red tsar", "Stalin as an opponent of his own political environment", "the betrayal and death of Stalin", "Stalin as the people's leader". Of all the elements of the mythological narrative in contemporary Russian cinema and television, such topics as the qualities, destiny and life of Stalin have been addressed.

The mythologeme "Stalin as the red tsar" comes to the fore in such works as *Stalin's Wife* and *Stalin Live*. In the former, Stalin's wife, Nadezhda Alliluyeva, asks Stalin about his desire to be crowned. He answers: "I was already crowned at the Sixteenth Congress. You are the queen, my darling". The same motif appears in the speech of the young seminarian Soso Dzhugashvili long before he became Stalin. Here is the scene from episode 34 of the TV series *Stalin Live*. The third minute of the film presents a conversation between Soso Dzhugashvili and a retired soldier of the Russian army. In response to his mother's words that Soso will be a priest, he says: "I will be the tsar". The retired soldier, rather nonplussed for a moment, continues the conversation: "Well, so be it! Let's drink to your making a good tsar!" In response to Soso's question of what makes "a good tsar", the soldier says: "The tsar doesn't have to be kind. The tsar has to be fair, otherwise, why do we need the tsar?" Thus, in the film, the well-known phrase that Stalin uttered to his mother about him being "the tsar of Russia", believed to date from 1936, is shifted to Stalin's childhood and gives special meaning to his whole path through life. The audience is made to believe that Stalin was aware of his special mission even in his youth.

Another interesting mythologeme is "Stalin the people's leader". In the third episode of *Comrade Stalin*, Stalin, for fear of being assassinated, orders a drastic change in the route of the automobile column along the streets of Moscow. As a result, his car almost runs over an elderly milk-woman, who is eventually offered a lift. Stalin apologises to her. In the car, Stalin starts a conversation with her: "We are very sorry to have upset you, dear. We will pay you for milk. Not from the state coffers, mind you. It will be deducted from my salary." The entire conversation between Stalin and the elderly woman is shown as a conversation on an equal footing. He listens to her attentively, hears out her abuse of authority and instead of giving any reply, keeps a pensive silence. Stalin says that the government is working to ensure that "an ordinary person can go shopping after work and buy some bread or milk without any problem". The same film draws attention to another mythologeme, that of "the betrayal and death of Stalin". All the top political figures of the USSR are shown to be waiting for Stalin's death. That is why the refusal to provide him with medical care in March 1953 is presented as the result of a chain of events and actions of members of the Politburo who betrayed Stalin for the sake of their own interests.

The mythology of the images of Joseph Stalin in modern Russian television journalism

The 2000s brought a spike in the number of journalistic TV programmes about Joseph Stalin. All in all, since 2000 there have been more than 20 Russian telecasts and other TV projects about the Soviet leader, the best-known including *Mysteries of Stalin: Versions of the Biography* by Edvard Radzinsky (Channel One, 1996–2001), *Historical Chronicles: Stalin* by Nikolai Svanidze (Russia-1, 2003) and *Stalin is with us* by Vladimir Chernyshev (NTV, 2013). Besides these serials, there have also been one-off television programmes about Stalin: *Stalin's Death: the Witnesses* (2008), *Stalin's Last Year* (2011), *How Did Stalin Get Killed?* (2013), *Stalin's Secret Speech* (2013), *Stalin: The Last Secret of the Red Emperor* (2013), *Joseph Stalin: How to Become a Leader?* (2014), *The Dark Business: Conspiracy against Stalin* (2015), *The Mystery of the Leader's Death: How Was Stalin Killed?* (2016), *The Man Behind Stalin's Back* (2016), *Why Do Russians Love Stalin?* (2016) and *Who Killed Stalin?* (2017).

Analysis of the telecasts reveals the absence of apparent criticism of Stalin on Russian television. One can distinguish between telecasts which avoid any assessments and interpretations and are based on presenting the factual information (for example, Svanidze's *Historical Chronicles: Stalin* and Chernyshev's *Stalin is with us*) and those which raise certain aspects of the mythological image of Joseph Stalin. It is the latter that dominate on Russian television, and they will be of particular interest to us here. The most popular mythologemes of Stalin's image on Russian television are those of "Stalin the strong hand", "Stalin the protector of the Russian State" and "the betrayal and death of Stalin". However, we are much more interested in the mythologised narratives in which these mythologemes are included. One of the most popular storylines on Russian television is the one which interprets the images of Stalin as an integral part and source of the USSR's development in the 1930s–1950s. It is within this context that the mythologemes "Stalin the strong hand" and "Stalin the protector of the country" are most in demand. The Soviet leader is not only opposed to the other leaders of the Revolution (Trotsky, Zinoviev, Kamenev) but is also portrayed as a statesman striving to preserve the historical continuity of power in Russia:

> The Soviet Union under Stalin gained such energy and such rapid development that it became an alternative system that might eventually defeat the system which Western bankers had begun to build in the other hemisphere of our planet. That is why it was necessary to eliminate the man who gave new meaning to the development of the ideas of socialism, the one who united the striving for justice inherent in the Russian people with those good ideas that were part of the concept of the socialist development of the State.[13]

Journalists even find a higher will in Stalin's actions, as did Alexei Pushkov on 20 April 2013, noting that "the ice axe of Stalin, swung into Trotsky's skull, was an instrument of divine retribution".[14]

Between memory and myth   237

The mythology of Stalin's images as a "strong hand" and "protector of the Russian State" turns out to be connected to the mythologeme "Stalin the earthly god". In one of his most popular television projects, Edvard Radzinsky portrays Stalin as the "earthly god": "What phenomenon is this, when even his victims were induced to write in their diaries about him as an earthly god. This impression of an earthly god even held sway among his enemies".[15] The narrative of Radzinsky's television project *Mysteries of Stalin: versions of biography* is forged as a portrayal of Stalin's life based on biographical data. However, the storyline itself is designed as a description of Stalin's majesty, showing him as "the master of Russia". Here the words about Stalin's "horrible Turukhansk exile", which turns out to be one of the hero's most terrible ordeals, sound grotesque. A special role is played by the mythologisation of Stalin's understanding of Marxism:

> He [Stalin] presented Lenin's body to the Party. And the delegates of the Thirteenth Congress . . . were to meet with his imperishable body. It was a symbol of the Bolsheviks' conquest of death itself. They did not realise that they were witnessing the dawn of a great religion, "Asian Marxism", in which Marxism would be the Old Testament and Leninism would become the New Testament; Lenin himself would be God the Father, and he, the former Koba, would naturally become the Messiah.[16]

It is characteristic that the tendency toward the sacralisation of Stalin is becoming more widespread in modern Russia. This has found expression in the appearance of several icons depicting Stalin. Not far from the Kremlin, in the Church of St Nicholas, there has long been an icon which depicts the Holy Matron of Moscow next to a full-length figure of Stalin in his military overcoat. The Holy Matron of Moscow is speaking to Stalin and blessing him.[17] Here is another example: on 28 May 2015, at Prokhorovka Field, in the Belgorod region, a church service was held with a "Mother of God" icon which depicts Joseph Stalin surrounded by Soviet marshals.[18]

Yet the most popular issue that has become the object of mythologisation and stirs debate about Stalin today is his death. The contradictory circumstances surrounding the death of the Soviet leader and the discovery of new documents in the 1990s generated various versions of mythologisation: from a global Jewish conspiracy to the direct involvement of Western countries in Stalin's death. "Stalin was poisoned as a result of a conspiracy at the top of the Soviet elite . . . who in any case had a connection with foreign special services and foreign agencies".[19] One of the arguments provided in this telecast is the fact that Winston Churchill's knighthood, in April 1953, is linked to the successful special operation to eliminate Stalin. "Stalin refused to surrender sovereignty and in response the Anglo-Saxon world immediately began to act".[20] Thus, the authors of several television projects bring home the idea that Stalin's death was the beginning of the disintegration of the Soviet Union, since all the subsequent leaders adhered to the wrong policy.

238   *Andrei Linchenko*

Conclusion

Even though analysis of the Russian Internet has remained outside the scope of our study, we are able to draw a number of conclusions. Stalin's mythology as a projection of a heroic myth turns out to be one of the most comprehensible and uniting images for the population of Russia, because it is associated with victory in the Great Patriotic War. It is the context of warfare that helps to sacralise the leader's image and conceals his less attractive features in popular historical awareness. The rationalisation of the myths about Stalin has rather lost impetus, which confirms the hypothesis of the crisis of anti-Stalinism in Russia.[21] Like the modern mythology described by Roland Barthes, the mythology of Stalin's images appears as a collection of separate, more or less interconnected, mythologemes. The images of Stalin which arose in the 2000s appear to belong to fundamentally different mythological narratives.

This analysis has revealed the dominance of such themes as the life of the Soviet leader, his qualities and his betrayal and death. Even though films and TV programmes give various plotlines to this mythologisation, we will try to reveal similar features. First, Russian cinematography and television journalism have both been displaying an evident surge of interest in Stalin's personality. Second, the proportion of negative and critical interpretations of Stalin's image is extremely low. It is interpreted either through a formal presentation of his life narrative or with the inclusion of the element of mythologisation. Third, the most popular themes in both cinematography and television journalism are those of Stalin's life, his special mission in Russian history, his struggle with internal and external enemies and his death. It is within the framework of these storylines that the mythologemes "Stalin the strong hand", "Stalin the red tsar", "the betrayal of Stalin as the most important cause of his death", "Stalin the people's leader" and "Stalin is the protector of the country" have been addressed.

Yet there are differences too. In cinematography, the reconstruction of the leader's daily life, especially in the latter years of his life, is more relevant. Unlike that of telecasts, the cinema image of Stalin appears less politicised. In the television projects of the late 1990s and early 2000s, Stalin's images are juxtaposed with that of the "earthly deity", and the most common issue discussed on television in relation to Stalin is that of his death (his betrayal and murder). In Russian cinematography, the most current themes were those of Stalin's life, his qualities and his special mission in Russian history. A special role within the framework of these narratives was played by such mythologemes as "Stalin the people's leader" and "Stalin the red tsar". The mythological images disseminated by Russian television journalism are somewhat different. Here, the themes mentioned previously are supplemented by the theme of Stalin's role in the fight against the enemies of Russia and the theme of his death. The dominant mythologemes include "Stalin the strong hand", "Stalin the protector of the country", "Stalin the earthly god" and "the betrayal of Stalin and his death".

The ban on the foreign comedy *Death of Stalin* in Russia in January 2018 summed up a certain outcome to the transformation of the mythology of Stalin in modern Russia. It is characteristic that these images cease to be only media and become important factors in political decision-making. The new millennium presents new challenges to Russian historical awareness, in which the images of Stalin and the mythologemes surrounding his epoch are destined to occupy an important, though not primary, place.

Notes

1 This article was prepared with the support of grant no. 20–011–00297 from the Russian Foundation for Basic Research.
2 Aleksandr Prilutsky, "The Stalin Myth in the Religious and Para-religious Discourses", *Vestnik Severnogo (Arkticheskogo) federal'nogo universiteta. Serija: gumanitarnye i social'nye nauki*, 2 (2016), 87–95; Boris Dubin, "The Stalin Myth", *Russian Politics and Law*, 4 (2010), 46–53.
3 Arsenij Roginskij, "Fragmentierte Erinnerung. Stalin und der Stalinismus im heutigen Russland", *Osteuropa*, 11–12 (2017), 81–88.
4 David Stone, review of Boris Gorbachevsky, *Generalissimo Stalin: The Myth of Stalin as a Great Military Strategist*, trans. and ed. Stuart Britton, *Journal of Slavic Military Studies*, 2 (2016), 319; André Bazin, "The Stalin Myth in Soviet Cinema", *Film Criticism*, 1 (1978), 17–26.
5 Roland Barthes, *Mythologies* (New York: The Noonday Press, Farrar, Straus & Giroux, 1991), 147.
6 Ibid., 107.
7 Prilutsky, "The Stalin Myth", 88.
8 Yuri Lotman, "Literature and Myths", in *Mity narodov mira: Jenciklopedija,* ed. Sergey Tokarev (Moscow: Sovetskaja jenciklopedija, 1980), 222.
9 Sergej Orlov and Dmitrij Chernyshkov, "Mythologeme 'Stalin': The Image of the Leader as a System-Forming Element of Russian Public Awareness", *Svobodnaja mysl'*, 12 (2011), 98.
10 Vladimir Propp, *Russian Heroic Epic* (Moscow: Labirint, 1999).
11 "The Recollections of the Victims of Mass Repressions. Do the Russians Remember the Victims of Repression? Do They Fear the Recurrence of Such Events?", Public Opinion Foundation, http://fom.ru/Proshloe/10675, accessed 25 September 2019.
12 "The Name of Russia", results of the project, www.nameofrussia.ru/, accessed 25 September 2019.
13 "Stalin – the Last Secret of the Red Emperor", www.youtube.com/watch?v=Pyz6 AcuIwWE, accessed 25 September 2019.
14 "Postcriptum, 20 April 2013", TV-Centre [video], www.youtube.com/watch?v= xKkbKoV9Loc, accessed 25 September 2019.
15 Edvard Radzinsky, "Mysteries of Stalin: Versions of the Biography. Part I: Koba's Secrets", www.youtube.com/watch?v=OupI6DMJOYk&list=PL1HQds2hezV_SgnP1MK z5TTK48bPAr9eW, accessed 25 September 2019.
16 Edvard Radzinsky, "Mysteries of Stalin: Versions of the Biography. Part II: Doubles", www.youtube.com/watch?v=KSKLqh73Oq4&list=PL1HQds2hezV_SgnP1MK z5TTK48bPAr9eW&index=2, accessed 25 September 2019.
17 The icon "The Matron and Stalin", https://ru.wikipedia.org/wiki/Матрона_и_ Сталин, accessed 25 September 2019.
18 Mikhail Poplavsky and Olga Alisova, "Icon with Stalin at the WWII Memorial: How Did it Happen?", *BBC*, www.bbc.com/russian/society/2015/05/150529_tr_prok horovka_stalin_icon, accessed 25 September 2019.

19 "Stalin – the Last Secret of the Red Emperor".
20 Ibid.
21 Kathleen E. Smith, *Mythmaking in the New Russia. Politics and Memory during the Yeltsin Era* (Ithaca: Cornell University Press, 2002), 89.

Index

Adamowicz, Tadeusz 199
Adams, George 211
Adenauer, Conrad 193
Adorno, Theodor 162, 215
Adriaansen, Robbert-Jan 105, 120
Adriani, Götz 222
Agamben, Giorgio 175
Agazzi, Elena 223
Agnew, Vanessa 120
Ahbe, Thomas 227, 230
Akker, Chiel van den 119
Alderman, H. Derek 133, 148
Alexander, C. Jeffrey 149
Alisova, Olga 240
Alliluyeva, Nadazhda 235
Alphen, Ernst van 20
Andrasz, Józef 39, 49
Andrzejewski, Bolesław 103
Ankersmit, Frank 118
Arendt, Hannah 20, 127, 129
Assmann, Aleida 7, 19, 162–164, 175–176, 214, 222–224, 230
Assmann, Jan 90, 137, 149
Avrech, Isaiah 175
Azoulay, Ariella 124, 129

Babiichuk, Roman 109, 119
Bacharach, Zvi 64
Bacon, Francis 104
Badger, Gerry 151, 160
Baeque, Antoine de 175
Bal, Mieke 2, 8, 20–21, 73
Baldwin, Craig 175–176
Balisz-Schmelz, Justyna 213, 222
Bałus, Wojciech 74
Bałzukiewiczówna, Łucja 45

Banach, Jerzy 200
Banach, Krzysztof 55, 64
Baranowa, Anna 103
Barasch, Moshe 81, 83
Baron, Jaimie 170, 176
Barthes, Roland 9, 20, 70, 74, 84, 91, 232, 238–239
Baselitz, Georg 213–223
Batory, Stefan (king of Poland) 31, 200
Baudelaire, Charles 122
Baudrillard, Jean 3
Baumeister, Martin 187
Baumeister, Willi 215
Bayer, Gerd 163, 175
Bazin, André 239
Bazin, Jérôme 223
Becher, Johannes 215
Becker, Wolfgang 226
Belting, Hans 48, 72, 74, 78, 83, 215, 222
Bem, Zachariasz Józef 211
Ben-Amos, Dan 20
Benjamin, Walter 2, 14, 17, 20, 127–129, 175
Bennett, Jill 21, 164–165, 174–176
Bergson, Henri-Louis 19, 21, 72, 74
Berleant, Arnold 103
Berman, Jakub 189
Bernatowicz, Piotr 222
Berry, M. David 118
Besenbruch, Walter 215
Białecki, Konrad 200
Bierut, Bolesław 189
Bistrovic, Miriam 63
Blamey, Kathleen 186
Boehm, Gottfried 77, 82, 104
Bois, Yves-Alain 104
Bollas, Christopher 9, 20

242   *Index*

Bolter, Jay David 175
Bonnard, Pierre 104
Bortkiewicz, Paweł 48
Bottici, Chiara 120
Bouchard, Donald 20
Bounarotti, Michelangelo *see* Michelangelo
Boyer, Dominic 227, 230
Boyer, W. John 63
Brandt, Józef 200
Branicki, Ksawery 31, 34
Brinkema, Eugenie 20
Britton, Stuart 239
Broch, Hermann 83
Brueggemann, Walter 130
Brussig, Thomas 226
Bryan, Julien 182–183, 187
Bryl, Mariusz 36, 48
Buchloch, H.D. Benjamin 222
Buckley-Zistel, Susanne 149
Buck-Morss, Susan 129
Buryła, Sławomir 64

Camus, Albert 201, 211
Carl, von Oestherreich (Erzherzog) 25–26
Carter, Erica 222
Carter-White, Richard 119
Caruth, Cathy 20
Catharine the Great (queen of Russia) 25
Challand, Benoit 129
Chanin, Clifford 69, 74
Chernyshev, Vladimir 236
Chernyshkov, Dmitrij 239
Chirac, Jacques 210
Chmielewski, Jakub 56, 64
Churchill, Winston 237
Cichocki, Bartosz 200
Cichońska, Barbara 48
Ciereszko, Henryk 43, 48–49
Cieślak, Stanisław 49
Clemenz, Manfred 77, 82
Clerc, Louis 161
Comerford, Vincent 148
Commane, Gemma 117, 120
Crampton, Nancy 68
Crewe, Jonathan 20, 73
Croft, Jennifer 63
Curdy, Mélanie 52
Cydzik, Maria Faustyna 50
Czaczkowska, Ewa Katarzyna 48–49

Czaplicka, John 90
Czarniecki, Stefan (Polish Hetman) 200
Czekalski, Stanisław 178
Czernik, Tadeusz 47

Damocles 61
Danieli, Ruvik 129
David (King of Israel) 12, 13, 53
Davoine, Françoise 12, 20
Dekel, Ayelet 176–177
Delbo, Charlotte 164
Deleuze, Gilles 19, 104
Derrida, Jacques 52
Desbois, Patrick 63
Descartes, René 14–21
Deumert, Ana 115, 118, 120
Diethe, Carol 222
Dijk, A. Teun 119
Dinhopl, Andja 106, 109, 118–119
DiSilva, Daniel 50
Dobrawa (Czech/Polish princes) 119
Dobrowolski, Tadeusz 191, 199
Douglas, Kate 117, 120
Drążek, Czesław (SJ) 49
Drozdovky, Petro 147
Dubas, Marek 65
Dubin, Boris 239
Duda, Stanisław 60
Duetz-Schroeder, Monika 230
Duller, Eduard 25–26
Dumoirez, Charles-François du Périer 25–26
Duńczyk-Szulc, Anna 63
Dunlap, Thomas 74, 83
Dzhugashvili, Soso 235
Dziurok, Adam 199

Ebbrecht-Hartmann, Tobias 165, 170, 175–176
Eckel, Julia 119
Elisabeth of Bohemia (Princess) 17, 21
Elkins, James 55, 64
Erdelyi, Matthew Hugh 91
Erdélyi, Stefan 211
Erll, Astrid 160
Eyerman, Ron 149

Fahlenbach, Kathrin 119
Farber, Stephen 211

Faustina (Saint) 36–39, 42–44, 46, 48–49
Fiedler, Milenia 176
Foot, Sarah 118
Forceville, Charles 108, 119
Forman, Harrison 182, 187
Foucault, Michel 9, 20, 86, 91, 109, 213, 222
Frąckowiak, Maksymilian 64
Frankowski, T. Marek 64
Freedberg, David 48
Freund, Sigmund 10, 12, 73
Fried, Michael 74
Friedländer, Saul 118, 175
Fuchs, Thomas 101, 104

Gadamer, Hans-Georg 115, 120
Gałęzowski, Marek 199
Gallinat, Anselma 231
Gamaker, Elan 13
Gamaker, Williams Michelle 12, 13, 20
Gardner, Alexander 70
Garnett, Jane 48
Gaskell, Ivan 48
Gatens, Moira 15, 21
Gaus, Günter 229
Germaine, Thomas 16
Gerson, Wojciech 194–195
Gierymski, Aleksander 191–192
Gilbert, Stuart 129
Giesen, Bernhard 149, 221–223
Gillen, Eckart 222–223
Giordan, Giuseppe 48
Glatigny, Pascal Dubourg 223
Glendinning, Nigel 187
Gobodo-Madikizela, Pumla 149
Godfrey, Mark 68, 70, 73–74
Godzic, Wiesław 170, 176
Gogol, Tetiana 138
Golik, Dawid 199
Gomułka, Władysław 192–193, 199, 211
Gorazdowski, Edward 195
Gorbachevsky, Boris 239
Gorczyca, J. Andrzej 49
Gorky, Maxim 190
Görömbei, András 212
Grabowski, Jan 63
Grasewicz, Józef 45
Gretzel, Ulrike 106, 109, 118–119

Grodus, Max 64
Groó, Diána 162–164, 171, 173–174, 176–177
Grottger, Artur 27–29
Groys, Boris 223
Grusin, Richard 175
Grzybowska, Katarzyna 57
Gucci, Santi 32
Guterman, Jakub 59–62, 65
Guterman, Symcha 60, 65
Guterman, Yaakov 65
Gutowski, Maciej 104
Gyimes, Miklós 207

Haake, Michał 189
Habsburg, Otto von 203
Halbwachs, Maurice 85, 90, 230
Hancock, L. Edward 176
Handro, Saskia 230
Hankowska-Czerwińska, Edyta 49, 50
Hansen, Oskar 1
Harari, V. Josué 20
Hariman, Robert 121, 129–130
Haring, A. Sabine 223
Haris, László 201, 203, 205–206, 211
Harris, Alana 48
Hart, M. Stephen 187
Hart, Onno van der 10, 20, 73
Hartmann, Geoffrey 174, 177
Haussman, Leander 226
Heffernan, Michael 149
Hegel, Georg Wilhelm Friedrich 82
Heidegger, Martin 35, 77
Heiferman, Marvin 129
Heinemann, D. Elisabeth 223
Henzel, Jana 226
Hinterkeuser, Guido 91
Hirsch, Marianne 20, 73, 163, 174–175, 177
Hirschberger, Gilad 149
Hitler, Adolf 171, 216
Hodgkin, Katharine 175
Hofmannsthal, Hugo von 78
Hoskins, Andrew 118
Howard, Richard 20, 74
Huberman-Didi, Georges 2, 52, 77, 82, 121, 126–130, 165, 175–176
Huizinga, Johan 115–117, 120
Hyła, Adolf 39–42, 44, 48–49

244   Index

Idzior, Aleksandra 187
Ingarden, Roman 3
Inwood, Joshua 148
Ionesco, Eugene 210
Irincheev, Bair 161
Ishchenko, Volodymyr 148
Iwanicka, Katarzyna 65

Jabłoński, Izydor 25, 35
Jagiellonka, Anna (Queen of Poland) 193
Jagiellończyk, Zygmunt (Saint
  Sigismundus) 197
Jamski, Piotr 69, 74
Janczewska, Marta 64
Janet, Pierre 10, 164
Jankowiak, Stanisław 200
Jankowska-Cieślik, Katarzyna 104
Janssen, Lindsay 148
Jarecka, Dorota 103
Jarnuszkiewicz, Jerzy 1
Jarocki, Robert 200
Jesus, Christus 38, 39, 42, 44–45, 48–50
Jirsa, Tomáš 20
John Paul II (Saint) 42, 44
Johnson, C. Nuala 148
Jokisipilä, Markku 160
Jonas, Regina 171–174, 176
Jordan (bishop) 193
Jóźwiak, Krzysztof 200
Julkunen, Martti 160
Jungingen, Ulrich von (Grand Master of
  Teutonic Knights) 193
Juutilainen, Antii 160

Kaczmarek, Jacek 222
Kádár, János 208
Kajda, Kornelia 64
Kallabis, Heinz 230
Kamiński, Łukasz 199
Kaminsky, Anna 149
Kansteiner, Wulf 105, 118
Kantor, Tadeusz 214
Kapliński, Leon 200
Kardos, György 212
Kasianov, Georgiy 148
Kaufmann, Dorothea 82
Kazimirowski, Eugeniusz 36–39, 42,
  44–48, 50
Kellermann, Natan 149

Kępiński, Zdzisław 103
Kern, Hans Georg 214
Khorolskaya, Maria 224
Kiefer, Anselm 223
Kiepuszewski, Łukasz 92–93, 103–104
Kinnunen, Tiina 160
Kirkconnell, Watson 211
Kiš, Danilo 210
Kiss, Földváryné Réka 210, 212
Kissinger, Henry 203
Kittel, Sabine 231
Kivioja, Virpi 161
Klapheck, Elisa 171, 174, 176
Klee, Felix 82
Klee, Paul 76–78, 82
Kleemola, Olli 151, 160–161
Klein, Matthias 82
Kluge, Alexander 213–214, 220, 222
Klymenko, Lina 148
Kobiałka, Dawid 64
Kobrynskyy, Oleksandr 163, 175
Kochanowski, Jan 31
Koenen, Gerd 223
Kołacka, Daria 82
Kölcsey, Ferenc 207, 211–212
Kolk, Bessel van der 10, 20, 73, 164
Komasa, Jan 162–164, 169, 170, 173–174
Köpeczi, Béla 209
Korhonen, Arvi 152
Korsak, Samuel 30
Kovács, László 201–203, 211
Kowalska, Faustina Maria see Faustina
  (Saint)
Kowalska, Małgorzata 104
Kowalski, Wiesław Józef 48
Kownacka, Dorota 75
Krajewski, Marek 222
Kramer, Hilton 79, 83
Krasicki, Michał 63
Krawczyńska, Dorota 64
Kress, Gunther 119
Kristina (Kristina Vasa, Queen of Sweden)
  17, 18
Krzysztofowicz-Kozakowska, Stefania 103
Kucharczyk, Jacek 230
Kudela-Świątek, Wiktoria 140, 148–149
Kulchytskyi, Stanislav 150
Kunert, Andrzej Krzysztof 186–187
Kunińska, Magdalena 74

Kurella, Alfred 216
Kurella, Hans 216
Kuscera, Gergely Tamás 201, 211

Laade, Clea Catharina 222
Laaksonen, Lasse 160
LaCapra, Dominick 71, 74, 175
Łada, Agnieszka 230
Lamb, Johathan 120
Lambroso, Cesare 216
Langiewicz, Marian 27
Lanzmann, Claude 163
Lavers, Anette 91
Lee, Kyoo 15, 20
Leeuwen, Theo van 119
Le Goff, Jacques 90
Lehmann, Janusz 200
Leite-García, Regina 119
Lenin, Vladimir 90, 195, 237
Leociak, Jacek 64
Leskinen, Jari 160
Leśniakowska, Marta 199
Lesser, Aleksander 194–195
Levchuk, Nataliia 148
Lifton, Jay Robert 138, 149
Lillis, B. Shane 129
Linchenko, Andrei 232
Linfield, Susie 122, 129
Lingis, Alphonso 83
Lipiński, Filip 67, 74
Littkemann, Jochen 218–219
Lloyd, Genevieve 15, 21
Lorentz, Stanisław 200
Losonczy, Géza 207
Lotman, Yuri 233, 239
Lucaites, John 121, 129–130
Łukasiewicz, Małgorzata 82

Mace, James 147
Machniak, Jan 36, 48
Majewski, Kazimierz 190, 199
Maléter, Pál 207
Malinowski, Kazimierz 199
Malpertu-Sibony, Yaëlle 21
Malraux, André 121, 124, 128–129
Manheim, Ralph 82
Manninen, Tuomas 159
Manovich, Lev 118
Mansfeld, Péter 207

Margalit, Ruth 118
Margitházi, Beja 162
Maritn, Hannah Meszaros 65
Mark, Ber 175
Markowska, Marta 199
Matejko, Jan 22–25, 27–31, 34–35, 195–196, 200
Matsäpelto, Armi Hillevi 154
Matvejev, Aleks 50
Mazali, Reia 129
Medveczky, Attila 212
Meek, Allan 175
Meis, Dzheims 149–150
Merleau-Ponty, Maurice 81, 83, 101, 104
Merve, Chris van der 149
Meusburger, Peter 149
Meyer, Richard 66
Michałowski, Piotr 200
Michelangelo 31, 33
Mickiewicz, Adam 23, 31, 35
Mieszko I (Polish prince) 193
Migasiński, Jacek 104
Mikołajczak, Stanisław 48
Miller, C. Judith 20
Miłosz, Jan 200
Minca, Claudio 119
Mirzoeff, Nicholas 114, 119
Misits, Éva 212
Mitchell, Arthur 21
Mitchell, Breanna 105
Mitchell, J.T. William 64
Mitscherlich, Alexander 215, 223
Mitscherlich, Margarete 175, 223
Molden, Berthold 63
Molotov, Vyacheslav 151
Mondzain, Maria-José 20
Montand, Yves 210
Moore, Henry 1
Morra, Joanne 13, 20
Moss, Caroline 118
Mruk, Antoni (Fr) 49
Mul, Jos de 115–117, 120
Münkler, Herfried 222
Murray, Derek 118
Musiał, Filip 199
Muzaini, Hamzah 119
Mydans, Carl 158

246 *Index*

Nader, Luiza 53, 64
Nagy, Gáspár 201, 206–209, 212
Nagy, Imre 207–208, 210
Naumann, Boaz 216, 220, 223
Nemes, László 162–166, 168, 176
Neumann, Bernd 228
Nevsky, Alexander 234
Nicolas (Saint) 237
Nietzsche, Friedrich Wilhelm 100, 213, 222
Nihtilä, Valo 152, 160–161
Noack, Christian 148
Nora, Pierre 86, 89, 90
Nordau, Max 216, 223
Norwid, Cyprian Kamil 176
Noszczak, Bartomiej 199
Nowicki, Michał 45–46, 50
Nowicz, Miriam 56, 64

Ogiienko, Vitalii 133, 135, 143–146
Oleńczak, Piotr 64
Olszewska, Anna 200
Orlov, Sergey 239
Orwell, George 84
Owens, Jesse 171

Pagé, Suzanne 104
Paget, Derek 176
Pągowska, Teresa 104
Palmer, Scott William 21
Pałka, Julian 1
Panofsky, Erwin 77
Partner, Nancy 118
Parr, Martin 151, 160
Paszko, Aleksander 56, 64
Patoharju, Taavi 152, 160
Patton, Paul 10, 20
Paul, Gerhard 160–161
Paul, Margaret Nancy 21, 74
Paul (Saint) 209
Payne, Lewis 70
Pellauer, David 186
Peschansky, Denis 52
Peterson, Jordan 149
Pfanzelter, Eva 118
Picasso, Pablo 222
Piechotka, Kazimierz 66, 69, 71, 73
Piechotka, Maria 66, 69, 71, 73
Pieczyńska-Sulik, Anna 82
Pierce, Charles Sanders 52

Pilke, Helena 152
Piotrowski, Piotr 222–223
Pitkänen, Silja 160
Plasota, Tadeusz 1
Plato 76, 122
Płoszewski, Leon 35
Poniatowski, Stanisław August (king of Poland) 25, 31
Poniński, Adam 29, 34
Poplavsky, Mikhail 240
Porębski, Mieczysław 196, 200
Potocki, Franciszek Salezy 25, 27–28, 30
Potocki, Szczęsny 25
Potton, Rebekah 117, 120
Potworowski, Jan 103
Potworowski, Piotr 92–95, 98–104
Pouvreau, Benoit 52
Price, Francis 129
Prilutsky, Aleksandr 233, 239
Propp, Vladimir 239
Pruszyński, Kazimierz 50
Przemysław I (King of Poland) 195
Przyłębski, Andrzej 103
Pugachev, Yemelyan 233
Pushkov, Alexei 236
Putin, Vladimir 232

Rabinow, Paul 222
Radstone, Susannah 175
Radzinsky, Edvard 236–237, 239
Raeber, Kuno 75–83
Rákosi, Mátyás 201
Rakowski, Stanisław 70
Rancière, Jacques 125, 129, 178, 186
Raphael 25
Raudvere, Catharina 19
Razin, Stepan 233
Rejtan, Tadeusz 23–25, 27–28, 30–35
Rembrandt 12
Remiszewski, Lech 55, 64
Repnin, Vasilyeich Nikolai 25
Ribbentrop, Joachim von 151
Richter, Józef *see* Rychter, Józef
Ricœur, Paul 107, 113–115, 118, 178–180, 186–187, 210
Riegl, Alois 81, 83
Rigney, Ann 107, 118–119
Rijn, Rembrandt Harmenscoon van *see* Rembrandt

Roberts, Len 207
Rodakowski, Henryk 200
Rodziewicz, Janina 45
Roginskij, Arsenij 239
Rollet, Jacques 91
Rose, Sala Rosa 223
Rosińska, Zofia 104
Rosiński, Lechosław 1
Rössing, Karl 78–81, 83
Rougle, Charles 223
Royer, Clara 165
Różycka-Bryzek, Anna 200
Rubens, Peter Paul 12
Rubin, William 73
Ruchatz, Jens 119
Rudnick, S. Carola 230
Rudnytskyi, Omelian 148
Rüsen, Jörn 107, 118
Rutkowska, Izabela 38, 48
Rybka, Małgorzata 48
Rychter, Józef 56, 58–59, 61, 64

Sabrow, Martin 227–228
Saergeant, Philip 118
Saltzman, Lisa 223
Sander, E. Gordon 160
Sander, Johen 13
Santi, Raphael see Raphael
Sárándi, József 208
Sarnecki, Fabian 200
Saryusz-Wolska, Magdalena 222
Saul (king of Israel) 12, 13
Savchuk, Alla 148
Scarry, Elaine 223
Schaarschmidt, Thomas 230
Schäfer, Stefanie 149
Schell, Maria 201
Schmidt, Werner 222
Schmitz, Hermann 96, 103
Schneider, Christoph 223
Schöler, Gabriele 230
Schrade, Ulrich 104
Schroeder, Klaus 230
Schüler-Springorum, Stefanie 187
Schulze, Ingo 226
Schütz, H. Erhard 223
Schwerfel, Peter 222
Schwind, Moritz von 25–26
Sedlmayr, Hans 215, 222

Seixas, Peter 118
Semper, Gottfried 81, 83
Sendyka, Roma 16, 52–54, 63
Serhei, Lefter 149
Shapira, Shahak 105, 117–118
Shein, H. Richard 148
Sheridan, Alan 222
Shevchenko, Taras 145
Shevchuk, Pavlo 148
Silberklang, David 63
Silverman, Kaja 9, 10, 20, 72, 74
Simon, Sherry 20
Sinclair, Stefanie 171, 176
Skaffari, Marja 18
Skarga, Piotr 25, 27, 31
Sleńdziński, Ludomir 42–44, 48
Ślizińska, Milada 187
Słodowska, Joanna 103
Smelser, J. Neil 149
Smilingytė-Žeimienė, Skirmantė 48
Smith, E. Kathleen 240
Sobieski, Jan III (king of Poland) 200
Sokorski, Władysław 199
Solus, Carol 69, 74
Solzhenitsyn, Aleksandr 210
Sontag, Susan 122–125, 128–129, 153,
    160, 174, 177
Sopoćko, Michał 36, 38–39, 42–45, 48–50
Sosnowski, Oskar 66
Sparschuh, Jens 226
Spencer, Catherine 63
Śpiewak, Paweł 63
Spiller, Jürg 82
Spinoza, Baruch 15
Spitzer, Leo 20, 73
Stalin, Joseph 202, 211, 232–240
Stańczyk 25, 27, 200
Stanisław of Szczepanów (Saint Stanislaus
    the Martyr) 197
Starzyński, Juliusz 190–191, 196, 199
Steege, ter Johanna 18
Steinberg, P. Michael 83
Stella, Frank 66–74
Stolypin, Peter 234
Stone, Dan 176
Stone, David 239
Stradling, A. Robert 187
Stryjkowski, Krzysztof 200
Suchocki, Wojciech 22

248 *Index*

Suchodolski, January 200
Suwała, Stanisław 49
Svanidze, Nikolai 236
Szabó, O. Ernő 212
Szakolczay, Lajos 204, 211
Szczęsny, Marek 103
Szemadám, György 206–207, 212
Szilágyi, József 207
Szmigielska, Helena 45
Sztompka, Piotr 149
Szujski, József 25
Szweda, Paweł 41, 48–49

Tagg, Caroline 118
Tanikowski, Artur 73
Tarnowski, Stanisław 35, 196
Tellkamp, Uwe 226
Tewerson, Heidi Thomann 82
Theweleit, Klaus 221–223
Tifentale, Alise 118
Timothy, (Saint) 209
Tokarev, Sergey 239
Tomann, Juliane 120
Traba, Robert 222
Trencsényi, Zoltan 205
Trojański, Piotr 63
Trotsky, Leon 236
Trypniak, Teodora 138
Turner, Chris 222
Turowski, Andrzej 67, 73, 103, 187
Turva, Maan 160
Tynkkynen, Vesa 160

Vaizey, Hester 230
Varga, László 205
Vasari, Giorgio 77
Vasy, Géza 212
Veselova, Olena 149
Vida, Ferenz 207
Volkan, D. Vamik 137, 149
Vörösmarty, Mihály 211

Wal, Vander Thomas 119
Wallenius, M. Kurt 157
Walter, Joahim 230
Warburg, Aby 2, 126–128
Way, Lori 120
Weigel, Sigrid 221, 223

Weiner, Allen 118
Weissberg, Lillian 20
Welzer, Harald 152
Wenerski, Łukasz 230
Wetzel, Juliane 63
White, Heyden 117–118, 120
Wiesel, Elie 163
Winders, Jamie 148
Winowska, Maria 49
Wirth, Sabine 118
Witkiewicz, Stanisław 23, 25, 27, 35
Witko, Andrzej 48–50
Wojciechowski, Przemysław 16, 17
Wojtyła, Karol (archbishop) *see* John
    Paul II (Saint)
Wolf, Christa 226
Wolovyna, Oleh 148
Wood, David 118
Woodhead, Linda 48
Worringer, Wilhelm 77–79, 82
Wróblewska, Hanna 222
Wrotnowski, Feliks 31
Wunder, Edgar 149
Wyrwa, Christiane 82
Wyszyński, Stefan (cardinal) 49

Young, E. James 71, 74
Yushchenko, Viktor 135–136, 142

Zagrodzki, Janusz 103
Zajczyk, Szymon 66
Żakiewicz, Zbigniew 50
Zappavigna, Michele 119
Zaprzalski, Zbigniew *see* Rychter, Józef
Zaręba, Zygmunt 178–180, 182, 184,
    186–188
Żarnower, Teresa 178–188
Zawadowska, Agnieszka 104
Zelizer, Barbie 177
Zhurzhenko, Tatiana 148
Zimmer, Thierry 52
Zinoviev, Grigory 236
Zohn, Harry 20, 129
Zsigmond, Vilmos 201–203, 211
Żuchowski, J. Tadeusz 84, 91
Zündorf, Irmgard 230
Żygulski, Zdzisław (jun.) 200
Zyrd, Michael 164–165, 171, 175–176

Printed in the United States
by Baker & Taylor Publisher Services